To Jason

Thanks for your support

[signature]

Frontiers of Globalization

Series editor

Jan Nederveen Pieterse
University of California
Santa Barbara, California, USA

With the onset of the twenty-first century, key components of the architecture of twentieth-century globalization have been crumbling. American hegemony has weakened politically and economically. Laissez-faire capitalism that shaped the neoliberal globalization has proved to be crisis-prone and is giving way to a plurality of ways of organizing and regulating capitalism. With the rise of emerging societies the driving forces of the world economy are shifting not merely geographically but structurally; industrializing societies, rather than postindustrial consumer societies, are again propelling the world economy. These changes involve major breaks: an era of multipolarity; the affirmation of the plurality of capitalisms; the emergence of new modernities; and the new patterns of East-South and South-South relations, in contrast to the North-South relations. These changes unfold on a global scale and cannot be properly understood on a national, regional or even international basis. They represent major trends breaks, although actual changes may well take shape through a thousand small steps. Understanding these changes requires interdisciplinary and kaleidoscopic approaches that range from global political economy to cultural transformations. The series welcomes contributions to global studies that are innovative in topic, approach or theoretical framework. Amid the fin-de-regime of the millenium, with globalization in the throes of dramatic changes, the series will cater to the growing interest in educational and study material on contemporary globalization and its ramifications. Proposals can be submitted by mail to the series editor: Jan Nederveen Pieterse, Mellichamp Professor of Global Studies and Sociology, Global & International Studies Program, University of California, Santa Barbara, CA 93106-7065, USA

More information about this series at
http://www.springer.com/series/14992

Phillip Kalantzis-Cope

The Work and Play of the Mind in the Information Age

Whose Property?

palgrave
macmillan

Phillip Kalantzis-Cope
New York City, New York, USA

Frontiers of Globalization
ISBN 978-3-319-64649-7 ISBN 978-3-319-64650-3 (eBook)
https://doi.org/10.1007/978-3-319-64650-3

Library of Congress Control Number: 2017952661

Cover image by Phillip Kalantzis-Cope

Printed on acid-free paper

This Palgrave Macmillan imprint is published by Springer Nature
The registered company is Springer International Publishing AG
The registered company address is: Gewerbestrasse 11, 6330 Cham, Switzerland

Foreword

Here is the paradox about the apparently neo-liberal turn of the late twentieth century: at much the same time as everything was meant to be privatized, information wormed its way out of the property form and started circulating for free. Owners of intellectual property did their best through technical and legal means to police and restrict its movement, and yet at the same time whole industries sprang up based on the technical capacity to reproduce and circulate information at minimal cost and the public's willingness to put in the free labor to make it so.

This is the starting point for Phillip Kalantzis-Cope in this stimulating and ground-breaking book on the geo-politics of intellectual property. The book explores a series of what he calls *propertyscapes*: copyright as a form of enclosure, the commodification of everyday life, the commercialization of knowledge within social media networks, and the patenting of forms of biological life. Putting these conflicts and processes at the center of the analysis moves our focus squarely onto questions of emerging forms of transnational regulation.

Not the least innovation of this book is that it draws a net of concepts over phenomena that might otherwise be distributed between different fields, ranging from legal studies to media studies to post-colonial and development studies. In this the book really does useful work in adapting and extending concepts, to show how parallel developments can be considered as part of a larger historical development. This might give us useful ways of identifying some of the tendencies along which capitalism has developed, or perhaps diverged, relative to received ideas about its form and destiny.

After this preliminary analytic and conceptual work, Kalantzis-Cope sets up the possibility of designing a different kind of international social and technical regime, one that might include several kinds of public-seeking divergent objectives. What he calls *Network Distribution* and *Ecological Decolonization* seem particularly promising and urgent forms of agency that might point toward ways of imagining a global social and technical regime in which the distribution of information might contribute to equitable and sustainable forms of life.

As I put it some years ago: information wants to be free but is everywhere in chains. Kalantzis-Cope gives us a nuanced and multi-dimensional approach to information as something produced in and by not only technical, economic, and legal institutions, but also social and cultural ones. It is a framework for thinking about a world that we might not only want to inhabit but also endure.

That might be preferable to the course it so often seems the ruling powers of this planet have embarked upon—a reckless gamble on an accelerated commodification of information, and through information, of every resource it could command. That is a path likely to undermine its own planetary conditions of existence, and to no greater aim than enhancing share-holder value. We will stand in the ruins, clutching our well-hedged portfolios, wondering why reality does not conform to their risk-assessments, but has taken a turn for the worse. Give that possibility, this is a timely book for thinking about information otherwise.

Las Vegas, NV McKenzie Wark
29 June 2017

Contents

1

Introduction: Becoming Property

Debates over property reveal some of the central antagonisms in modern political philosophy. In the broad landscape of modernity these tensions, and the social lives to which they have given meaning, have tended to coalesce around two general positions: one defined by private property and the other defined by collective ownership. After the fall of the Berlin Wall, advocates from one of these camps claimed that the question of the meaning of property, at least in its material manifestations, was now settled, and in their favor. Private property, they supposed, came out victorious. Positions advocating common or collective ownership of material property became increasingly viewed as outdated or outmoded, their conceptual language burdened by the collapse of the political regimes of communism, discredited as a variant of totalitarianism. By the late 1990s this victory seemed hyperreal, exaggerated to the point where the world might be considered to have reached an "end of history."[1] The world, in this view, had become a completely interlinked marketplace of private property, with capitalism solidifying its position as the pre-eminent economic, social, and ideological system. Notions of collective ownership of property as the foundation of political, economic, or social life, all-but faded away as politically viable alternatives, or retreated into isolated

P. Kalantzis-Cope, *The Work and Play of the Mind in the Information Age*,
Frontiers of Globalization, https://doi.org/10.1007/978-3-319-64650-3_1

islands of dictatorship. The centuries-long property debate had, it seemed, subsided from its place in the center of mainstream political discourse.

However, through the 1990s we also experienced the intensification of the case for, or living realities of, another kind of epoch-defining shift, a shift toward a post-industrial information age. Interpretations of the distinctive character of this age were focused on a move toward knowledge work, and research-based production, and the emerging social and productive practices associated with digital technologies and communication networks, now becoming the core engines for social, political, and economic development. Although holding a privileged starting position, private property is no longer taken to be the default property logic for mediating the production and ownership of the defining good of this new age, a form of labor that I will term in this book, *the work and play of the mind.* In fact, in this so-called information age, private property becomes just one among several significant alternative conceptions, each defining the work and play of the mind as a different kind of property. These alternatives did not simply present themselves as theoretical propositions, but are embedded in, and argued through, real lifeworlds and knowledge production ecologies. Moreover, these alternative conceptions defining the work and play of the mind as property do not solely speak to the nature of property, but to what kind of world we were going to create. Who did we want to *become* as agents of human culture and knowledge? What kinds of opportunities for *becoming* is history now affording us? This book presents an account of the origins of four alternatives to the production and ownership of the work and play of the mind in the post-industrial information age. I will call these Information Privatization, Information Exceptionalism, Transformative Distribution, and Ecological Decolonization. I will ask how each model attempt to grapple with this question of human social *becoming.*

I use the phrase *work and play of the mind* to establish a particular starting position. The work and play of the mind need not be property. But it may be construed as property, it may *become property*, and this construal may take different paths. This starting point is motivated by a desire to allow that the historical emergence of each approach occurs in the practices of knowledge and cultural production themselves, activities of work and play, that only in certain historical circumstances *become property*, and then property of specific and varied kinds. Thus, my focus is on a certain kind of constitutive collective political action, the social action that of *becoming property*.

Another reason for this phraseology is to invoke the simultaneously *disembodied* and *embodied* nature of the work and play of the mind. The work and play of the mind is disembodied in a temporal sense. Its immaterial residues reach us from the long history of the human cultures and knowledge, disembodied in the disconnection from their original creators. It is also disembodied in a spatial sense: the vectors of cultural and epistemic production that do not fit naturally within any formal frames of territoriality. Knowledge and ideas flow without geographic friction, as if the distant were close, and vice versa. At the same time, the work and play of the mind is embodied in the same way that the mind is embodied. Mind touches the ground of material space with our bodily forms and our media productions. For these reasons, *becoming property* offers a basis to explore an antinomy in the framing of global space, defined by *disembodied* and *embodied* flows of culture and knowledge, or in opposition to them.

I am interested in the constitutive collective political action of *becoming property* at a normative level because the right to the work and play of the mind is today a central mediator of power and authority in our everyday lives. In the context of today's increasingly machine-mediated relations to nature and each other, this role is destined to increase in significance. I am also normatively motivated by a diagnosis of our current historical condition. From about 2008 there begins a wave of co-producing global crises. One of these is an economic crisis, where across the globe people have experienced the effects, or live in the ideological shadow, of a rationalism of austerity, at once fabricated and in its effects, real. Another is a crisis of culture and economic identity with the rise of nativist and populist movements, in part a reaction to the rigors of austerity. Yet another is an environmental crisis, presenting the challenge of climate change and the contestation of truth claims over our species effects on the pace and nature of that change. In at times unexpected and unassuming ways, the constitutive collective political actions represented in the models of *becoming property* that I will explore in this book offer a microcosm of the story of how we got to the difficult place we find ourselves today, the current *state of emergency*.

But there is also something about *becoming property*, a unique generative quality, that also makes it a useful site to think about collective political action, and possible emancipatory potentials within the work and play of the mind. The generative quality is as follows: theoretical moorings of the social utility of property come to demand an institutional form of some shape—a law, regime, or common set of accepted norms. Until recently, the jurisdictional geography for *real property* was framed by the modern nation-state. Asserting the meaning and rule of property has in large part defined the purpose of the modern nation-state as the pre-eminent form of political community in global politics. Today's alternative interpretations and regimes of the work and play of the mind uniquely challenge this conventionally modern framing of global space. So, my questions become: what might be the new coordinates, and demands, for understanding political community as constitutive collective political action within the context of our age? My ambitious claim is that embedded in all four models for *becoming property* are the nascent logics for *becoming political community.* New opportunities emerge for political community as modes of collective political action, representing fundamental, democratic-constitutive acts. Will one or several come to dominate? Or will the future be one like the present, where paradigmatically different kinds of political community co-exist, albeit in difficult, mutually defining tension?

Political Community as Constitutive Collective Political Action

Modes of political community have provided one of the dominant interpretative coordinates from which we have made sense of global space. The Westphalian age is defined by reference to the modern nation-state. At the most elementary level the emergence of the modern nation-state was a certain kind of *constitutive collective political action.* Within its original historical context this political action evolved to include an ideal of a shift in power to *the people*—popular sovereignty, where affinities are ostensibly based on shared historical experience and community is bound together by common institutions. The institutional legitimacy of the modern nation-state is established in a series of relational obligations to its members: their security, economic well-being, and sense of belonging.

It is now almost taken as a given that technologies of interconnection—modes of transport, markets, and communication—increasingly challenge the central meaning-making functions and institutional authority of modern nation-state. If we commonly accept these global historical changes are taking place, the normative purpose and institutional shape of the modern nation-state may not align with the demands of the lives of its *people*. If that is the case, what is the future of popular sovereignty? If there is decay in this mode of social organization, then what is replacing it? How does the spatiality of shared historical experience map the new realities where global institutions shape everyday life?

These challenges to the framing of global space are uniquely, and productively, born out in production and ownership of the work and play of the mind. Looking through the *production* of the work and play of the mind, these challenges are brought to the surface in the realities of experiences of life mediated by digital communication systems. These communication systems have connected spaces of information, knowledge, and cultural production in ways that generate new kinds of de-territorialized shared meanings, allowing the production of new kinds of affinities and relations of global social life. Moreover, the form of the production of informational goods reveals a new labor spatiality, not primarily defined by the physical boundaries of territoriality, but a new kind of lived labor, symbolically and materially rendering obsolete the boundaries of life and labor understood previously through the modern nation-state. Looking through the *ownership* of the work and play of the mind, processes guaranteeing the right to the work and play of the mind also represent a destabilization of the traditional frames of global space. At one extreme we see the emergence of global legal frameworks that undermine the *property sovereignty* of the modern nation-state from above, and at the other, common regimes that undermine the *property sovereignty* of the modern nation-state from below.

Within the study of global politics, particularly in the fields of International Relations and Political Geography, a series of epistemological conundrums tend to ossify our thinking on the nature of political community, as constitutive collective political action.[2] For positivist approaches, as well as the Realist, Neo-Realist, or Behaviorist traditions, the challenge of reconceiving the nature and form of political community is compromised, to the extent that these traditions posit the modern nation-state as integral to their conception of global politics. The modern nation-state is the epistemological mooring for claims to the significance of empirical phenomena, with the law-like behavior and predictive capacities of analysis based on the relationships established between modern nation-states. Visions of political community outside of the modern nation-state, while not entirely discredited, are nonetheless relegated to the less significant normative "ought." The effect is to reify the modern nation-state as the telos of political community.

Critical approaches in the form of Critical International Relations Theory, Constructivism, Post-Modernist, or Feminist Theory have attempted to reconsider the fundamental nature and traditional forms of political community. However, in pursuing their various agendas they face a strategic dilemma: whether the primary locus of analysis must scale up and be generalizable to the global, or scale down to grounded, localized, or specific communities of practice. This strategic dilemma, on one hand, directs our attention to the exclusionary and deterministic nature of scaling up and, with such scaling, a need to resort to universalizing and thus homogenizing accounts of reason, ethics, morality, and justice. On the other hand, while emphasizing identity and differences as critical denominators in a normative geopolitical landscape, scaling down to specifics and the contingencies of difference directs our attention to the implications of narrowing our attention to the scope of affinity beyond the specifics of stratified groupings. This strategic dilemma of normative and institutional scale generates a rich debate about the future of political community at a normative theoretical level, at times falling short of providing a meaningful explanation of what makes political community as collective political action, as an institutional form and embodied in political organization. The local and specific may be described empirically, but often this is at the expense of generalizable interpretation.

These established theoretical models can create path dependencies that produce unintentional blindness to emerging alternatives, embryonic forms, and new kinds of political community that do not fit the Westphalian model. These may be camouflaged by divergent discourses and complex realities in the thick of global life. Not to simply rehearse old arguments, or to create a property reductionism, but if guaranteeing the right to property was so important in the definition of political community of the Westphalian system and its primary unit, the modern nation-state, what impact do new frames for regulating the work and play of the mind, whether sourced from above and below the level of the nation-state, have on the "old order"? To return to my more ambitious line of questioning, what are the constitutive collective political actions represented by each of the approaches that I will describe on this book, of *becoming property?* What traces of nascent political communities, as theoretical propositions or as empirical phenomena, do they reveal? To approach these questions and dust off the telos of the nation-state, I offer the perspective of *propertyscapes.*

Propertyscapes

In discussing the concept of "propertyscape," I must begin by recognizing the work of Arjun Appadurai.[3] Within the context of globalizing forces, Appadurai's "scapes" were an attempt to understand the flows of cultural phenomena or the operations of power in the production of global social imaginaries. When looking at the transformation of the work and play of the mind into property—*becoming property*—there is a direct connection to the "scapes" whose power Appadurai is attempting to understand and explain. Each of the propertyscapes I will define represents a distinguishable social imaginary, grounded in a specific reading of the essential nature of the work and play of the mind. This essential nature is situated within specific readings of history and understanding of the nature of the post-industrial information age. Nevertheless, the unique *generative* power in *becoming property* is where I distinguish the frame of propertyscapes from Appadurai's *scapes.* This generative power tightens the connection between *becoming property* and *becoming political community* as constitutive collective political action.

Two actions of *becoming*—property and political community—demand realization in specific institutional forms. These institutional forms tell us something about formal systems of relational obligation:

duties, responsibilities, economic rights, and avenues for justice. The distinguishing element of the propertyscape framework I am presenting is this emphasis on the necessary generation of institutions. My working hypothesis is that the production of these institutions, regimes of the work and play of the mind, implicates the nature of future forms of political community as constitutive collective political action.

I will define each propertyscape of the work and play of the mind, and the framework of propertyscapes more generally, through a tri-partite rubric: its *ontological ordering principle*, a relational set of *normative presuppositions*, and its *institutional topology*. This tri-partite rubric serves to construct an ideal type in the form of an origin story that I retell for each propertyscape. The ontological ordering principle serves to ground each propertyscape in its essential understanding of human action. This understanding of action combines a specific reading of history, based on the characteristic practices of the work and play of the mind in an information age, with longer views of the nature of human action found in the act of becoming property in general. The normative presuppositions animate a social imaginary, associated with essential assumptions about human motivation, again based on the combination of historically specific reading of the practice of the work and play of the mind in an information age and aligning with a longer view of the nature of human motivation. Finally, the institutional topologies of each propertyscape illuminate its ontological ordering principles and its action logic, motivated by normative presuppositions in its social imaginary, producing a regulatory order of some form, and at some scale. These topologies speak to already existing, living propertyscapes in global space.

The purpose of this propertyscape frame is not just to understand a geo-politics of intellectual property. The purpose of the propertyscape notion is an attempt to not begin with questions of the order: *Is the state disappearing?* or *Is the nation still relevant as a locus of political community?* Rather it is to offer a lens sufficiently capacious to capture the emergence of alternative configurations of political community, either as empirical realities or as normative propositions. It also represents an attempt to create a rubric that can be used to make sense of the modern nation-state. Be they traditional and established or alternative and newly emerging, political communities have ontological ordering principles that define their legitimacy as sovereign entities; they have normative presuppositions that inform systems of order and regulate social practice; and they have institutional topologies marking their boundaries, defining their outsides and insides. In this way, the modern nation-state can be read through this rubric, but the modern nation-state does not define the rubric. Moreover, the frame is meant to be useful in a more expansive way, to connect the *making* of these propertyscapes of the work and play of the mind, to the *making* of political community.

My intent here is not only to illuminate the institutional terrain of the work and play of the mind, in its own right and in the variety of its manifestations. I also want to explore how these institutional orders, as grounded readings and manifestations of collective political action, also reveal nascent models of political community, so directing us to the challenges to, and of, political community as a frame of political life in a post-industrial information age. The aim is to understand and reclaim political community as a possible, generative, and speculative site for constitutive collective political action.

Whose Political Community?

In what might seem a tautology, political communities are political. The productive parallel between the act of *becoming*, *property* and *political community*, is not happenstance. Nor is it directed toward simple theoretical restructuring of notions of the one or the other. The imbricated questions of *whose property?* and *whose political community?* underlie the normative thrust of this project. For whom does each propertyscape seek to secure economic benefit, allow space for social participation, and frame political representation? What is the territorial scope of the work and play of the mind found in each propertyscape? Whose work, and whose play, is considered demanding of consideration for the realization of social, political, and economic justice? These questions provide a basis upon which to evaluate the actualities of power within each paradigm, as well as the institutional mechanisms now appearing on the geopolitical landscape for the enforcement of that power. As an *interested project*, in the spirit of Critical Theory, I am motivated by a desire to find the emancipatory potentials within the global politics of the production and ownership of the work and play of the mind. My hunch, my working hypothesis, is that reframed notion of political community might offer a way of doing this, and along with this the creation of a new political geography.

My approach owes a conceptual debt to the work of Nancy Fraser. Fraser has offered a searing critique of the conditions of life in global space. She argues that the Keynesian-Westphalian model is "losing its aura of self-evidence."[4] As the dominant "constitution of social space" the model has become increasingly riddled with "nodes of abnormality," reflecting "the destabilization of the previous hegemonic grammar."[5] For Fraser, this historical reality demands that we consider the *framing* of global space. This must begin with *who*: "who counts as a subject of justice in a given matter? Whose interests and needs deserve consideration? Who belongs to the circle of those entitled to equal concern?"[6] Then we need to consider the framing of the *what.* Fraser believes that our current condition creates an "absence of a shared view of the 'what' of justice" in which "the very what is up for grabs."[7] Finally the *how*, "the political dimension of representation."[8] If the Keynesian-Westphalian model is becoming outmoded, collapsing as a political project, what was coming in its place? What kind of new political order might follow?

My interest in the work and play of the mind, and the propertyscapes constituted by its variant forms, is to engage with Fraser's diagnosis of our historical condition and the very problem of framing that condition. I am also interested in how Fraser pivots from diagnosis to prognosis via her *transformative approach.* This approach "aims to challenge the deep grammar of frame setting in a globalized world."[9] The agenda that emerges entails a politics that must "aim to democratize the process of frame-setting." In her words, "what turns a collection of people into fellow subjects of justice is not geographic proximity, but their co-imbrication in a common structural or institutional framework, which sets the ground rules that govern their social interaction, thereby shaping their respective life possibilities in patterns of advantage or disadvantage."[10]

In approaching these propertyscapes via the lens of political community, representing as it does a fundamental, democratic, constitutive act,

I also want to consider the kind of actions that political communities themselves represent. If the *becoming* of political community inherently demands institutional forms, and so not just as principled, discursive, or theoretical ways of articulating political action, then we are addressing the practicalities of making order. So, key questions arise, such as who can participate in this constitutive collective political action? What does *becoming property* tell us about the opportunities and limits of constitutive collective political actions in the post-industrial, post-Westphalian age? This book interrogates the embodied and disembodied production and ownership of the work and play of the mind in a way that might challenge our conventional ways of seeing political community in global politics, be that already existing in some forms, embryonic, or merely at this stage speculative. By examining this particular mode of collective political action, *becoming property*, I want to explore how this might offer us unique insights into the *doing* of political community in the information age. Then, more expansively, we may be able to reclaim *becoming political community* as an emancipatory project within global space.

Notes

1. Francis Fukuyama, *The End of History and the Last Man* (New York: Maxwell Macmillan International, 1992).
2. Phillip Kalantzis-Cope, "Geopolitical Structuring in the Age of Information: Imagining Order, Understanding Change," *Alternatives: Global, Local, Political* (2017).
3. Arjun Appadurai, *Modernity at Large: Cultural Dimensions of Globalization* (Minneapolis: University of Minnesota Press, 1996).
4. Fraser. p. 71.
5. "Abnormal Justice," *Critical Inquiry* Spring (2008). p. 400.
6. Ibid. p. 398.
7. Ibid. p. 398.
8. "Reframing Justice in a Globalizing World." p. 73.
9. Ibid. p. 81.
10. Ibid. p. 82.

2

The Private: *Whose Equilibrium?*

In the late 1990s neo-liberals boldly proclaimed two victories: that the free market had become the pre-eminent method of resource allocation and that liberal democracy had risen to be the only viable mode of political organization. Conceptually connecting these victories was a belief that the aspirations and rationality of this political project played itself out, naturally, without the heavy hand of state regulatory intervention. The promise was market-based equilibrium and political stability. The whole of humankind was on track to be incorporated into a completely interlinked, democracy-inducing, global marketplace.

This chapter offers an account of the ways in which the production and ownership of the work and play of the mind comes to be imbricated within this history of economic neo-liberalism. This result was the extension of private property and the free market into a wider range of global social spaces. I call this the propertyscape of "Information Privatization."[1] While Information Privatization will be only one of four propertyscapes defined in this book, in many ways it is the most important.

Information Privatization's ontological ordering principle, normative presuppositions, and institutional topology operate in concert to define and regulate the work and play of the mind, on a global scale, in the

P. Kalantzis-Cope, *The Work and Play of the Mind in the Information Age*, Frontiers of Globalization, https://doi.org/10.1007/978-3-319-64650-3_2

form of *private* property. The constitutive collective political action of *becoming private property*, within the context of broader forces of capitalist development, provides the focal object of critique for my entire project.

I will in this and subsequent chapters use the device of a "living story" to demonstrate, by way of case illustration, the ways in which each propertyscape plays out in practice. The living story through which I critically engage the propertyscape of Information Privatization centers on the creation of the Great Firewall by the People's Republic of China (PRC). The Great Wall of China was built and extended over time by successive emperors to keep warlike barbarians out of China. The Great Firewall is another kind of spatial construction, again an attempt to protect Chinese interests from an outside world. It is both a response to and itself an aspect of the propertyscape of Information Privatization. In connecting the propertyscape of Information Privatization to the Great Firewall I want to uncover one of the ways in which the production and ownership of the work and play of the mind has become a foundational rubric by means of which to articulate mechanisms of global order in a post-industrial information age, complicating the narrative of equilibrium at the center of the neo-liberal zeitgeist where this propertyscape finds greatest historical traction.

The Diagnosis: Piracy and Theft

Regimes designed to protect intellectual property as private property trace their beginnings to the very first copyright laws. Foundational markers within the modern nation-state include in England, the Statute of Anne of 1708, and internationally, the Berne Convention established in 1886. The specific propertyscape I am defining here—Information Privatization—while part of this history, began its unique gestation period in the late 1980s and early 1990s.

By the 1990s there was no doubting the importance of the post-industrial economy, as an ideological proposition or economic reality. The US-based lobby group International Intellectual Property Alliance (IIPA) claimed that:

> Between 1977 and 1996, the core copyright industries grew nearly three times as fast as the annual rate of the economy as whole—4.6% vs. 1.6%, in 1996, 3.5 million Americans worked in the core copyright industries—about 2.8% of the entire U.S. workforce, and in 1996, the U.S. core copyright industries achieved foreign sales and exports of $60.18 billion, surpassing, for the first time, every other export sector, including automotive, agriculture and aircraft.[2]

However, there was something troubling about the character of the post-industrial moment for copyright-based industries. Greater access to digital reproductive technologies, coupled with the rise of global information and network platforms, in particular the Internet, meant that the knowledge basis, and/or material manifestations, of their products could be reproduced with greater ease. *Sharing* and *distributing* became understood through a language of moral approbation as "piracy" or "theft." These kinds of acts were a real threat to the future "bottom lines" of the copyright industries. Jack Valenti, then Chairman and CEO of the Motion Picture Association, claimed that "international piracy of American creative works" had "reached a level of some $18–20 billion annually."[3]

In patent-based industries, multinational companies, and in particular the pharmaceutical companies, were similarly worried about a comparable trend: the ways in which generic replicates of their products were being created and sold, in developing markets. A growing chorus of intellectual property-based industries came to see that something had to be done to protect the intellectual property that underwrote the immaterial and material commodities that these industries were creating, from movies to drugs.

The primary problem was one of scale. The social life of piracy and theft of copyrighted goods was facilitated in large part by digital communication networks that are inherently transnational; the design and manufacture of copycat generic pharmaceuticals in developing nations was beyond the reach of legal processes in the countries of their original invention. While corporations could lobby their own national governments to restrict these violations with some success, it was difficult to enforce intellectual property rights across national borders. To compound matters, there was a general consensus in the business world that the World Intellectual Property Organization (WIPO), the primary UN regulatory body for intellectual property rights, was failing to protect the rights of these corporations in the global marketplace.[4]

Thus, multinational corporations felt there was no choice but to lead the global agenda for the protection of intellectual property rights. James Emhart, then Director of International Affairs for Monsanto, pronounced, "if war is much too important a subject to leave to generals, as Bismarck said, the rules of international commerce are far too important to leave up to government bureaucrats."[5] To "define the rules" these interests rallied behind several lobbies and coalitions. The most important was the US-based Intellectual Property Committee (IPC). Founded in 1986 the IPC was made up of a cross-section of the multinational world: Bristol-Myers, CBS, Du-Pont, General Electric, General Motors, IBM, Johnson and Johnson, Merck, Monsanto, and Pfizer. It became necessary for this coalition, and other similar groups, to develop a unified account of why global enforcement of private intellectual property rights was so important.

Unquestionably the key move made by these lobbies was to align their diagnosis of piracy and theft with the rules of global trade. Tapping into a neo-liberal zeitgeist, these private interest groups found their rationale for the global protection of their intellectual property. As Peter Drahos writes, "the belief that the *absence* of intellectual property protection" was "an impediment to free trade" was the most "important rhetorical victories" of these lobbies[6] (italics added). This argument led multinational corporations, along with their state trade representatives, to formulate the regulation they needed, The Agreement on Trade-Related Aspects of Intellectual Property Rights (TRIPS).

Established in 1994, the TRIPS Agreement was a founding element of the World Trade Organization (WTO), itself a defining figurehead of 1990s processes of economic globalization. The agreement defined a single scheme of regulation that covered patents, copyright, trademarks, geographical indications, industrial design, and integrated circuit layout design. We engage with these forms of property everyday as painting, literature, music, machines, software, genetic material, seeds, brand names, logos, the name of one's region, and so on. In other words, these cover the full gamut of the work and play of the mind that we as a species create.

Information Privatization

The Agreement

In the TRIPS Agreement we find the ideational and institutional markers of Information Privatization as a propertyscape of the work and play of the mind. The opening statement of the agreement "recognizes" that "intellectual property rights are private rights."[7] In this statement there is a definitiveness that resonates with the "end of history" thesis proselytized by neo-liberals in the 1990s. By merely recognizing the private nature of these rights, the defining act of *becoming property* is taken as a given, a supposedly natural connection between *real* property and material goods with *immaterial* property and the work and play of the mind. As the Motion Picture Association of America asserts, protecting intellectual property rights is "no different from the importance of protecting any other property rights such as those in manufactured products, homes and buildings."[8] This assertion situates the agreement within a particular property ontology. Here we will pause to understand the ontological ordering principle of Information Privatization as a propertyscape of the work and play of the mind.

This reading of property has a conceptual pedigree found in the classical liberal ontology of private property. The mixing of one's labor anchors the foundational claim to ownership. *Becoming property*, making that property exclusive and thereby rivalrous, is at the moral core of related labor theory of value. Simultaneously *becoming property* is central to the articulation of human action: the free will of the producer, as both economic and social agent in this ontological system. In the "recognizes" claim, a transposition of this ontology occurs, from the fruit of one's labor, the production of material goods, to the fruit of one's mind or the production of immaterial goods. I want to stay focused on the nature of Information Privatization as a propertyscape with its own internal logic, as a placeholder for the analysis that will occur in subsequent chapters. However, it must also be noted that this supposedly "natural" *becoming property*, a move to define the right to the work and play of the mind as a *rivalrous* economic object, is fundamentally at odds with non-rivalrous interpretations of the work and play of the mind.

The social purpose of this private right becomes crystallized in Article 7, which defines the Objectives of TRIPS. The agreement asserts that enforcement:

> Should contribute to the promotion of technological innovation and to the transfer and dissemination of technology, to the mutual advantage of producers and users of technological knowledge in a manner conducive to social and economic welfare, and to a balance of rights and obligations.[9]

By extension, the ontology of private property is the basis of a set of normative presuppositions about the nature of social and economic development. Here we see a certain kind of anthropological assumption about human motivation. As the Business Software Alliance, a powerful intellectual property lobby group, argued, private property "inspires creativity."[10] The assumption is a belief that *becoming property*, in this case becoming *rivalrous property*, incentivizes innovation and stimulates processes for the transfer of knowledge. The *rivalrousness* of private intellectual property becomes analogous to Adam Smith's "invisible hand" of the market where individuals act to serve their own self-interest, but inadvertently generate a social logic. In this way, immediate private motivations, to protect *my* original intellectual property by granting me an exclusive right, are seen to produce social benefit through the motivations of the market. With TRIPS the work and play of the mind become compartmentalized as trade objects within a global marketplace. The defense of these trade objects becomes integral to normative defense of the free market itself.

The TRIPS Agreement was not just a theory of intellectual property; it was, and is, a global regulatory framework. Defining a particular institutional topology, the agreement also provides a kind of "constitution," if you will. The agreement defines the *relationship* between members: "each member shall accord to the nationals of other members treatment no less favorable than it accords to its own nations with regard to the protection of intellectual property."[11] It defines the *character* of rights holders, who can be "federations and associations having legal standing to assert such rights."[12] Unlike many other global legal frameworks, the agreement has real enforcement teeth. On a global level this enforcement comes in the form of the WTO dispute settlement procedures and the Council for TRIPS; on a national level it demands aligning regulation be embedded within national rules of intellectual property.[13] Finally it legitimizes and creates the space for the seizure of intellectual property, as per Article 61: "remedies available shall also include the seizure, forfeiture and destruction of infringed goods and of any materials and implements the predominant use of which has been in the commission of the offense."[14] Thus not only does TRIPS legitimize the seizure of property across borders; the agreement allows for the confiscation of the means of production of intellectual property.

In total, this institutional topology produces both norms and enforceable rules to an extent never seen before in a property regime within the international system. As Christopher May writes: "for the first time a multilateral trade agreement has required, not merely changes in the manner in which imports and exports are regulated at national borders, but has also required significant undertakings in regard to national legislation for non-internationally traded products."[15]

The Maximalist Agenda

The TRIPS Agreement was presented as setting no more than minimum standards for the global protection of the production and ownership of the work and play of the mind as a private right. For some, these standards immediately proved too harsh and inflexible. For others, they seemed too soft and flexible. The latter argument came most often out of developed nations, as the principal exporters of private intellectual property; the former from developing nations, primarily importers of intellectual property.

A critical language of flexibilities emerged: one set of arguments focused on the timeframe within which countries had to adopt TRIPS minimum standards, another on a critique that rigid enforcement was not in fact conducive to economic and social welfare. Far from promoting technological innovation, evidence suggested that TRIPS was creating cycles of technological dependency for developing nations. As Keith Maskus and Jerome Reichman explain: "for poor countries to take advantage … they need to absorb implement and develop new technologies."[16] This is because for developing countries the technological innovation and knowledge base that is privileged is imported. This is what is called in the literature the problem of "latecomer development."[17] As a result of these global structural imbalances, key elements of TRIPS were contested. Or, at a minimum, the integration of TRIPS into domestic regulatory regimes of developing nations was stalled. As Carolyn Deere's detailed analysis of "the implementation game" highlights, countries did take advantage of the "safeguards, options, and ambiguities in TRIPS" with various levels of success.[18] The most prominent example has been in the area of public health, specifically around generic pharmaceuticals and perhaps most famously in the case of antiviral AIDS medications.[19]

Taking these points of contestation into account, nevertheless, I want to focus on those who believed that the TRIPS Agreement was not strong enough and too easy to get around and who, as a consequence, sought to extend and deepen what is known as the "maximalist" agenda of the work and play of the mind as a private right. As a historical marker, this is often referred to as the "TRIPS plus" era. It is here we see the embedding, diffusion, and "order" characteristic of the expanding propertyscape of Information Privatization.

Armed with the normativity of "free trade," the legal teeth of TRIPS private sector watchdogs became increasingly important in the intensification of the privatization agenda. For example, the IIPA was, and remains, heavily involved in reporting violations to national governments and international regulatory bodies.[20] The violation reports that the IIPA compiles were very important data sets used in public policy and by advocates of a maximalist interpretation of private intellectual property rights alike, thus providing their own ideational knowledge base within the intellectual property discourse.

Not only has a web of enforcement steadily expanded and deepened as a consequence of these private initiatives, developed nations increasingly began to embed intellectual property clauses in other kinds of bilateral or multilateral agreements; what is known as "forum shifting" or "forum shopping."[21] As the world's leading exporter of intellectual property, it comes as no surprise that the United States has been the most aggressive in this kind of action. When TRIPS did not provide the protection needed, the Office of the United States Trade Representative (USTR) pushed forward with "vigorous campaigns" of bilateral and multilateral free-trade agreements.[22] And the United States was, and is, not alone in these kinds of actions; we see, for example, the European Union and Japan acting in similar kinds of ways.

The TRIPS Agreement also sets in motion a more general framing device informing understandings of global "development." The development agenda intersects with issues of the ownership of the work and play of the mind around questions of indigenous knowledge, the processes of technology transfer, and the abuse of patent monopolies. These manifest themselves as questions of access, participation, economic development, and human rights.[23] A prime case illustrating the kinds of dilemma that TRIPS creates is to be found in WIPO practices.

TRIPS produced a "strategic dilemma" for WIPO.[24] The dilemma arises because WIPO is the largest provider of technical and legal assistance for nations attempting to align their national standards with global standards. However, the structural parameters set by the TRIPS Agreement enforce a one-size-fits-all approach to the production and ownership of the work and play of the mind. Thus, the assistance that WIPO provides must be directed, in some ways, toward the eventual assimilation of national regimes into the TRIPS logic. As such the "relationship between WIPO and the WTO has taken the form of merely a de facto division of labor."[25] Since 1996, there has been a formal agreement between the two to align their agendas. WTO does the enforcement; WIPO the "socialization and norm building."[26] In effect WIPO becomes an active player in extending the private logic of TRIPS. Those working in and with WIPO are conscious of this tension: "there are dangers in WIPO's technical assistance activities over-emphasizing the benefits of intellectual property over the costs and the need to use TRIPS flexibilities."[27]

These kinds of tensions spread throughout the development agenda. For example, the United Nations Conference on Trade and Development issues regular "Creative Economy Reports" that consistently argue for the need for flexibilities. However, it still operates within the realities of the dominant paradigm by arguing that developing nations can harness "the socio-economic potential of the creative economy for development gains" by seeking to "optimize the trade potential of their creative products in both domestic and international markets."[28] The World Health Organization tries to find ways to minimize the negative effects of the TRIPS regime, but again does not contest the overall logic of the propertyscape TRIPS represents.

Outside of the development agenda other global bodies are also explicitly helping to extend the enforcement the "maximalist" agenda. For example, the International Medical Products Anti-Counterfeiting Taskforce (IMPACT), The World Customs Organization,[29] and Interpol all become policing mechanisms enforcing "global minimum standards."[30] These enforcement and regulation measures, as Ruth Kediri argues, have "the effect of calcifying the pervasive ideology of maximalist property rights on a global scale."[31] This steady trajectory of embedding and diffusing "order" in rules and norms of global institutions and actors continues today. As Drahos wrote in the midst of first wave of these developments, "there appears to be no end in sight to the use being made of this global intellectual property ratchet."[32]

The point here is not to argue that the embedding and diffusing of "order" happened without moments of contestation. Nor am I trying to deny that there were not some moments of effective resistance to the encroachment of the propertyscape of Information Privatization. My aim is to define Information Privatization as a *living movement*. TRIPS was the foundational move, providing the genesis of both the ideational and institutional aspects of the propertyscape. Nevertheless, by highlighting the spread of this logic of "order" throughout a web of global institutions, practices, and norms, I want to reveal a more general political agenda based in a particular reading of the nature and purpose of the social activity underwriting the work and play of the mind, demanding regulation, enforcement, and rule setting. While the ontological foundation remains steely clear, the institutional form is more fluid and less singularly expressed, but nonetheless implicitly coordinated.

The Propertyscape of Information Privatization as an Ideal Type

Now, to summarize the propertyscape of Information Privatization as an ideal type. The ontological ordering principle of the propertyscape of Information Privatization is found in private property and its logic of rivalrousness. This understanding of the work and play of the mind is grounded in a naturalization of the connection between material and immaterial property. *Becoming property*, in this case becoming rivalrous private property, is associated with a fundamental act of human autonomy. The moral utility of this act is tied to the ability to determine one's economic destiny based on the fruits of one's labor.

Defining the work and play of the mind as *rivalrous* is integral to the normative presuppositions of this propertyscape, not just at the level of individuals, but as an anthropological assumption about human motivation in general. The social purpose of private property is found in the belief that rivalrousness motivates action: to create, to build, and to innovate. Moreover, a related normativity of making private property is to protect the work and play of the mind of an "inventor" by means of a monopoly.

The ontological ordering principle and normative presuppositions described here are not new to the debates on intellectual property rights. Nevertheless, these debates had previously predominantly operated within state-based regulatory orders. The regulation of the work and play of the mind, through the right to property represented, as May argues, is "an explicit bargain" between the "creator" and the "nation-state," "balancing ownership and disclosure allowing both for individual reward and social use."[33] These were, at least in theory or ideological justification, democratically vetted and by accountable state actors and articulated in specific cultural interpretations of the social role of knowledge within the state. What TRIPS and the ensuing regulatory meshwork represent are global forums in which these bargains take place. This is a major shift from the nation-state-based regulation of domains of knowledge production. A global regulatory framework has been established that is further removed from the lands of supposed democratic accountability that had been originally associated with the property bargain.

In a wider view, I am positioning the propertyscape of Information Privatization as an expression of the Neo-Liberal project, with its ideal of equilibrium. A belief that the aspirations and rationality of this political project played itself out, naturally, without the heavy hand of regulatory intervention. In this way, the propertyscape represents a more general vision of a kind of globalism. Nevertheless, fundamentally, at the property level, there is nothing inherently rivalrous or exclusive about the work and play of the mind. Moreover, in making this supposedly natural connection between material and immaterial property, as a private right, a long history can be misrecognized. Within the framework of the modern nation-state private property was not a natural condition, but something established and maintained through a regulatory agenda. As I have tried to exemplify here, rivalrousness is imposed and necessarily regulated through private property.

I now turn to the Great Firewall to flesh out some of the implications of the propertyscape of Information Privatization. The Great Firewall is by no means the archetypal place to explore the ways in which the propertyscape of Information Privatization shapes the world we live in. In fact, each of the following chapters in this book documents the effects of, and searches for alternatives to, the march of private property into the production and ownership of the work and play of the mind. The prima facie tangential relationship of this living example serves a purpose, to begin with an example that draws attention to the ways in which the production and ownership of the work and play of the mind is at times an unseen force shaping global politics, not just at a surface level, but fundamentally guiding actors, actions, and meanings.

The Great Firewall of Information

In late 1970s the PRC embarked on a project of modernization. At the heart of this project was *economic* modernization. Economic modernization held two major challenges: to transform a predominantly rural economy into an industrial economy and to become a fully participating member of the global economy. These challenges shared a meta-challenge: to reconcile the entrance of the "market" into a communist society without destabilizing political order. Modernization had to be on terms that spoke to the principles of an evolving legacy of Marxism-Leninism, a distinctive Communism with Chinese characteristics. Thus, the history of *modernization* is defined by a certain kind of balancing act between *opening* and *control.*

As a logical extension of the process of industrial economic modernization, China recognized early that the Internet was critical to a "third wave" of post-industrial modernization. As such the Chinese Government spent an enormous amount of money to commit to building the infrastructural foundations of the Internet in China.[34] A 2008 White Paper records that from 1997 to 2009, 4.3 trillion Yuan was invested.[35] In early 2001 the government committed to spending another "US$14.5 billion on building up this Internet infrastructure in the autonomous regions, including Tibet, Xinjiang, and Inner Mongolia."[36] Not only did the PRC invest heavily in infrastructure, the Internet became a frame of reference for broader state agendas. For example, 1999 was called the "year of online government" and 2000 "the year of online enterprise."[37]

During this first wave, Internet usage grew exponentially. The World Bank reported from 1997 through the early 2000s usage went from 0% to 22.5% of the population.[38] The China Internet Network Information Center claims that by 2012 the number of "net citizens" reached around 560 million.[39] In 2016, the number of Chinese Internet users was estimated at around 721 million people.[40] As an important counterfactual, from 2013 to today (2016) Internet access growth in China has slowed to around 5% annually.[41] Furthermore, while the number of Internet users in China on face value looks large, this is in large part because of the size of China; there should also be recognition of the lack of access, with a population of over 1.4 billion people only 50% had Internet access in 2016.[42]

That being said, the Internet now holds a central place in contemporary Chinese society. Patterns of growth parallel the rise of a young relatively affluent middle class, the so-called little emperors/empresses or new radicals, a generation that has lived its entire life in a mixed economy, with a degree of social freedom not previously afforded, where private property is permissible and a commodity culture is prevalent. This is a generation that, in their lifeworld experience, mediates the tension of *opening* and *control*: opening in the desire for western brands, control in a sense of pride in national identity, and the hope for an economically strong China.[43]

Online life in China is primarily on domestically produced platforms. There are Chinese equivalents of all major western-based social media platforms. For example, the search engine Baidu—a Google equivalent; video hosting platforms like Youkan or Tudor—the equivalents of YouTube; photo-sharing platform Bababian—like Flickr; Nice—similar to Instagram; the social networking site Renren—the Facebook equivalent; the microblogging platforms like Sina Weibo or WeChat—a Twitter/Facebook hybrids. There is even now a "social" venture capital platform for Internet startups in China—"Chuangyepu"—similar to Kickstarter.

Internet-based businesses have also become an important factor in Chinese economic development. Three of US-based Fortune Magazine's 2016 "unicorn list" (private technology companies valued at $1 billion or more) are Chinese. Bar one Indian company, these are the only non-US companies in the top 15. As a gauge of the sheer economic weight of these businesses, in global perspective, one can turn to the Shanghai-based Alibaba Holdings Group. Alibaba is a Chinese e-commerce platform connecting producers to consumers. In its 2014 initial public offering (IPO) the total amount raised was around $25 billion dollars.[44] This was the largest IPO in *global* history.

Within a broader history of *modernization* one could say that the "third wave" of post-industrial economic development in China has been by enlarge a success. There has been strong economic growth associated with the rise of an Internet-based industry, running primarily on market principles, integrated within a global economy, without the ultimate destabilization of the political system of China. Moreover, China has met a political target: via participation on the Internet, the lives of Chinese people in a shared social experience with a global experience of *modernity*. The key regulatory mechanism of this balancing act of *opening* and *control* is found in the Great Firewall.

Three Perspectives of the Great Firewall

The Great Firewall is not a single object. It is the name for multifaceted regulatory mechanisms aimed at controlling what information comes into China, what information is produced in China, and how content is distributed on the Internet in China.[45] It represents a move to *protect* Chinese Internet users against a global flow of information objects and interests.

There are a number of government departments dealing with "public security" that monitor the Internet in China. The PRC's "Provisions on the Administration of Internet News and Information Services" clearly states the parameters of the regulation of the Internet in China: at an organizational level who is approved to use the Internet to transmit content and the nature of that content. Explaining their purpose, the State Council Information Office and Ministry of Information states:

> Internet news and information services entities shall abide by the Constitution, laws, and regulations, by persisting in providing service for the people and serving socialism, and guiding public opinion to protect the interests of the nation and the public … the state shall encourage Internet news and information services entities to transmit healthy and civilized news and information beneficial to improve the qualities of the people, to spur economic growth, and to promote social development.[46]

The Internet Society of China, a leading professional association for the Chinese Internet industry also calls for its use to be in accordance with the "fundamental interests of the nation." There must be "patriotic observance of law, equitableness, trustworthiness and honesty." Internet businesses should not produce, post, or disseminate "pernicious information that may jeopardize state security and disrupt social stability." The Internet must be "consistent with and carry forward the rich cultural tradition of the Chinese nation and the moral code of socialist spiritual civilization."[47]

There are three perspectives through which I will frame interpretations of the Great Firewall, as a model of regulatory control for the Internet. Within the broader context of the project of modernization in China, each reading of the nature of control reveals a complicated and coded terrain on the broader implications of the social utility of the Internet and its relationship to broader processes of globalization. These perspectives serve to lay the groundwork for situating the shape-shifting ways in which the regulation of the work and play of the mind creeps into political use of these interpretations.

The first perspective I will call the *not free* argument. This argument emphasizes the degrees to which the Internet in China should be a "concern" for "anyone who believes in participatory democracy."[48] The core thesis here is that "threats to social stability," as defined by the Chinese government, provide an unbounded charter to control speech and communicative practices within the digital domain.[49] This argument simultaneously rests on an a priori assumption about the capacity of the Internet as a unique kind of communication platform, with a supposedly inherent democratic potential. Thus, the Great Firewall is antithetical not only to the principles of liberal democracy, but also to an ideal based on the supposed inherent qualities of the Internet.

At a symbolic level this argument plays out by framing the communicative practices of the Chinese Internet as an "ideology" or "information" war between the Chinese government and its people, contextualized within a global informational sphere.[50] This thesis supposes the cunning of the Chinese state, disseminating information on the Internet to dupe citizens, to "neutralize critical online opinion," moderating debate through Internet "police forces." In a representative example, Zhang Fenglin, a deputy director from an "Information Department" of a Chinese province, said "in the information age and the internet age, the most important and critical mission in front of us is how to seize the initiative on internet opinion and how to seize the high point of internet opinion."[51] Proponents of the *not free* augment emphasize the "steady crackdown" of communication in China in which "authorities have taken a series of harsh steps to control and suppress political and religious speech on the Internet, including the jailing of Internet critics and bloggers for peaceful political expression."[52]

In the global sphere the *cause célèbre* has been the activism of Chinese artist Ai Weiwei. The work that first brought Weiwei to attention was the Sichuan Earthquake Names Project, a response to the 2008 earthquake. Domestic unrest arose in reaction to the response of Chinese Authorities to the earthquake, in particular, the failure to record and recognize the actual number of deaths and to seek accountability for the number of people, predominately children, who died in poorly constructed public buildings. Along with the parents who lost children and a team of volunteers, Weiwei documented the names of those who died. He used the

Chinese-based social media platforms, in particular Sina Weibo, and international social media platforms, in particular Twitter, to document the results. "I'm doing this because every incident in China, whether it's an earthquake or a mine collapse or a fire, they never release the names," he argued.[53] The response of the Chinese government was swift and heavy-handed. They began a regime of intimidation designed to silence the artist, which Weiwei documented and shared on the Internet. In the end Weiwei was imprisoned for unrelated, and unsubstantiated, reasons, most prominently a tax evasion claim. When he was released from prison he installed a webcam in his house to keep a public watch on his personal activities 24 hours a day. This played on live on a blog weiweicam.com. Again, it did not take long for the Chinese authorities to censor the site and its content.

Outside of China, Weiwei is seen as "one of China's boldest political activists," an "evangelical believer in transparency."[54] In his own words, "openness and transparency are the only way to limit these dark powers."[55] Speaking directly of the Great Firewall he argues "the government computer has one button—delete."[56] Nevertheless he sees the Internet as capable of producing a radical change in Chinese society. These are technologies that "put the government on trial." The Internet as "a miracle gift" for "human struggle."[57]

In sum the *not free* argument predominantly presents the Internet in China, in its totality, as a site of repression and control, with the Great Firewall as the meta-narrative for China's Internet experience. Such an augment is imbricated in a more expansive claim about *freedom* in Chinese society. It implicitly presents a historical legacy of a communist society that seeks to enslave the minds of its people. Again, the argument critically rests on a certain set of assumptions about the inherent qualities of the Internet as a communication platform, as if there were a natural yearning for the kind of freedom that the Internet, as a communication system, inherently produces.

A second perspective on the Great Firewall focuses on *acts of rebellion*. This perspective presents Chinese online public spheres on their own terms: as information ecologies, more complex than simple spaces of oppression. Using examples of communicative practices, this perspective is unified by an attempt to illuminate a constant and consistent counter narrative to the states' attempt at control.

The most often cited examples are the language games between Chinese netizens and censors. These games are played out via the use of differing phraseology or memes, revealing lifeworlds shaped by attempts to circumvent the shifting rules of censorship. For example, people use phrases like "river crab" to talk about the Chinese government's attempt at "harmonization," which itself is the code word of censorship.[58] "50 cent party" refers to people who are "allegedly and secretly" paid 50 cents RMB "per post/comment that praises, supports, or defends from criticism/attack the country, government, or Communist Party." Or "netizens who are very nationalistic are often accused of being part of the '50 cent party,' spreading propaganda or 'guiding' public opinion."[59] Sometimes people use similarly pronounced words, homonyms, or other replacement terminology with implicit cultural associations: "Great Cultural Revolution" with "Mosquito Flower Hiccup Mandate"; the "Communist Party" with "Provide Shovel Party."[60]

These communicative lifeworlds speak to an Internet in China, that even in formal political discourse, is full of play, humor, and satire, thus complicating the *not free* control narrative. These kinds of critical communicative lifeworlds are also not necessarily in overt political discourse but in other cultural spaces, for example, discussing literature or film in the culture industries.[61] While nonetheless influenced in differing ways by censorship, these practices reveal the general ubiquity of such spaces of contestation and the nature of these contestations as a particular experience of the Internet China.

Within this perspective there is a strong narrative stressing the futility of attempts at control. This thesis is strongest when looking at the "cat and mouse games" played in the blocking of access to censored platforms from outside of China, for example, Facebook or YouTube. We see a lot of analysis on the use, for example, of Virtual Private Networks (VPN) or of the Tor Network to access content or news from outside of China and the resulting attempts at the Chinese government to block access.[62] Again the emphasis is on the futility of the actions of the Chinese state, too large and bureaucratic to keep to with the technical skills and everyday tools available to a technically savvy youth.

The *acts of rebellion* perspective, nonetheless, does share with the *not free* perspective an understanding of inherent communicative potentials of the Internet, as an information production and distribution system. This connection is also found in the language of Weiwei. "Since we got the net and could write blogs—and now micro blogs—people have started to share ideas, and a new sense of freedom has arisen."[63] "It is a unique, treasured moment. People have started to feel the breeze. The Internet is a wild land with its own games, languages, and gestures through which we are starting to share common feelings."[64] Weiwei argues that even the restricted Chinese versions of the Internet "still offer a certain kind of freedom this nation has never seen before."[65]

While the Great Firewall serves the context-shaping of communicative practices, the *acts of rebellion* perspective does not present it as the singular meta-narrative of Chinese Internet experience. The Great Firewall is used as an insight into the futility of control, to reveal an already existing freedom in online life in China. While taking critical position on state-based authoritarianism, rebellion is seen as part of the everyday life of a "Chinese netizen."[66] A lot of the research is also keen to point out that there has been activism and circumvention of censorship since the first entry of the Internet in China. While the inherent communicative potential of Internet may be seen to be an "import," the *act* of rebellion is not foreign to Chinese people and Chinese culture, and so there is a distinct continuity in the history of Chinese Internet activism.

A third perspective centers on a *culture-based* perspective. This perspective investigates the Internet in China primarily as a space where everyday life happens. Rather than being viewed as a draconian sphere of controlled communication, the Internet in China is presented as a "vibrant cultural realm."[67] It is a cultural realm that is uniquely Chinese, with distinct "user habits"[68] and "family and social pressures"[69] informing its use. Moreover, we see research revealing an everyday life that also includes the politics of social causes: saving trees in a park, or the lives of stray dogs, which have led to actions by the government at local and national levels, evidencing some degrees of accountability in the political system of China.[70] Within this perspective there is a foundational argument for the high rate of adoption of the Internet that is not due to the "import" of the communicative practices inherent to the Internet, or the essential lure or a western modernity, rather drawing from communicative practices that have long historical foundations in Chinese culture.

The *culture-based* perspective represents a fundamental turning of the table, not associating the kind of control represented by the Great Firewall with the negative connotations with which it is often associated. Rather, within a spectrum of nationalism and cultural empowerment, we find neutral or even positive views of the role the Great Firewall plays. Some Chinese people, particularly young people and so-called digital natives, see censorship as a "necessary brake on change."[71] Others use social media platforms to promote the "party" and its actions. In part these positive associations with the Great Firewall are motivated by a weariness of the west trying to exploit or suppress the rise of China.

Within this perspective there is a unifying attempt to grapple with the historical flux of a China searching for "indigenous modes of modernity."[72] This grounds a counter argument to the default logic of a submissive East wanting to break out of its *un-freedom*. Rather, through the construction of the idea of a "Chinese Exceptionalism,"[73] the attempt at "control" represented by the Great Firewall is assessed within deeper historical currents, contemporaneous political forces, and strategic understandings of political, social, and economic development. For example, there is an idea of an "authoritarian informationalism" which "combines elements of capitalism, authoritarianism, and Confucianism."[74]

In sum, the *culture-based* perspective breaks the default "good versus evil" reading the Internet in China.[75] The *culture-based* argument is unified by an attempt to paint a picture of the Internet in China as a space unique in its social life, practices, and form. It demands an understanding of the Internet in China on its own terms: "network service with Chinese features," calling for the need for "Chinese social-network (fundi) theory."[76] It also allows for the Great Firewall to be seen as either a necessary regulatory move or even in a positive light.

On face value, the mapping of these perspectives brings out a simple point. Perspectives on the nature of *control* are motivated by underlying political, social, and economic presuppositions. But in the specific richness of the research that defines these perspectives we get a complex picture of the social utility of mechanisms and interpretations of *control*.

This complex picture also serves as the context for understanding a doublespeak implicit in the global regulation of the right to the work and play of the mind and the unsatisfying alternatives we are left with when understanding the place of the Internet in the construction of the rules and principles of the global under the logic of Information Privatization.

The Doublespeak of Neo-Liberal Equilibrium

In 2007, the then head of global public policy for Google, Andrew McLaughlin, proclaimed: "it is fair to say that *censorship* constitutes the single greatest trade barrier we currently face."[77] Eric Schmidt, Google's CEO, states: "the Internet has created this remarkable set of free markets and open competition. We need to keep it free and open—if it goes the other way then we've got a serious problem."[78] How is *censorship* a *trade* barrier? In what way has the Internet created *free markets* and *open competition?* In their interrelation, these questions bring clarity to a doublespeak permeating the discourse of neo-liberal equilibrium, connecting the Great Firewall and its responses to the propertyscape of Information Privatization as one of the meta-narratives of globalization.

This doublespeak begins in a set of assumptions, intimately connected, and mutually generative. These assumptions share a relational juxtaposition: *equilibrium* versus *control*; the equilibrium of markets versus the control of a state in economic affairs; the equilibrium of a liberal democratic model of communication and action versus state control of communication and action. Intensifying these assumptions is the claim about a historically specific post-industrial equilibrium drawn from a reading of the inherent democratic nature of the Internet, as a platform for information production and distribution. The juxtaposition takes the form of an equilibrium manifest in the democratic communication potential of Internet, versus a regulatory, or authority-based, network model of communication.

Adding another dimension to these assumptions is a related reductionism: *free trade* with *free speech*. In speaking directly to the PRC, the United States has a long history of this kind of reductionism. James Baker in 1991:

> No nation has yet discovered a way to import the world's goods and services while stopping foreign ideas at the border. It is in our interests that the next generation in China be engaged by the Information Age, not isolated from global trends shaping the future.[79]

Madeline Albright:

> There is no question that with the spread of the Internet and globalization, the spread of information, there is no way to keep that out of China. If China is going to compete economically, the two go together. They need to have the kind of technology in order to be able to be part of the international economic system, and it can't be stopped.[80]

Hillary Clinton:

> New technologies do not take sides in the struggle for freedom and progress, but the United States does. We stand for a single Internet where all of humanity has equal access to knowledge and ideas. And we recognize that the world's information infrastructure will become what we, and others make of it. Now, this challenge may be new, but our responsibility to help ensure the free exchange of ideas goes back to the birth of our republic.[81]

The conflation of *action* in the marketplace with *action* in speech is possible because the work and play of the mind can be free speech itself. In this way, it is possible for equilibrium *of markets* to shape-shift into understanding equilibrium *of free speech.* When we return to the statement of how *censorship* is a *trade barrier*, with the framing of the Internet as a space inherently associated with *free markets*, *open competition*, and the enactment of *global liberal democracy*, we gain a clearer picture of the nuances of the doublespeak and what it implicitly and explicitly obscures.

It would be uncontroversial to say the Great Firewall has been economically positive for China. By one measure it is estimated that "China's tech sector raised $7.2 billion in private funding deals" in 2015.[82] This has provided a space for Chinese Internet-based technology industries to grow without the competition of western companies. This protection in large part is a "trade barrier." In the words of a founder of Innovation Works, a Beijing-based innovation incubator, "if I were an entrepreneur

... I would still feel mostly grateful for government censorship because it keeps international giants from entering the market."[83] In the West this effect has not gone unnoticed: "in a country well-known for copying and mass-producing the ideas and products of other countries, from automobiles to movies, a new economic tool has been invented: an insidious, uniquely twenty-first century form of protectionism."[84]

The systems logic and expertise of creating and maintaining the Great Firewall has also become an exportable product for the China. Often this is cloaked in the disguise of aid packages to other nations. For example, exporting expertise and technical capacity for building communication infrastructures to developing countries, as China provided for Ethiopia.[85]

Thus, *control* has been a double positive. It has nurtured the development of a strong Internet-based economy within China. China has not only kept up with post-industrial development; it has become an information economy powerhouse. It also ideologically strengthened the role of the party as to "maintain a socialist spiritual society." The legitimacy of state control is based in the rise of such an industry and positioning China on par globally with other nations in the development of Internet tools and platforms.

In this context, at the surface level the doublespeak of *free markets* and *free speech* permeating the broader ideal of neo-liberal equilibrium can obscure real economic interests. China represents the largest single communications market in the world. The Internet in China presents a cascading set of value propositions for western Internet-based communication and information services: new users to add to their user base, building the market value of their platforms under the logic of shareholder benefit; enlarging databases of social activity to sell as advertising companies; and the ability to target material and information commodities to users of these platforms based on this data. Thus, the "free exchange of ideas" obscures the symbiotic connection with the free capture and exchange of information commodities.

These economic interests force western companies to tread a fine line. They need the normative argument of free markets as an overarching logic to gain entry to the market, while determining what level they can get into the market by abiding by its system of control. Western companies have a history of profiting from the system of control. In fact, Cisco played a large role in creating much of the Great Firewall's key infrastructure. US corporations have also worked with the Chinese state operating under the rubric of "threats to public security." Yahoo "handed over user information on four Chinese government critics to the Chinese authorities resulting in their trial and conviction."[86] Google, as a condition of entering the market with Google.cn, blocks certain search results too.[87] Facebook "has quietly developed software to suppress posts from appearing in people's news feeds in specific geographic areas, according to three current and former Facebook employees, who asked for anonymity because the tool is confidential. The feature was created to help Facebook get into China, a market where the social network has been blocked, these people said. Mr. Zuckerberg has supported and defended the effort, the people added."[88]

At a deeper level the ideal of neo-liberal equilibrium, expressed in the principles of *free markets*, *open competition*, and the enactment of *global liberal democracy*, can obscure a fundamental contradiction in the very notion of equilibrium itself. This is where the global regulation of the work and play of the mind productively re-enters the conversation. Tim Wu writes: when "internet *content* can be reached from anywhere," it makes "nearly everyone on the internet a potential importer or exporter of services (and sometimes goods). Hence, almost by accident, the WTO put itself in an oversight position for most of the national laws and practices that regulate the Internet," which necessarily also relates to the content flowing and produced on the Internet.[89] What is more, the requirements of both the WTO and TRIPS call for an equal playing field in the global telecommunications industry based on "non-discriminatory processes," again relative to the intricately embedded nature of platform, services, and content, as layered intellectual property production and dissemination goods. In the view of the global regulation of communication space via the mechanisms of intellectual property, China's *censorship* becomes a violation of its *free-trade obligations*, as it blocks access to the Chinese information market and to the flows of informational goods from non-Chinese content distributors. As I have attempted to show, this global regulatory regime, and the demand for it that is at the motivational core of the propertyscape of Information Privatization, was not a natural given but something that necessarily structured and enforced by global regulation. Thus, in the creation of the global information market there was nothing *natural* about its regulatory framework, nor its principle of order. For this reason, the contestation is essentially over jurisdictional geographies. What we have here is not a binary of "equilibrium" versus "control" but "control" versus "control."

The point is not to argue that this doublespeak is a "secret" language, but rather this doublespeak is part and parcel of the shape-shifting neo-liberal project and its contradictory nature. On one hand, we are presented with a case for the natural equilibrium in markets and communication. But on the other hand, we witness the creation of global regulatory power necessary to enforce the right to private property.

Two Unsatisfying Alternatives

When we think about the kinds of responses to the Great Firewall, as described earlier, and interface them with the doublespeak of neo-liberal equilibrium, we are left with two unsatisfying alternatives. The first operates in the connection between the "not free" argument and the propertyscape of Information Privatization. To restate the key thesis of the "not free" augment, the Internet in China taken as a whole is a site of repression and control. The Great Firewall serves as the meta-narrative of understanding China's Internet experience. But without a *conceptual firewall* between the notions of free speech and free trade, how do we extract the *not free* thesis from simply being something that is not good for western economic interests? How are notions of free speech not simply reduced to a free market principle of traded epistemic and discursive objects? Are institutions like the WTO going to be the arbiter of these interests? How do we untangle a defense of free speech, from the defense of information-based corporations like Google? In sum, what is the language of critique that does not mean we also must concur that the Internet is necessarily also a production and delivery mechanism for the work and play of the mind as private property?

The second alternative operates in a thin connection between *every day acts of rebellion* and a thick connection between the *culture-based Internet* argument and the propertyscape of Information Privatization. Within broader historical context, China is searching for an indigenous modernity, a capitalism with Chinese characteristics, a Chinese exceptionalism. But what is its place in the global magma? Economically, what right does China have to protect its domestic market from foreign multinational *information* corporations? How do we account for jurisdictional sovereignty of China and its right to control the integration of the global into the domestic? Can we recognize an Internet with its own rules of action, that might in one interpretation seem authoritarian but in another as culturally specific? At the same time, might we fall into the trap of defending state-based authoritarianism, with the culture-based thesis as a cover? Recent reports indicate that China is about to roll out a comprehensive online-based "social credit system," where access to public services is based on evaluative criteria connected to "a history of monitoring and control of people's private lives."[90]

In a final destabilizing element to the "control" narrative, it would be remiss not to mention the debates over the privacy of data collected by western governments and corporations. In the wake of WikiLeaks and the whistleblowing of Edward Snowden, it has become common knowledge that the public sector monitors large parts of our everyday lives and these practices are legitimated under the rubric of national security. At the same time, the private sector monitors large parts of our everyday lives under the supposed lemmatization of the logic of the information economy, to deliver personalized services.

The larger take away in this living example of the regulation and response to the Great Firewall is there is no natural equilibrium. There is no natural move to the free market and private property, and regimes like TRIPS are necessary for establishing *order*. In the case of the work and play of the mind, a global trade regime, including intellectual property agreements, has become the center of a regulatory discourse—a framework of control. The legitimization of this global regulatory framework operates under the normative umbrella of the *global*—the actions of supposedly a global shared authority, rather than a single nation-state, or select group of corporate lobbyists as was the case with the TRIPS Agreement. Simultaneously, we are offered a grammar where private property becomes the language of communicative freedom, as a symbiotic enforcement. But who is this *global* that legitimizes?

Whose Equilibrium?

I will close this chapter, and the chapters that follow, by starting to develop thinking about "propertyscapes" as models of economic distribution, social participation, and political representation. By asking the question of *whose equilibrium*, my aim is to start to overlay an evaluative rubric of the *who*, *what*, and *how*, with a view to analyzing this propertyscape as a nascent model of political community.

The *who* of this nascent model of political community is ascribed to a universal global subject. The scale of the *who* is demanded, at a historical level, by the inherently global nature of the work and play of the mind and the need to bring global order to this domain of social activity. Supposedly all producers of the work and play of the mind are equal subjects in the ideational and institutional scope of the propertyscape. There is no outside in this framing of global life; it is on a planetary scale.

The *what*—a rivalrous, exclusive, and private definition of the work and play of the mind—is taken as a given. This *what* extends a longer history of private property, irrespective of the differences raised by the immaterial aspects of knowledge, culture, and ideas. The ethics and morality of the right to private property are naturalized and universalized via an anthropological assumption about human motivation writ large. The historically specific aspect of the *what* is prescriptive, namely the opportunity, indeed the necessity, for the work and play of the mind to become an engine in the next wave of capitalist development, with *becoming private property* the necessary cornerstone of this development.

At a regulatory level, addressing the question of the *how*, what is powerfully revealing in the propertyscape is the necessity of global order for this domain of social activity. While the trajectory of privatization has been dominated by a neo-liberal vision of free trade, its institutional topology stands in direct contradiction with the anti-regulatory, anti-statist roots of this agenda. In this case, we find that what was initiated under the auspices of neo-liberalism necessarily spawns institutions that contradict its guiding principles as ideology and political practice. Contrary to appearances, the highly regulated nature of global rights to the work and play of the mind provides evidence of the emergence of a regulated global system of social production. Despite its pretense to anthropological universality, this global regime favors a narrow range of interests. In the final analysis, this movement is not about de-regulation and the market, but re-regulation, exclusion, and monopoly.

The question of *whose equilibrium* draws our attention to a process of globalization dominated by a corporate global ruling elite, in collusion with state actors even though their jurisdictional power is waning. The result is an inherent democratic deficit in the making, enforcement, and participatory feedback loops of the WTO/TRIPS framework. Only diffused avenues are available with which to contest this global regulatory framework. If we look at the WTO and global trade regulation as the cornerstone of this nascent model of political community, we get democracy for the few both in its making and its enforcement. There may be institutions that adjudicate disputes, but their meaning making power is determined by private interests, under the cover of global institutions, detached from systems of grounded accountability.

Notes

1. Kalantzis-Cope.
2. International Intellectual Property Alliance, "New Economic Study Shows U.S Copyright Industries Pass $278 Billion Mark and Account for over 3.5 Million U.S Jobs," (Washington D.C.: International Intellectual Property Alliance, 1996).
3. Ibid.
4. See: Peter Drahos, Braithwaite, John, *Information Feudalism: Who Owns the Knowledge Economy?* (New York: W. W. Norton & Company, 2003); Xuan Li, Correa, Carlos, ed. *Intellectual Property Enforcement: International Perspectives* (Cheltenham: Edward Elgar, 2009); Keith Maskus, *Intellectual Property Rights in the Global Economy* (Washington D.C.: Institute for International Economic, 2000); Christopher May, Sell, Susan, *Intellectual Property Rights: A Critical History*, ed. Renee Marlin-Bennett, Ipolitics: Global Challenges in the Information Age (London: Lynne Rienner Publishers, 2006).
5. Sell. p. 96.
6. Drahos. p. 36.

7. World Trade Organization, "Agreement on Trade Related Aspects of Intellectual Property Rights," World Trade Organization, http://www.wto.org/english/tratop_e/trips_e/t_agm0_e.htm.
8. http://www.mpaa.org/contentprotection.
9. World Trade Organization.
10. Business Software Alliance, "About Us," Business Software Alliance, http://www.bsa.org/about-bsa.
11. World Trade Organization. Article 3(1).
12. Ibid. Footnote to Article 42.
13. Ibid. Article 41 (5).
14. Ibid. Article 61.
15. Christopher May, *The World Intellectual Property Agenda: Resurgence and the Development Agenda* (New York: Routledge, 2007).
16. Keith Maskus, Reichman, Jerome, "The Concept of Public Goods in the Expanding Knowledge Economy," in *International Public Goods and Transfer of Technology under a Globalized Intellectual Property Regime*, ed. Keith Maskus, Reichman, Jerome (Cambridge: Cambridge University Press, 2005). p. 5.
17. Banji Oyelaran-Oyeyinka, Sampath, Padmashree, *Latecomer Development: Innovation and Knowledge for Economic Growth* (New York: Routledge, 2010).
18. Carolyn Deere, *The Implementation Game: The Trips Agreement and the Global Politics of Intellectual Property Reform in Developing Countries* (Oxford: Oxford University Press, 2009). p. 2.
19. For a detailed analysis of these 'flexibilities' see: Charles Collins-Chase, "The Case against Trips-Plus Protection in Developing Countries Facing Aids Epidemics," *University of Pennsylvania Journal of International Law* 29, no. 3 (2008).
20. International Intellectual Property Alliance, "About the International Intellectual Property Alliance," International Intellectual Property Alliance, http://www.iipa.com/aboutiipa.html.
21. For a detailed explanation of this strategy see: John Braithwaite, Drahos, Peter, *Global Business Regulation* (Cambridge: Cambridge University Press, 2000). Chapter 24.
22. Susan Sell, K., "Intellectual Property and the Doha Development Agenda "in *The WTO after Hong Kong: Progress in, and Prospects for, the Doha Development Agenda*, ed. Donna Lee, Wilkinson, Rorden, (London: Routledge, 2007). p. 57.

23. May. p. 30.
24. Sisule Musungu, Dutfield, Graham, "Multilateral Agreements and a Trips-Plus World: The World Intellectual Property Organisation (WIPO)," in *TRIPS Issue Papers*, ed. Geoff Tansey (Geneva: Quaker United Nations Office, 2003). p. 11.
25. May. p. 34.
26. Ibid. p. 34.
27. Musungu. p. 2.
28. Creative Economy Report. p. xxiii.
29. World Customs Organization, "Global Congress Combating Counterfeiting and Piracy: Outcomes and Recommendations," World Customs Organization, http://www.ccapcongress.net/Recommendations.htm.
30. INTERPOL, "Database on International Intellectual Property," INTERPOL, http://www.interpol.int/Public/FinancialCrime/IntellectualProperty/DIIP/Default.asp.
31. Ruth Okediji, "Public Welfare and the Role of the WTO: Reconsidering the Trips Agreement," *Emory International Law Review* 17, no. 2 (2003). p. 822.
32. Peter Drahos, "Bits and Bibs: Bilateralism in Intellectual Property," *The Journal of World Intellectual Property* 4 (2001). p. 800.
33. Christopher May, *The Global Political Economy of Intellectual Property Rights: The New Enclosures* (London: Routledge, 2010). P. 10.
34. Lokman Tsui, "An Inadequate Metaphor: The Great Firewall and Chinese Internet Censorship," *Global Dialogue* 9, no. 1 (2007). p. 61.
35. Information Office of the State Council of the People's Republic of China, "The Internet in China," Information Office of the State Council of the People's Republic of China, http://news.xinhuanet.com/english2010/china/2010-06/08/c_13339232.htm.
36. Randolph Kluver, "Us and Chinese Policy Expectations of the Internet," *China Information* 19 (2005). p. 303.
37. Christopher Hughes, R., "China and the Globalization of ICTS: Implications for International Relations," *New Media & Society* 4, no. 2 (2002).
38. The World Bank, "2010 World Development Indicators" (Washington D.C.: The World Bank, 2010).
39. China Internet Network Information Center, "Statistical Report on Internet Development in China.," China Internet Network Information

Center, http://www1.cnnic.cn/IDR/ReportDownloads/201302/P020130221391269963814.pdf.

40. Internet Live Stats, "Internet Users in China," www.internetlivestats.com, http://www.internetlivestats.com/internet-users/china/.
41. Ibid.
42. Zhan Zhang, Negro, Gianluigi, "Weibo in China: Understanding Its Development through Communication Analysis and Cultural Studies," *Communication, Politics & Culture* 46 (2013).
43. Ruby Murray, "China's Digital Natives Behind with the Great Firewall," thesaturdaypaper.com.au, https://www.thesaturdaypaper.com.au/2016/01/23/chinas-digital-natives-behind-with-the-great-firewall/14534676002803.
44. Liyan Chen, "Alibaba Claims Title for Largest Global IPO Ever with Extra Share Sales," Forbes, http://www.forbes.com/sites/ryanmac/2014/09/22/alibaba-claims-title-for-largest-global-ipo-ever-with-extra-share-sales/#e57f7bf7c26d.
45. Lena Zhang, "Behind the 'Great Firewall': Decoding China's Internet Media Policies from the Inside," *Convergence: The International Journal of Research into New Media Technologies* 12, no. 3 (2006). p. 279.
46. State Council Information Office, "Provisions on the Administration of Internet News and Information Services," State Council Information Office, http://www.china.org.cn/business/2010-01/21/content_19281869.htm.
47. Internet Society of China, "Public Pledge of Self-Regulation and Professional Ethics for China Internet Industry," Internet Society of China, http://www.isc.org.cn/20020417/ca102762.htm.
48. Open Democracy, "The Great Firewall of China," Open Democracy, http://www.opendemocracy.net/print/2524.
49. Hughes. p. 207.
50. George Chen, Dickinson, Steve, Schleshiner, Qiang, Xiao, Creemers, Rogier, Wertime, "China's Great Firewall Is Rising," Foreign Policy, http://foreignpolicy.com/2015/02/03/china-great-firewall-is-rising-censorship-internet/.
51. Jonathan Watts, "China's Secret Internet Police Target Critics with Web of Propaganda," The Guardian, http://www.theguardian.com/technology/2005/jun/14/newmedia.china#article_continue.
52. Human Rights Watch, "Race to the Bottom: Corporate Complicity in Chinese Internet Censorship," (New York City: Human Rights Watch, 2006). p. 3.

53. Malcolm Moore, "Ai Weiwei Starts New Openness Campaign," The Telegraph, http://www.telegraph.co.uk/news/worldnews/asia/china/8159401/Ai-Weiwei-starts-new-openness-campaign.html#.
54. Ibid.
55. Ai Weiwei, "China's Censorship Can Never Defeat the Internet," The Guardian, http://www.guardian.co.uk/commentisfree/libertycentral/2012/apr/16/china-censorship-internet-freedom.
56. Ibid.
57. "Ai Weiwei: The Internet Vs. The Chinese Government," Big Think: Smarter, Faster, http://bigthink.com/experts-corner/dispatches-from-the-police-state-nil-1-the-internet-is-constantly-putting-the-chinese-government-on-trial.
58. Ow Wei Chow, "Songs About 'Mother' at the Verge of Being 'Harmonised': Propagation of Resistance against the Great Firewall of China," in *Music and Mind*, ed. Jahnichen Gisa, Made, Mantle Hood, Chinthaka, Meddegoda (Selangor: Universiti Putra Malaysia, 2014).
59. Bruce Sterling, "Web Semantics: Popular Chinese Internet Slang Expressions and Acronyms," Wired.com, https://www.wired.com/2010/09/web-semantics-popular-chinese-internet-slang-expressions-and-acronyms/.
60. Astrid Nordin, Richaud, Lisa, "Subverting Official Language and Discourse in China? Type River Crab for Harmony," *China Information* 28, no. 1 (2014). p. 57.
61. Giorgio Strafella, Berg, Daria, "A Decade of Blogging in China," University of Nottingham, https://blogs.nottingham.ac.uk/chinapolicyinstitute/2015/08/31/a-decade-of-blogging-in-china/.
62. Tom Simonite, "Browser Plug-in Punches an Unfixable Hole in China's Great Firewall," MIT Technology Review, https://www.technologyreview.com/s/543711/browser-plug-in-punches-an-unfixable-hole-in-chinas-great-firewall/.
63. Weiwei, "China's Censorship Can Never Defeat the Internet".
64. Ibid.
65. "Ai Weiwei: The Internet Vs. The Chinese Government".
66. Jordan Sullivan, "China's Weibo: Is Faster Different?," *New Media & Society* 16 (2014).
67. Goubin Yang, "Technology and Its Contents: Issues in the Study of the Chinese Internet," *The Journal of Asian Studies* 70, no. 4 (2011).
68. "A Chinese Internet? History, Practice, and Globalization," *Chinese Journal of Communication* 1, no. 6 (2012).

69. "Technology and Its Contents: Issues in the Study of the Chinese Internet."
70. "A Chinese Internet? History, Practice, and Globalization."
71. Murray.
72. Yang, "A Chinese Internet? History, Practice, and Globalization."
73. Feng Zhang, "The Rise of Chinese Exceptionalism in International Relations," *European Journal of International Relations* 12, no. 2 (2011).
74. Jiang Min, "Authoritarian Informationalism: China's Approach to Internet Sovereignty," *SAIS Review* 30, no. 2 (2010).
75. Goubin Yang, "Technology and Its Contents: Issues in the Study of the Chinese Internet," *The Journal of Asian Studies* 40, no. 4 (2011). p. 1043.
76. "A Chinese Internet? History, Practice, and Globalization."
77. Jon Garvie, "Trading Free Speech," *Index on Censorship* 4 (2007). p. 43.
78. Ibid. p. 43.
79. James Baker, "America in Asia: Emerging Architecture for a Pacific Community," *Foreign Affairs* 70, no. 5 (1991/92). p. 16.
80. Madeleine Albright, "Sustaining Democracy in the Twenty-First Century," in *The Rostov Lecture Series* (School of Advanced International Studies, Johns Hopkins University, 2000).
81. Hillary Clinton, "Remarks on Internet Freedom," United States Department of State, http://www.state.gov/secretary/rm/2010/01/135519.htm.
82. Gorden Chang, "China's 'Internet Plus' Strategy, a Net Minus," Frobes, http://www.forbes.com/sites/gordonchang/2015/04/19/chinas-internet-plus-strategy-a-net-minus/#6f5734227ac4s.
83. Bao Beibei, "How Internet Censorship Is Curbing Innovation in China," The Atlantic, http://www.theatlantic.com/china/archive/2013/04/how-internet-censorship-is-curbing-innovation-in-china/275188/.
84. Jordan Calinoff, "Beijing's Foreign Internet Purge," *Foreign Policy* (2010).
85. Endalk, "Ethiopia: Netizens Outraged as Ethiopia Steps up Internet Censorship," GlobalVoices.org, https://globalvoices.org/2012/04/27/ethiopia-netizens-outraged-as-ethiopia-steps-up-internet-censorship/.
86. Human Rights Watch. p. 5.
87. Wook Kim Sung, Douai, Aziz, "Google Vs. China's "Great Firewall": Ethical Implications for Free Speech and Sovereignty," *Technology in Society* 34 (2012).
88. Mike Isaac, "Facebook Said to Create Censorship Tool to Get Back into China," NYTimes.com, http://www.nytimes.com/2016/11/22/technology/facebook-censorship-tool-china.html.

89. Tim Wu, "The World Trade Law of Censorship and Internet Filtering," *Chicago Journal of International Law* (2006). p. 287.
90. The Economist, "Big Data, Meet Big Brother: China Invents the Digital Totalitarian State," TheEconomist.com, http://www.economist.com/node/21711902/.

3

The Exceptional: *Whose Creativity?*

In the mid- to late 1990s it was commonly argued that a technology had emerged to consolidate the decades-long emergence of a new age, a post-industrial information age. This technology, the internet, was set to disrupt all aspects of life. With it came new utopian imaginations about the way we might come to work and live. One such imagination interpreted the nature of the age through the *creative act*. In this imagination of the age, digital communication technologies were going to allow us to be, *exceptionally* in this era compared to earlier ones, the makers of our own culture. The information age portended a fundamental disruption of how knowledge and culture could be produced, uniquely allowing a move away from the traditional hierarchies with their restrictive gatekeepers of common knowledge. In this imagination, digital communication technologies were understood, again *exceptionally*, to afford a new kind of economic autonomy: the possibility that anyone could become an independent cultural producer in a new information-based economy. The platform defining this disruption, the internet, was not territorially constrained. Nor was the imagination of space. This imagination was on a planetary scale. In this interpretation of the *creative act* we encounter a propertyscape that I will call Information Exceptionalism.[1]

P. Kalantzis-Cope, *The Work and Play of the Mind in the Information Age*,
Frontiers of Globalization, https://doi.org/10.1007/978-3-319-64650-3_3

The first half of naming speaks to the object of this propertyscape, *information*. This serves as a framing device for the diverse social activity of the work and play of the mind: knowledge, culture, and personhood. The second half of the naming, its *exceptionalism*, refers to a particular reading of a unique historical confluence of a technology and the kind of creative activity that technology supported. This exceptionalism arises from inherent nature of information as a non-rivalrous good, where one person's use does not exclude use by another. While I am using, or possessing, a material good, another cannot. Such is the nature of rivalrous goods. While I use an idea, another person can use the same idea without limiting in any way the access to the idea on the part of the first user. In this sense, information is a non-rivalrous good, an immaterial good quite unlike any of the other goods in the world.

Specific historical conditions frame the production and ownership of the work and play of the mind in a post-industrial information age. These serve to intensifying this fundamentally non-rivalrous character of information goods, because of the capacity of digital communication technologies to reproduce information at near-zero marginal cost. So, there emerges a broader *exceptional* economy built on the foundation of non-rivalrous goods. This exceptional economy has a new generative core for economic development, unleashing the true productive potential of the age. As Kevin Kelly, self-proclaimed techno-utopian and founding editor of *Wired* magazine, proclaims, in contrast to the property logic of economic development for the industrial economy, "don't seek refuge in scarcity … far greater wealth will be made by exploiting plentitude."[2] By following this exceptional property path, a new economy affords radical new ways of being, where *becoming creative* and the realities of *becoming property* share a common path.

In explaining the boundaries of Information Exceptionalism, I am attempting to capture a distinctive moment. This is apparent in the kinds of sources from which I draw, principally activism and scholarship from the mid-1990s to the early 2000s. This is not to imply that the movement is over, but to historicize the idealism and headiness of the idea of an exceptional economy, and the prevailing sense of optimism that something *exceptional* was on the horizon. This notion of exceptionalism is the groundwork for what would become a widely pervasive world view.

In the living story with which I want to illustrate this propertyscape, I turn the focus of my attention to the photographic act, as a paradigmatic kind of creative act in the exceptional economy. Looking at the digital, internet-mediated photographic act through a longer history of the medium, a more complicated relationship between the old and the exceptional economy is revealed. This adds a critical perspective to the *value of participation* in the exceptional economy and complicates the normative underpinnings of Information Exceptionalism.

The Diagnosis: Centralization and Control

In 1998 the United States Congress introduced the Digital Millennium Copyright Act (DCMA). The DCMA was presented as an effort "to implement United States treaty obligations and to move the nation's copyright law into the digital age." It was a regulatory means by which the United States could navigate the "relationship between technological change and U.S. copyright law."[3] It sought to restrict, by making illegal, any action to "decrypt an encrypted work, or otherwise to avoid, bypass, remove, deactivate, or impair a technological measure" that protected the intellectual property of the owner of that property, "without the authority of the copyright owner."[4] It also made illegal services that "traffic … any technology, product, service, device, component, or part thereof, that is primarily designed or produced for the purpose of circumventing protection."[5] In plain words, the DMCA was targeted at the kinds of content reproduction and sharing activities that were made possible by digital technologies and the internet.

The act of "piracy" was the moral trigger for this law, an important personalization of responsibility and accountability of a generalizable social phenomenon. But there was a deeper worry concerning the digital disruption that lurks behind the DMCA, and similar regulatory moves appearing at the same time in other national settings. The availability of a pirated information good—a song, a book, or a movie, for example—fundamentally undermines the commercial market for that good. By introducing to the market a free reproduction of the proprietary original, the market value of the original good is reduced or eliminated. In breaking the exclusive relationship of the owner of the good to the market, the entire property basis of the information industries is undermined. More broadly, piracy, one act at a time, hollows out the very principle of a market-based capitalist economy where the exclusive right to make an information good scarce is a base assumption.

Rather than viewing the disruptive qualities of digital technologies and the internet as a threat, the diagnosis defining the propertyscape of Information Exceptionalism centers on a view of the DMCA, and regulatory orders like it, as being the real threats. The DMCA was diagnosed as a relic of the old economy, a fundamental misreading of the affordances of the digital disruption, the social activity that underwrites the work and play of the mind in the new economy, and with this, the emergence of a new kind of *exceptional* market logic associated with these transformations.

The DMCA was diagnosed to have misread the productive potential of the digital technologies and the internet. Digital disruption, in this view, has *afforded* new kinds of scope for social action: the ability to create, remix, view, and share a spectrum of information goods. By protecting a *rivalrous* understanding of the information that is being produced and reproduced by digital technologies and distributed via the internet, the effect of DMCA was to restrict the use and reuse of these information objects, to limit the creative activity of those who through the internet have been given unprecedented access to information and creative power. This question of *use* and *reuse* is a matter of the use of information objects in everyday communication. More broadly conceived, it is the basis for creating new information products in the new economy. The making of them non-rivalrous via the act of socially sharing information is not the threat, but source of the unique affordances of the age—so the Information Exceptionalist argues. Thus, while aiming to stop piracy, the Act was far more consequential because of the ways it attempted to curb broader social and communicative affordances of the internet. And at the core of this *diagnosis*, is the individual right of action or the *maker's right* in the creative act. It is here we see the first foundation of the diagnosis, a posture toward attempts to restrict the generative social and economic potentials in the creative act.

The DMCA was also diagnosed to represent a misreading of the organizational affordances of the internet. Via the regulation of information goods, the DMCA is seen as an attempt to control what happened on the internet. But the essential architecture of the internet, what makes it unique, is a move away from this kind of centralization of control. This is what makes it the basis of an exceptional platform for the making of the social. The internet is a social platform that has not been built by the state. Nor is it regulated by the state. Rather, it is a collection of individual acts of production and distribution of the work and play of the mind. However, as Laurence Lessig warns, while "the architecture of the original Internet minimized the opportunity for control," this space is progressively becoming controlled and enclosed.[6] Tarleton Gillespie frames DMCA within a broader framework of order as emergent "techno-regulatory control system."[7] Yochai Benkler calls this "a battle over the institutional ecology of the digital environment."[8] A broader social regulatory mechanism is determining the scope of creative action. This regulatory move has implications not only for individual creative action, but also for the dynamics of social activity in the new economy. Here we see a key foundation of the diagnosis, an attitude toward the regulatory control over the creative act.

There are two final contextual prefaces necessary for situating the diagnosis defining Information Exceptionalism. First, it is important to say that both the DMCA and Information Exceptionalism are in large part a conjoined American story. The DMCA is an attempt at a regulatory mechanism for US corporations to maintain their competitive advantage as global leaders in cultural production. Even the application of similar regulatory moves in other national settings is influenced by the US interests in the global sphere. It is an American story also in the way that Information Exceptionalism has become the mainstream counterargument. This alternative propertyscape is also an American product.

A second preface, and maybe the most important for understanding the uniqueness of the propertyscape of Information Exceptionalism, is its implicit stance toward capitalist development. The critique of the DMCA is not a critique of capitalism writ large. Nor is this an argument about the desired end of capitalism. Rather the diagnosis is about a fundamental misreading of the market and the emergence of a new kind of *exceptional* market in the age of information. The diagnosis is centered on what is considered to be a misguided attempt at the regulation of an emergent information market, under principles that do not make sense in terms of the unique characteristics of its fundamental productive object: *information*. This initiates a critical dichotomy, between the *old* economy and the *exceptional* economy. In the definition of this propertyscape there is always present a historical point and counterpoint: the industrial and the post-industrial; an economy of material property; and an economy of immaterial property. For short, I will use the naming of the *old* versus *exceptional economy* to speak of these historical epochs and their imbricated production and property logics. As a point of qualification, the *old* economy is both past and present; past as it defined an epoch, present as the logic still persists in the new economy. In what follows I explore the nature of the digital disruption, the affordances of digital technologies and the internet, and how the production and ownership of the work and play of the mind is essential to understanding the productive potential of the *exceptional* economy.

Information Exceptionalism

Becoming Creative

In the logic of the old economy, information production is dominated by capital-intensive industries dedicated to these purposes. This is due to the high entry cost of the technical tools and the professional skills needed to use these tools—in the culture and knowledge industries, printing factories, film studios, audio recording and disk manufacturing facilities, television recording and transmission stations, and the like. The epoch-defining character of the exceptional economy is materially grounded in the reduction of the cost of these tools of information production and distribution—personal computers, digital cameras, audio recording devices, storage media, and the distribution mechanisms of the internet. Yochai Benkler proclaims: "capital has been put in the hands of a billion people around the globe who are connected more or less seamlessly."[9] This shift in access becomes the basis for an argument for significant new opportunities to *become creative*. In the words of Laurence Lessig, access to digital technologies "enable an extraordinary range of ordinary people to become part of a creative process."[10] Not only do these tools open out the means of information production, they also give people the capacity to become independent distributors or broadcasters of information. Gillespie declares that "mass distribution, once the near-exclusive domain of institutions, now becomes available to the individual."[11] Clay Shirky heralds a new world where "everyone is a media outlet."[12] The digital disruption, defined by greater access to the tools of production and distribution of information, allows for everyone to *become creative*. This is presented as a wellspring for a newfound personal autonomy. Access to the tools of information production and distribution *affords* an awakening of the *self*.

While an argument about greater access to digital technologies and the internet is used to explain the exceptional material conditions of the information economy, a network logic is used to explain its organizational principles defining the digital disruption. The exceptional network logic is that of the *distributed* network. The internet, the defining social platform of the age, operates under this *distributed* logic. The qualities of the internet as a distributed network, in layman's terms, are as follows. Rather than being a single network, the internet is a network of networks that nonetheless functions as an integrated system. The network is the aggregation of a mesh of interdependent nodes, for example, a personal computer or a server, connected end to end. The transmission of information within this system is not dependent on one node. Information is broken up into packets; these packets flow through the network along different routes and are put back together when they reach their destination. The rules that govern these flows, or the movement of information between dispersed nodes, are known as protocols. Together, these distributed qualities govern relations of social interaction on the internet. The internet is seen to be exceptional for the following qualities: it is *scalable*, a network only determined by the actions of those creating new layers to the network; it is *decentralized*, end to end meaning a network that does not inherently demand control from hierarchy-creating mediation; and it is *resilient* because the network is not dependent on one node, but rather a multiplicity of interchangeable backup nodes guaranteeing the flow of information if one node fails.

Distribution serves as metaphor for a more expansive claim about the unique organizational principles of the social life. Foundationally, the creative act is coded with a view of the internet as being inherently built on the workings of free and equal producers, a distribution of social power. As an organizing principle, one *node*, the placeholder for the individual, is the creator of the network, but not dependent on the network. The autonomy of this individual, as the cornerstone of this social power, is guaranteed by the distributed character of the network, as the network is not depended on any one individual or centrally located individuals for its existence. Thus, control of the production of information is in the hands of the creator, communicating independently and directly to an audience. Moreover, in the end-to-end qualities of the network, the creative act can be freed from the hierarchy-creating mediators of knowledge and cultural production that characterize the old economy. This notion of distribution presents an organizational principle for the social that opens another element of this awakening of the *self*. But this is not now a *collective-self*, the accumulation of numerous individual acts, each dependent on their independence. The *distributed* nature of the defining network of the new economy, the internet, *affords* a new found collective autonomy as the prerogative of its makers.

This awakening of the *self*, and the production of the *collective-self*, provides the backdrop for the ontological ordering principle of the propertyscape of Information Exceptionalism. Greater access to the tools of information production and distribution, and the *distributed* organizational model of the internet, are the *exceptional* historical conditions for which creative action becomes a disruptive force for the new economy. A property thesis is imbricated in this awakening of the *self*, and the production of the *collective-self*, where *becoming creative* and the realities of *becoming property* in the exceptional economy share a common path.

In the *old* economy, rivalrous property is the *norm*. This understanding is situated within the material nature of that economy. The exceptional economy is an information-based economy. For this reason, *becoming property* can operate under exceptional principles. The Information Exceptionalist reading operates within a longer view of the economic and normative character of information.

As a general modern economic principle, a rivalrous good exists when one's use of a good excludes the simultaneous use by another of that good. The work and play of the mind—information—is an *exceptional* kind of good because of its essentially non-rivalrous character. One's use of information does not exclude its simultaneous use by another. Moreover, there has been a consistent understanding of the social utility of the informational good that transcends modern left-right political frameworks, that intensifies its exceptional quality. The convergence of these aspects is found in the often-referenced Thomas Jefferson quote:

> If nature has made any one thing less susceptible than all others of exclusive property, it is the action of the thinking power called an idea. He who receives an idea from me, receives instruction himself without lessening mine; as he who lights his taper at mine, receives light without darkening me. That ideas should freely spread from one to another over the globe, for the moral and mutual instruction of man, and improvement of his condition, seems to have been peculiarly and benevolently designed by nature, when she made them, like fire, expansible over all space, without lessening their density in any point, and like the air in which we breathe, move, and have our physical being, incapable of confinement or exclusive appropriation.[13]

With this confluence of the fundamental economic character and the social utility of information, the question of *becoming property* becomes rooted in an *exceptionality*, in a contrast with the norm of the material and the rivalrous.

The action of *becoming property*, from social activity of the work and play of the mind to intellectual property, can take a very different course from that of material property in the exceptional economy. To be specific, the digital disruption, its tools, and network logic have given rise to a new, exceptional property movement, exemplified, for instance, by Creative Commons and Free and Open Source Software. This is not a movement that is singular in its political agendas, but its proponents and practitioners do share a property perspective. As a basic definition, "open source" is a model of software development where the underlying code of the software is visible, accessible, and reusable by other software programmers. Such a development is supported by licenses that give software developers the opportunity to guarantee the openness and accessibility of these software tools. "Property in open source is configured fundamentally around the right to distribute, not the right to exclude."[14] Lessig argues the movement is "democracy brought to code."[15]

Steven Weber states: "the open source phenomenon is in some ways the first and certainly one of the most prominent indigenous political statements of the digital world."[16] Software is important because it is an infrastructural aspect of the internet. This movement in software becomes the basis for a more expansive revelation about the nature of the creative act in digital environments. Replacing software with information we raise the following possibility: if we keep the right to the work and play of the mind accessible, then it will be reusable, by other producers of information. Therefore, information goods born on, or distributed by, the internet come to afford new kinds of potential for the creative act.

Proponents of the exceptionalist thesis point to many sites in the digital economy to show that this idea of non-rivalrousness, both at the software and at the content level, is not simply in the minds of those theorizing technologies, but pervasive in the lifeworld of the internet. It is not that the new economy might produce this rupture, but that it has. As Benkler argues, there are key sectors of the information economy that already operate against the "dominant thesis that (private) property and markets are the roots of all growth and productivity."[17]

Peers, Reputational Economies, and Free Labor

The exceptional economy is characterized by an epoch-defining mode of production: *peer* production. One of the quintessential examples of the transformational potential of peer production, and its qualitative difference from the information production logics of the old economy, is Wikipedia, counterpoint of the print encyclopedia. Wikipedia is an ideal entry point to this discussion, because it illustrates so clearly the duality of information; it is a storehouse of facts about our collective-selves, while the production of this knowledge simultaneously provides a feedback loop, revealing the systems of authority that influence the production of representations of our collective-selves. In understanding the production of the representation of our collective-selves in the exceptional economy, we bring into sharp focus the normative presuppositions of Information Exceptionalism.

In the industrial model of information production, the old economy, the print encyclopedia was produced in a rivalrous context by private enterprise. It required heavy investment in printing plants, warehousing, distribution, and sales infrastructures. As a physical object, it was expensive to make and expensive to purchase. From a knowledge industry perspective, it is the laborers in this industry who were paid, not only for production but also for editorial, and the experts who wrote. Each entry was written in the singular voice of an author, name signed at the end, and their work was overseen by a waged editorial bureaucracy. The encyclopedia's taxonomy of epistemic salience was determined by the expertise of the publisher.

In contradistinction, peer production offers an exceptional way to construct an encyclopedia, to do the business of the work and play of the mind. Because of the unique affordances of the platform upon which it was built—the internet—an encyclopedia came into being that is "free, open and neutral."[18] Wikipedia is free in the sense that anyone with a computer and internet can access it and at no charge; it is open because its content is written by anonymous authors in the communities of practice, perhaps professional knowledge workers but perhaps not; and it is neutral because a public of peers vets its own knowledge creation processes. Anderson argues, "Wikipedia is simply a different animal to Britannica. It's a living community rather than a static reference point."[19] The so-called Wikipedia revolution is more than a matter of building an encyclopedia. It is emblematic of a fundamental disruption of how we produce information and our relationship to that information in the new economy. This social frame of *community* and *living* is critical to the understanding of what the fundamental causality of motivation in the exceptional economy of peers.

Scaling up from the Wikipedia example, digital technologies and the internet have allowed for important reference points defining the meanings of our collective-selves produced in everyday contexts, not only by established experts, but open to anyone with a computer and an internet connection. The ability to participate in this construction of social meaning is based on an assumption that peers are free and equal producers. This is an expression of the distributed nature of the platform that defines the new economy, the internet.

Intensifying this participatory normativity, peers not only produce information; communities of peers are offered the tools to be able to validate representations of their collective-selves. Within this context we are presented with a kind of democratization within these systems of validation; an idea of the "wisdom of crowds" or "collective wisdom."[20] This is one of the exceptional characteristics of the technologies of the age. This notion of the crowd has an aura of Adam Smith's classical argument about the invisible hand of the market. Through a myriad of separate acts by individuals, community is created. Such community, as an abstract living body, validates systems of knowledge production in ongoing discursive manner. This allows for new kinds of knowledge authority to emerge, supposedly in an organic manner from the bottom-up.

Within this process of production there is a causality of motivation grounded in a normative principle of self-actualization. As Benkler argues, peer production offers "a series of indefinable improvements" on how "we perceive the world around us, the extent to which we can affect our perceptions of the world, the range of actions open to us and their possible outcomes, and the range of cooperative enterprises we can seek to enter to peruse our choices."[21] The last clause, "the range of cooperative enterprises we can seek to enter to peruse our choices," is where a crucial shape-shifting occurs, in the confluence of epistemological self-actualization and economic self-actualization.

Making this distinction between the old and exceptional economies, in the old economy, it is assumed that motivations to produce were directly relational to the market, its rationality of profit and accumulation, operating under the logic of rivalrous property. There is a material reality to these kinds of primary motivations. For example, there is a direct cost of means and tools of industrial cultural production and the need to pay for this infrastructure. And there is a need for labor to earn an income for its work. But in the new economy, building off the principle of peer production as the cornerstone of social activity in the work and play of the mind is an exceptional economic motivational logic—or so it is argued. In the exceptional economy, motivation is seen to derive from primarily non-market desires, operating within the shadow of the *social*.

The primary motivation in the exceptional economy is essentially connected to a view of the labor of the creative act. The exceptional economy is idealized by the input of *free labor* on the part of the volunteer or the amateur. The creative act is rewarded by attention, in reputational or status economies. The motivation for the creative act is thus seen to be primarily associated within different first-order motivational desires: personhood, affirmation, status. These are connected normatively to the production of the social in the aggregation of creative acts. In this way, the social of peer production can be normatively characterized as the essential *freedom* to become creative. Speaking specifically to the creation and editing of Wikipedia entries, Lessig argues, "it just turns out that when you invite the world to participate, there are enough volunteers in a range of categories of work to make the whole thing function quite well."[22] The creative act is positioned as *free labor*, in the sense it is distanced from traditional wage laboring. It is free of the pressures of laboring, in the industrial sense. Its motivation is on the part of creative agents to participate in the making and validation of their cultures.

This understanding of *non-market* motivation is also influenced by a fluidness between work and play in the exceptional economy. The creative act is happening in what have been non-traditional spaces of labor, outside of formal labor time, in people's *free* time. Clay Shirky presents this *free* time as "novel resource"[23] that should be viewed as a "social asset," or the idea of a "cognitive surplus … as the world's cumulative free time."[24] Again *free time* intensifies this association with the creative act being *free of labor*, because of its normative social loading.

These normative presuppositions underwrite an imagination of the social, intensifying the exceptional ontological ordering principle of non-rivalrousness as a general characteristic of the work and play of the mind. Rivalrous interpretations of the right to the work and play of the mind lead to the problem of monopoly, and this monopoly exemplifies the normative character of the work and play of the mind. As Gillespie states, "because the commodity in question is information, abuse of this monopoly position would not merely inflate prices or make a worthwhile product hard to acquire; it might deplete public debate, disable democracy, or starve art and culture."[25] This is a tendency not only in the economic sense, but also in the sense of a cultural monopoly.

In the context, that of the economy of peers striving to extend their reputations, rivalrous intellectual property rights act as a *friction*, a constraint on a freer, more creative, more innovative, and so more dynamic markets. Kevin Kelly argues that it should be "plenitude, not scarcity" that "governs the network economy."[26] If we are to embrace this epoch-defining model of peer production, where digital networks are destined to fulfill their potentials as "possibility factories," one should not "seek refuge in scarcity." Rather, in a revealing turn, he claims that "far greater wealth will be made by exploiting plenitude."[27] What he means is that building upon the collective aggregation of acts *free of labor*, understood in the first instance as property-less creative acts, we develop productive foundations for the general economy. It is important to stress the point that this exceptional economy is not aimed at the destruction of the market, but understanding new entry points in the production of value, in the form of primary and second-order desires. In this reading, the primary desire is assumed with non-market motivation, but secondary desires can be developed with a view to the market. Reputation and status can lead to income in the market.

Michael Heller argues that making information rivalrous property in the exceptional economy produces an "economic gridlock." Revealing of the connection between the exceptional economy and modes of capitalist development, Heller states, "gridlock is a paradox. Private ownership usually increases wealth, but too much ownership" of information "has the opposite effect." For information goods, rivalrous property "wrecks markets, stops innovation and costs lives."[28] This is not to say that private rights are inherently destructive, but that in the exceptional immaterial domain they are counter-productive to social and economic growth. As Benkler proclaims, peer-to-peer production "is as rational and efficient given the objectives and material conditions of information production at the turn of the twenty-first century as the assembly line was for the conditions at the turn of the twentieth."[29] In other words, because of the decreased cost of the tools of information production, the social imagery of peers, free labor, reputational economies, and non-rivalrous property is not *irrational*. In fact, these represent the rationality of the new economy.

At the core of this social imaginary is a vision of the individual agent. By imposing the logic of private, rivalrous property creativity is hampered and freedom restricted.

The Exceptional Commons

I will go on to describe several commons models in the subsequent propertyscapes of Transformative Distribution and Ecological De-Colonization. In fact, all the property alternatives to Information Privatization are based on differing kinds of commons model. The framing context for the *exceptional commons* follows the pattern established: a reading of the exceptional quality of information as a good, and the exceptional affordances of the age as understood via the internet and digital communication technologies.

The exceptional commons model has a number of co-defining principles. These principles open with an a priori belief in the natural and inalienable right to the work and play of the mind. We have this right because of the normative quality of the work and play of the mind; what makes it inherently exceptional. It is the culminating point of our collective-selves, the "great and ancient storehouse of human innovation."[30] Understanding this fundamental connection to the human good is the basis of a reading of "cultural citizenship,"[31] one that constructs a notion of the commons on a model of citizenship defined by *self-dominion*. Grafted on to this understanding of *self-dominion* is the critique of the permissions required in the propertyscape of Information Exceptionalism. Lessig argues there is a "character text" to assess the resource natural connection to a commons model "anyone within the relevant community has a right without obtaining permission of anyone else."[32] Thus, aligning perfectly with the ontological ordering principle and normative foundations of the exceptionalist model, the right to participate is anchored in an ideal of individual autonomy. It is the elementarily basis for self-actualization, the cornerstone of the constructing of the collective-self. Benkler argues that within the domains of the work and play of the mind, the commons are a "core institutional component of freedom of action in free societies."[33]

Self-dominion is the stepping stone to the next core principle of the exceptional commons: *self-governance*. Lewis Hyde argues that the *making* of the commons unlocks a kind of liberty that might be characterized as collective autonomy, where "liberty means self-governance, and self-governance is a common pursuit."[34] The "common pursuit" as the cumulative acts of individuals in concert is the centerpiece of understanding the basis of sovereignty for the exceptional commons. Translating these principles into the realities of history, the internet affords for these forms of *self-governance* through the ability to simply assign the legal rights contracts. Such contracts define the relationship of participants to the work and play of the mind. This is the centerpiece of the free and open source movement and Creative Commons. In an important reminder of relationship of this model to modes of capitalist development, Lessig writes, "to support open source software is not to oppose copyright."[35] At the heart of the critique is the burden of regulation, or law, on the creative act. As Lessig argues, this is the difference between a "free culture" and a "permission culture."[36] "The charge I have been making about the regulation of culture is the same charge free marketers make about the regulation of markets."[37] This critique is thus primarily focused on how law can restrict the newfound autonomy, facilitated by digital tools and modes of production, understood as the creative act.

Finally, this interpretation of *self-governance* is fully realized through the possibility of "cooperation-enhancing exit." In explaining "why exit matters," Heller argues that "exit stands for the right to withdraw or refuse to engage: the ability to dissociate, to cut oneself out of a relationship with other persons."[38] The right to enter and exit communities is a fundamental matter of free choice and consent.

The exceptional commons model finds its pre-eminent expression in the Creative Commons Project, founded in 2001 by Lessig and others. Creative Commons stated intervention is as follows: "to achieve the vision of universal access, someone needed to provide a free, public, and standardized infrastructure that creates a balance between the reality of the Internet and the reality of copyright laws. That someone is Creative Commons."[39] Creative Commons provides a set of copyright licenses that people can attach to the digital products of their creative acts. There are six types of licenses. All license types share the baseline of attribution, the personhood that is so important to the self-actualization of the exceptional economy. They then provide options based on three variables: whether or not you will allow derivatives of your work; whether or not you allow commercial works to be produced from yours; and whether or not you share alike, meaning you guarantee openness of your work in the commons. The aim is to make "creative, educational, and scientific content instantly more compatible with the full potential of the Internet."[40] By these means, Creative Commons licenses "provide tools that allow work to be placed as squarely as possible in the public domain."[41]

Key to the alternative institutional model of social production is a distinctive understanding of individual autonomy. As Creative Commons states, "our users build the commons itself."[42] In this model of the commons, the exceptional commons, the public sphere of information forms on a piece-by-piece basis, one contract at a time, and so is wholly dependent on individual actions. Underwriting Creative Commons is the idea of legal equality, or individuals capturing ownership of their labor power and sharing it through contracts established between free and equal subjects—one creator and one reuser at a time. The work and play of the mind is committed to the public domain, but one contract at a time rather than as a matter of social principle or policy. The idea of the public is built out of individual choice and private realms of autonomy. Understanding duty in the exceptional economy, looking at copyright, Boyle says, "in the 1950's none of this would have mattered. Unless you were in some related business—as a publisher, broadcaster, film distributor, or what have you—it would have been hard for you to trigger the rules of intellectual property law."[43] But in the post-industrial age, these triggers are ubiquitous in the production spaces of the networked social economy, making this connection to duty close to everyday action.

The production of the exceptional commons is not some fringe element on the internet. There are currently "1.1 billion works and counting" that have assigned Creative Commons licensing.[44] At the core of Wikipedia is a Creative Commons license. The Public Library of Science, which has come to be one of the largest alternatives to the traditional journal system for publishing medical and scientific research, uses Commons licenses. Even corporate giants in the tech industry, like Google, support the use of these licenses by making them a search variable.

The Propertyscape of Information Exceptionalism as an Ideal Type

The ontological ordering principle of the propertyscape of Information Exceptionalism is found in the principle of non-rivalrousness. Non-rivalrousness, it is argued, is anchored in the fundamental nature of information; knowledge, culture, and ideas, reflecting the inherent social utility of information as a good. This is a statement of trans-historical principle. And at an historical level, the new economy intensifies the connection with information and the principle of non-rivalrousness. It does so as a consequence of the infinite reproducibly of information goods via digital technologies and the internet. To make an information good rivalrous has implications beyond simple economics. A digital disruption, characteristic of the information age, affords opportunities for new kinds of actions in the production of information. This deeper disruption implicates the nature of defining our individual and collective personhood. *Becoming creative* is an exceptional affordance of the exceptional economy.

The social production of the representations of our collective-selves sets the context for the normative presuppositions of the propertyscape of Information Exceptionalism. Through the participatory grammar of peers, interrelating in communities of living producers, each motivated by human desire, personhood, and reputation, the exceptional economy provides a normative conceptual distance from the operations of the old economy. This establishes an epistemological normativity as these principles align with an authenticity of being able to make one's culture. There is a personal relationship to this information, from creation to validation, a personal and collective affirmation. There is also an economic normativity associated with an exceptional logic of motivation. The old economy singularly motivates via systems of profit and private accumulation; the new economy is motivated by individual and communal self-actualization. It is near impossible to separate these two normative aspects, generating as they do a relational meaning to each other—the making of one's self and the making of one's economic prospects. The emphasis on cooperative enterprises is essentially about the individual right, motivation, and desire for self-actualization at core of the act of *becoming creative.* Within this context the creative act is focused on an individual as a kind of information-peddling small business.

The exceptional commons model has three principles: self-dominion, self-governance, and cooperation-enhancing exit. Self-dominion connects the normative quality of the good, with our natural right to its use. The ability to access this good is fundamental to the freedom of action, both within a longer view of history and as understood through the productive potential of the exceptional economy. Self-governance, the making of the commons, is the ultimate principle of expression for this self-actualization. Aligning with the methodological individualism of Information Exceptionalism, the first principle is an individual's right to self-governance. The internet has afforded these possibilities by offering the individual the ability to choose rights regimes regulating to their creative acts. The creation of the exceptional commons is about the right to define the regulation of one's life, and without having to ask for "permission." Finally, cooperation-enhancing exit rounds out this model of the commons. To choose to enter and leave is the meta-assertion of self-dominion and self-governance.

In sharpening the propertyscape of Information Exceptionalism, the exceptional economy thesis is not aimed at making a case the case that all goods must be understood through the principle of non-rivalrousness, or that should be situated in the commons. Nor is it in opposition to a wider system of private ownership of the fruits of human labor. Steven Weber: "open source code does not obliterate profit, capitalism, or intellectual property rights."[45] Laurence Lessig: "free resources have nothing to do with communism."[46] In this way the exceptional economy is not a counter economy, but a parallel economy. The charge is that information works in a fundamentally different way from other goods. Private intellectual property rights act as friction, restricting the ability of action in the exceptional economy. The *creative* act is a political act, the act of an autonomous economic agent. This is not only productive for the individual but for the entire economic system. Intellectual property should be shared in the commons, a non-market space that subsists beside the market—the labor market and the market for material goods. Without ever saying this so clearly, the case being made is for a new kind of capitalism, a capitalism in tune with the affordances of the information age.

The Photographic Act

The number of images captured by digital cameras and uploaded to, displayed on, and distributed by digital communication networks is simply staggering. A quick review gives insight into the scale and velocity of this deluge: on Facebook over 200,000 images are uploaded every minute; on Instagram over 80 million photos a day; on Flickr over 1 million photos a day.[47] In 2014 over 1.8 billion images were uploaded to the internet.[48] This exponentially expanding mass of visual communication provides an archive of our contemporary times, the digital age, or what we one day might come to call in a history of visual communication, the age of the image.

In this living story, I will focus on a specific creative act, the *photographic act*. The photographic act is unavoidably defined by the affordances of its media, and its media by technological tools. In the longer history of the photographic act, there are two media moments: an original *analogue* media moment and new *digital* media moment. The historical context for the "original" new media moment of photography is an industrial moment; the digital moment is post-industrial. In navigating this history, there is a complicated framing relationship to the old and new economy. This helps to illuminate the *new* of the exceptional economy and the specificity of the *disruption*.

Photography's New Media Moments

Photography's *original* new media moment begins with glass plate cameras in the nineteenth century, is brought to a mass market with the Box Brownie of 1900, then extends to the last decades of the twentieth century with advent of the 35 mm camera. This long original moment is marked by a specific technology, the *analogue* chemistry-based camera. The relative affordability and ubiquity of the analogue camera was made possible by the advances and efficiency of industrial mass production. Associated production technologies and processes—photographic film, light sensitive papers, the darkroom, the chemicals of emulsification and developing—are tied to modes of cultural production made possible by industrial technologies. This material foundation, along with the mechanical nature of the camera itself, aligns with visions of modern technological progress, paralleling other kinds of material technological objects also at the same time transforming the practices of everyday life. At a socio-technological level, the analogue camera embodied a shift toward the automation of everyday life. The original slogan for Kodak Eastman was, "you press the button, and we do the rest."[49]

As a consequence of its relative accessibility to the masses, the analogue camera enlarged the scope of who could *make images*. As art critic and photographer Franz Roth wrote in the 1930s, "all vital and expressive activities can be divided into two classes: those that can be practiced only by the view few, and those that are basically open to everyone. Photography belongs to the latter category, and therein lies its far reaching sociological importance."[50] The analogue camera and its *affordance*, the photographic act, are commonly argued as democratizing the private record of what could be *seen*. Families were able to capture personal moments once only previously possible for those who could afford painted portraiture. Reportage was able to represent local, national, and international events, once only open to experience or interpretation by spoken word or written text. Non-human life forms, like animal movement, could be captured in ways never before possible, and formerly impossible places, such as outer space, or the record of empirical nature in scientific method. These kinds of photographic acts become visual interventions on social life in general: visualizing people, places, and conflicts. Realities once sectioned off in human experience or left to the imagination, increasingly becoming represented and reproduced as *real* by virtue of their visualization. Intensifying the relationship of the analogue camera to the *real* as a mechanism of empirical representation, it came to be thought that the photographic act stripped of interpretation, the ideal that what is *seen* is the *real*—hence, the truth-in-fiction that "the camera never lies." As John Tagg explains, due to its technological nature, the analogue camera becomes understood as "an instrument of evidence."[51]

As an amalgamation of different practices, analogue photography symbolizes what the Hungarian Bauhaus artist László Moholy-Nagy called the birth of a "modern lens."[52] There is a double meaning to this idea of a *modern lens* as it comes to define photography's original media moment.

It is a lens that affords a scaling down of communicative power in the representations of *self*, a personalized truth function. The photographic act also marks the birth of a visual media culture, as a generalizable sociological phenomenon, a visual culture in the slipstream of industrial capitalist development. Sontag famously writes "industrial societies turn their citizens into image junkies."[53] The photographic object, the image, and the act become the vessel of *truth* for an industrial age.

Photography's *second* new media moment also begins with a specific technology, the *digital* camera. Digital photography is similarly characterized by a material shift in access, again based on the affordably of the material object, the digital camera, and its related equipment, memory cards and storage media. Moreover, associated production technologies and processes, as they shift toward automated or easily usable software manipulation and rendering, become more affordable and thus more accessible. There is no marginal cost in taking another image. There is no direct cost in post-production. The advent of the digital camera and software applications for editing and manipulation does not revolutionize the medium. Rather the material shift in access expands the scope of who can make images and how easily they can be made. On a path of intensification, expanding the scope of who can make images, the digital photographic act accelerates the association of the act with a sense of expanding visual democratization. Nevertheless, there are some very important shifts transforming the nature of the photographic act in its second media moment, with implications for how we must read the image, and photographic act, as a vessel of *truth* for an information age. These, as I will argue, are not so unproblematically democratic.

Symptomatic of the digital photographic act, the traditional camera is no longer the instrument on which images are predominantly being made. The photographic act is happening using other kinds of technologies, most often mobile communication devices. Mobile telephones now dominate as the tool of choice for the production of images, to the degree that the camera and the phone have become synonymous. Evidence of this shift is the fact that the iPhone has become the most used tool for the making of images found on the Flickr, one of the largest and oldest image social media spaces found on the internet.[54] Instagram is exclusively designed for photo archiving from phones. This re-normalization of the photographic act moves it into a more general kind of communicative action. Accelerating this perception of everydayness, the image is aligned with other communication forms: words in a Facebook post, with a hashtag in a tweet, or a caption for an Instagram picture. Lev Manovich asserts that "to know how to communicate via photographs shared on social media is becoming a basic social skill."[55]

The digital photographic act is simultaneously characterized by a shift in audience. At a personal level, the photographic act in analogue photography was a matter of private and domestic production. The audience was family, acquaintances, or the circle of people you closely knew. The development of these images happened in private commercial transactions with the "lab." As Pierre Bourdieu famously wrote, the act was integral to the production of the "domestic cult."[56]

Digital communication technologies have today allowed for the sharing of images with a broader audience. No longer are these images kept in photo album books or boxes in attics. This once private domestic practice becomes part of the magma of a visual public, contributing the creation, image by image, of a collective digital social space, a "socially mediated publicness."[57] In a general sense these individual image practices embody a new "culture of connectivity."[58] This relationship to an audience changes the motivation of the creative act, "no longer … capturing a fleeting reality or special occasion; it is about the public display of everyday situations that construct a self."[59]

Another defining characteristic of digital photographic act is a fluidity of the distinction that once was more clearly made between the amateur and the professional, and the consumer and the producer. Such fluidity presents a number of opportunities for the creator of the photographic act. For the amateur wanting to enter the domain of the professional, we have the proliferation of affordable software and web-based post-production editing tools with functionality on par with professional studios. This has opened the door for many to participate in spaces that were once open only to the professional culture industries. In parallel, the capture on image of everyday life can make every consumer of images in equal measure a producer, and their photographic act when shared via the internet can be (re)used by the mainstream culture industries. As imbricated forces we see the effects of fluidity most keenly in the world of photojournalism and the rise of what has been called the "fifth estate."[60] This fifth estate is an amalgam of everyday practices, *becoming journalism*, for example, "mobile conflict journalism,"[61] or citizen journalism. There is a belief that fifth estate journalism embodies a democratic accountability, a check and balance on authority, and a proximity to truth. This fluidity has, from a culture industry perspective, some negative externalities as manifest in the decline of traditional professions associated with the photographic act. On the one hand, this presents an economic challenge, displacing the paid labor of a professional photographic image-making class. On the other hand, this also presents an epistemological challenge. What is becoming of the formal knowledge that is associated with membership in this professional image class? Speaking to the professions of photojournalism we get a sense of threat to professionalism, expressed in these terms by Ritchin: "instead of being presented with iconic photographs made by experienced photojournalists, we are increasingly seeing images made by people without photographic training and who primarily attempt to capture information, not to create symbolic images."[62]

Finally, a defining characteristic of the digital photographic act is its imbrication in other kinds of related information production vectors, and in particular the metadata that accompanies the photographic act. This metadata can be created in indirect ways—indirect in this sense it is not the primary reason for the photographic act and its recording is incidental and mostly unnoticed, for example, the automatic recording of date, time, camera settings (e.g., aperture, shutter speed, ISO). This metadata can be put to use in direct ways. For example, geo-tagging an image posted to the internet enhances search, or adding meaning-contextualizing tags to the image, sometimes informally in what is known as "folksonomies." There is also a community production, a sense of making, in the metadata of the photographic act in the digital network. Considering the production of folksonomies, at "the collective social organization and description of information at the metadata level … a folksonomy does not follow a predetermined organization or indexical structure, but is, instead, a socially and collectively produced alternative."[63] Metadata is used to tell something about who we are, and sociological generalizations made in a context that is often today characterized as big data.

The purpose of framing the photographic act within this longer view of a history of photography is to situate a productive continuity. The continuity between these two media moments is that photographic act is in some respects essentially unchanged. There has always been something *exceptional* about the photographic act, and this exceptionality is tied to the material affordances of specific technologies and the age in which they are produced. The photographic act has both in its analogue and digital moments been the harbinger of new historical practices, the vessel of certain kinds of *truth*.

Nevertheless, in comparison, we can see sharply what *is* new in the digital. What is new is how the act now becomes embedded within other communication forms, dissolving the separation from the photographic act from what it means to be communicative in general. Moreover, the ideal of digital image communication is intimately associated with the construction of a public via personal representation, with the *self* at the center of the *collective-self*. The photographic act, aggregated on digital communication platforms, produces a "diverse tapestry of doings."[64] This aggregation of communicative acts as image and associated metadata not only indicates the way in which the *self* is the center of the meaning-making authority the post-industrial information age. It also points to the development of "new capacities for self-organized representation"[65] that are intensely participatory and thus democratic, or so it is supposed.

What is *new* is an ethic or spirit of the age, a kind of *protestant ethic* for the *exceptional economy*. The motivation for action is in the ideal of self-actualization as the *modus operandi* of the production of the collective-self and the ability to produce the collective-self. Sometimes there is a given assumption that a *technology*, as an abstract historical force, has demanded this change. Technologies, in this case of image-making devices, gave us the means and tools to disrupt. These are their affordances, as technologies. Infused in this dismantling argument is a normative presupposition. These technologies have afforded us the ability to participate, to act. Together in our individual and collective actions *we* are dismantling the old economy: by geo-tagging your selfie at the festival; or checking in at your local coffee shop; tagging your travel photography; or photographing ourselves in the latest hashtagged fashion; or capturing a local protest with an incidentally linked geo-tag. There is a seductiveness to the argument of the breaking of the old order of knowledge production or the idea of dismantling mass media corporate media oligarchies. This has appeal across the political spectrum and poses a powerful general normative thrust.

The Value of Participation

Mark Rothenberg, one-time head of Flickr at Yahoo, says, "what we are trying to do at Flickr ultimately is to use all these new technologies to get back to that rich storytelling experience—and to do it in the only way it can be done, with the technologies of today."[66] In this statement we have a microcosm of the splitting of parallel economies, the conventional and the exceptional, vital to the presentation exceptional economy. By asking what is the *value* of participation as "experience," we can start to tease out the true nature of this political economy, and in so doing get to the heart of the contradictions that constitute the propertyscape of Information Exceptionalism.

The essential base for these parallel economies is found in a foundational shift in the *business* of the mass media. The *business* of the traditional mass media was primarily the production and distribution of *content*. The *business* of the exceptional new media economy, on the other hand, is primarily service based, the production of platforms facilitating the production of content created by consumers. Thus, the evaluative criterion for the *value of participation* can reside in how these services facilitate the production, and *productiveness*, of the social. This move allows for these platforms to be essentially associated with being a *social service*, with the principles of their social played out within the broader ideal of *public benefit*, rather than a transaction between a content creator and content distributor. Intensifying this association with a *social service* or *public benefit*, social media platforms, like Facebook and Twitter, or image-centered social media, like Flickr or Instagram, are free or offered at little cost to users. As such, the *service* can be understood as a social utility, again giving distance from a commercial transaction.

Within this fundamental framing of a *social service* or *public benefit*, the value of participation is reframed via other kinds of non-market association. The value of participation is primarily grounded in the ability to express personhood. As stated in the prospectus for the Facebook initial public offering (IPO), "people use Facebook to stay connected with their friends and family, to discover what is going on in the world around them, and to share and express what matters to them to the people they care about."[67] The photographic act is deeply tied to the production of online personhood. In turn this production of online personhood is connected to a public representation, connecting personal experience with audience. The result is the production of "the intimate public" in a "co-constitutive manner."[68] The process is intimate in the sense that each image of one's life helps to build a visual community embedded in everyday life, essentially anchored to the storytelling of an individual. This is a kind of a self-directed "intimate surveillance."[69] When connected with the logic of the attention economy there is de facto democratization of who is seen. This confluence between the production of personhood and a reframing of new media platforms as a *social service* or *public benefit* creates the legitimizing distance from parallel commercial economies, while underlying value resides in non-commercial spheres.

Intensifying the non-market association of the value of participation in the exceptional economy takes us back to the primary motivation for the photographic act, or the social nature of digital networks. This motivation is associated with social desires for fame, notoriety, attention, and status orders within these specific networks. In each social network the photographic act is socially contextualized by scales and metrics in the non-market economies of "followers," "shares," "likes," or in Flickr's case, the patented and secretive workings of "interestingness." In this way, the *experience* of the photographic act is situated within a primarily social experience. So too is the network in which it is shared. The tactic of users in these motivational ecologies is like "fishing for followers … using hashtags like bait."[70] These attention economies also encourage users to participate in the social network itself: uploading, commenting, tagging. Here it is not just the image that is part of the status order, but also the social dynamics of commentary. As a Flickr user notes, "when an image depends on the actions of others to push it through the Flickr Explore page algorithm, contributors who are as good at networking as they are at photographing are going to have a distinct advantage. Great photographers who prefer to shoot, then sit quietly while admirers tell their friends about their fantastic imagery will struggle to achieve results."[71]

The take away here is simple. The *value of participation* in the exceptional economy primarily resides in normative economies, communicative capacities, or service logics. Cultural production, in this case the photographic act, is ripe for a kind of normativity of this kind, aligning with a spirit of cultural production—the purity of an artist's production, or the insight of the photojournalist, or images of everyday life. But there are many ways in which the sharp autonomy of these parallel economies, the *exceptional*: the non-rivalrous, non-market, normative motivations to act, and the *norm*: the rivalrous, the market, and profit motivations, are blurred. In fact, they co-exist, are essentially co-productive, without contradiction.

For the creator of the photographic act there can be a desire for market-based economic value from their creative act. There are stock image platforms through which images can be bought and sold. Photographers can also use the attention economy, leveraging status orders to become established creative workers in *real* life. Caterina Fake, co-founder of Flickr, offers revealing advice when arguing that these social production spaces are for the "self-directed, self-motivated and *self-employed* [emphasis added]."[72] She offers the following social media tip: "When somebody posts on your [Facebook] wall or responds to you on Twitter, think of them as customers standing in front of you in your shop. If you ignore them, they won't come back. Respond the same way online as you would offline. Engage with them and be yourself."[73] These kinds of motivations are perfectly legitimate, and not at all contrary to the *exceptional* motivations of the new economy. They are evidence of the *value of participation*. In fact, this intensifies such claims to the extent that these kinds of economic action embody a fundamental ability to act freely in the marketplace. In this interpretation, creators are positioned as small culture/knowledge businesses, metaphorical or real, and so as autonomous economic agents. Whether or not the creator extracts economic value from their creative act, they are idealized as being agents of the new digital age, now empowered as economic agents as well as cultural producers.

Within a broader context, the photographic act is located in a market-based environment economic value extracted by social network businesses. The aggregation of social action and the ability to interpret interests and preferences become data for targeted advertising. As the Center for Digital Democracy argues, "digital dossiers ... have become the primary currency for the global digital advertising industry."[74] For example, Facebook's principal source of revenue is advertising. Facebook claims they offer "advertisers a unique combination of reach, relevance, social context, and engagement to enhance the value of their ads."[75]

Consumer data companies also extract market-based economic value from participation. They collect metadata through deals with social networks, from cookies in web browsers, or collect independent data sets from already existing census or survey data. The databases of one of these companies, Acxiom, are said to contain "an average of 1,500 items of data on the 96 percent of Americans currently in its databases."[76] They have "more than 23,000 computer servers collecting, collating and analyzing consumer data," constituting "a stealth engine of consumer espionage."[77] In their *Moment of Truth White Paper*, Acxiom heralds "the age of the connected consumer." Their commercial purpose, using their proprietary "business intelligence analytics software," is to analyze social interaction in order to optimize "value at every interaction."[78]

Moreover, analyzable data, and the size of the social network, are also ingredients in a speculative economy, not only trading in the New York, London, and Tokyo stock exchanges, but also serving as the motivational logic for venture capital investing in the information economy. A journalist at the *Wall Street Journal* attempted to quantify returns during the 2012 Facebook IPO to calculate the value of each individual user's social activity, the *value of their participation*. "The results show that you are worth about $81 to Facebook. Your friendships are worth $0.62 each, and your profile page could be valued at $1,800. Put another way, Facebook's nearly one billion users have become the largest unpaid workforce in history."[79]

Information Wants to Be Free of Labor?

When we put the photographic act in the context of labor, dual conundrums come into view. One half of the intellectual property conundrum is associated with the right to the product of the photographic act, the image itself. Instagram's terms of use state that they do not "claim ownership of any content that you post." However, by agreeing to the terms of use "you hereby grant … a non-exclusive, fully paid and royalty-free, transferable, sub-licensable, worldwide license to use the content." Furthermore, this content will be "non-confidential and non-proprietary."[80] Facebook, the parent company of Instagram, uses a similar approach: "you grant us a non-exclusive, transferable, sub-licensable, royalty-free, worldwide license to use any IP content that you post on or in connection with Facebook (IP License). This IP License ends when you delete your IP content or your account unless your content has been shared with others, and they have not deleted it."[81] On Flickr, the default is "all rights reserved." Nonetheless, they give you licensing options, including a Creative Commons license. They also say that, in using their *service* you also grant the parent company, Yahoo, a royalty-free sublicense.

In these agreements a pattern emerges. Ostensibly it seems that one owns the right to one's images. To the untrained eye, we are assigned the property right to the photographic act. Moreover, by signing the contract when you create an account, you are coming to an agreement with these platforms, in a pervasive *click-through contractualism*. In these agreements one is assigning a *royalty-free* sublicense to the platform, allowing your work to be used on supplementary services such as advertising and the sale of personal demographic and preference data to third parties. As an act of labor, your imaging work is *free labor*. "Our photo albums, dating preferences, porn habits, and most random and banal thoughts have all become profitable data sets, mined for advertising revenue. We are encouraged to see ourselves as pieces of human capital that must ceaselessly enhance our value—optimizing our feeds and profiles, hustling for follows and likes and swipes."[82] For the everyday photographic act we are presented an argument that we should be satisfied enough with the non-market value of participation, that it is *free of labor* self-positioning. Nevertheless, for someone in the creative industries the conundrum is as follows: in using these platforms to display work, as a necessary space for exposure, one loses the right to earn an income directly from the creative act. Meanwhile, someone working for an income in the creative industries is often competing with "free" copies of the same cultural good, collaterally devaluing their labor activity.

The other half of the conundrum is the indirect aspect of the labor in the photographic act, the associated metadata. And as I detailed earlier, it is not just the photographic act that is on-sold, but the metadata linked to the image, for example, time, place, and tag. As an example of the general stance by mainstream social media companies, Bryce Glass, Senior Interaction Designer at Yahoo, argues that "there's nothing especially proprietary about the information or opinions embedded in the patterns."[83] In a stark and revealing position, the metadata associated with the photographic act is not seen as the property of the creator at all. Moreover, public access to this data, asking these platforms for our raw personal data or the aggregation of our data as social activity, is nearly impossible. Yet the ability of corporations to read patterns on this data is a critical factor in assessing the comparative value of these social platforms.

If the photographic object, the image, and the act of its creation, becomes the vessel of *truth* for differing ages, what is the truth found in the images of the information age? The truth resides in the parasitic nature of the exceptional economy. The incentives to produce in the networked settings of community production are strong because these settings style themselves as being outside of pure market conditions. The ideology tells users that they produce for a common good, in defense of the public sphere, and to realize their selves as autonomous cultural beings. But where does free labor for the pleasure of self and friends and production of esthetic value end, and the web of commercial interests that encircle, produce, and underwrite these spaces of social activity begin?

In the exceptional economy, free labor is idealized through notions of free association and autonomy in self-actualizing cultural production. Users (as agents of the age) might be considered to be transgressors of market logic, harbingers even of a post-market economic frontier. And by giving away their labor, people are contributing to the production of a de facto public domain.

Nevertheless, the free labor associated with the image in digital spaces, the products of which are collected and pooled as information capital, become the bedrock for speculative markets in the technology domain. The market, the *norm*, and non-market, the *exceptional*, become completely dependent upon each other. The use-values of the work and play of the mind are used to obscure or hide the realities of exchange-values in the realms of markets and capital where these image artifacts also reside. The work and play of the mind is palpable in the use-values constituted in the immaterial economy and in the status orders of social life established in digital spaces, such as identity, voice, personhood, esthetic vision, and visible difference. This has conveniently been called *peer* production. But beneath the everyday phenomenal experiences of users, exchange value is harvested by corporations that host this social activity.

Free labor also represents a political economy that devalues intellectual and cultural labor, putting intellectual work that is for sale in punishing competition with free offerings. The devaluation operates at the individual worker level with a move away from the wage earning in a material world of industrial cultural production to the free labor speculative economy of digital production. It also operates at a societal level as the embedded benefits of wage earning are stripped out of the social system in which this labor operates.

While aggregators in this network economy extract surplus value from the epistemic and cultural actions of the crowd, the immaterial worker is at the mercy of the attention economy. Free association is driven by bondage to an immaterial property system. One's free time is devoted to social production in the digital economy with no guarantee of economic return. But this labor in the realm of immaterial production is not without its costs. There is always a material basis for immaterial labor in the form of mortgages, rent, and food, and the material digital infrastructure of immaterial production such as computers, smart phones, and an internet connection. As such, there is a material labor foundation that undergirds the very ability to be an immaterial producer. Moreover, access to this newly constituted public space, as expressed in the digital domain, is wholly dependent upon access to information communication technologies, or being on the affluent side of the digital divide.

This gets to the heart of the problem with the separation of the norm and the exceptional. The implicit argument has been that material production, with its output in the form of rivalrous commodities, is fundamentally different from immaterial production. Immaterial products are essentially communicative. By implication, the material commodity is not communicative. Material production is not subject to the imperatives of free speech in the way that communicative work is. Rather, it is an expression of a mute, ahistorical reality. According to this logic, the products of material production are inherently exclusive, and my use or ownership excludes yours.

While there is something empirically true about the relative immateriality of the work and play of the mind in the regime of Information Exceptionalism, it is also a political statement about the constitution of the social world within the historical frame of capitalist development. In the industrial era, the material, as expressed in the car and road system for instance, was used to communicate a kind of freedom, mobility, and individuality. By the same token, there is also an inherent material reality to the means of production of communication, knowledge, and culture in the information era: the e-book reader, the instrument playing the tune, or the screen on which an image is reproduced. As communicative expressions, culture and knowledge are grounded on the very same material existence that situates life in general. Importantly they are equally the fruits of human labor. So why should the work and play of the mind be classified an exceptional property? Why, on this basis, should we insist it be made available for free? Conversely, one could ask the same question of material property; why should it not also be free?

Whose Creativity?

In the closing of this chapter, I want to make inroads in thinking about this propertyscape as a model of economic distribution, social participation, and political representation. By asking the question of *whose creativity*, my aim is to start to overlay an evaluative rubric of the *who*, *what*, and *how*, with a view to analyzing how this propertyscape reveals the emergence of a nascent model of political community.

The *who* of this nascent model of political community is ascribed to a universal global subject. The *who* is constituted at an historical level by the fact that our shared lives are becoming further and further imbricated in information communication systems in the form of the shared spaces where our work and play co-exist. These exceptional technological affordances of the age allow for a certain kind of awakening of the self, *becoming creative*, and on a planetary scale.

The cornerstone of the *what* is the non-rivalrous nature of the work and play of the mind. Non-rivalrousness represents a self-evidence: a confluence of the fundamental economic character of immaterial goods, the social utility of these goods, and the imbrication of the production and dissemination of information with digital communication systems. In contrast to the supposed natural tendency to privatize or to make rivalrous the work and play of the mind, the economic character of information and the affordances of digital communication technologies allow individuals and collectives to self-determine the very character of the *what*. The exceptional quality of the age is to define our own property meanings, to determine the very nature of regulatory authority over our individual and social lives. Within the *what* is not simply an understanding of the right to the work and play of the mind, but a more fundamental space of self-actualization. This supports an argument for a democratic model of order embedded in the production and ownership of the work and play of the mind. The answer to the question of *whose creativity?* is in the maker's right.

The institutional model of exceptionalism, the *how*, seeks to emphasize the autonomy associated with the act of contractualism, opting out of the default regime of private intellectual property and making alternative rights agreements to produce the exceptional commons. On this account, the institutional guarantee at the core of the production of social, and the nascent model of political community that it spawns, is an essentially private act. This is a model of political community that happens in a piecemeal way, one act of rights reassignment at a time, one work at a time. Creative Commons licenses over-ride, from below, copyright laws with their default state-instituted guarantees of private property. They replace the public law of private property with apparently public licenses—however, these are based on the law of private individual contract, one license at a time, and can be withdrawn by creators at any time. Thus, in trying to locate the geo-political scale of this propertyscape, the jurisdictional geography of its nascent model of global political community, we must consider the presence of an at least minimal state capable of enforcing these private contracts.

When we ask the question of *whose creativity*, new dilemmas present themselves. Looking specifically at "creative labor" there are restrictions on who can participate, who can *become creative*, who is afforded the *maker's right*. The catch for creative labor is that these new spaces of *social* work encourage openness of ownership, and this openness is essential for the visibility of your labor in the social economy. But this openness also demands a devaluation of paid creative labor, mostly to zero, creating the economic question of who can afford to participate in this new exceptional economy.

Digital communication technologies are presented as platforms that define our global common bond. But when *participation*, social activity at its most elementary, is where value is extracted from digital networks, what in the language of *participation* is oppositional to post-industrial capitalist development? While we are presented with an ideal of self-actualization, is this notion a mystifying veil for the parasitic nature of a new mode of capitalist development? Are we left with nothing but a false hope, a naive optimism, and vulnerable to cynical doublespeak where *participation* motivates social labor, but with great profit to corporations but without compensation to creators?

Notes

1. Phillip Kalantzis-Cope, "Whose Data? Problematizing the 'Gift' of Social Labour," *Global Media and Communication* 12, no. 3 (2016).
2. Kelly, p, 49.
3. U.S Copyright Office, "Executive Summary, Digital Millennium Copyright Act, Section 104 Report," copyright.gov, http://www.copyright.gov/reports/studies/dmca/dmca_executive.html
4. US Government, "Digital Millennium Copyright Act (DCMA)," ed. 105th United States Congress (1998).
5. Ibid.
6. Laurence Lessig, *The Future of Ideas: The Fate of the Commons in a Connected World* (New York: Vintage, 2002). p. 140.

7. Tarleton Gillespie, *Wired Shut: Copyright and the Shape of Digital Culture* (Cambridge: MIT Press, 2007). p. 11.
8. Yochai Benkler, *The Wealth of Networks: How Social Production Transforms Markets and Freedom* (New Haven: Yale University Press, 2007). p. 2.
9. Ibid. p. 462.
10. Lessig. p. 9.
11. Gillespie. p. 35.
12. Clay Shirky, *Here Comes Everybody: The Power of Organizing without Organizations* (New York City: Penguin Press, 2008). p. 55.
13. Thomas Jefferson, "Thomas Jefferson to Isaac Mcpherson," University of Chicago Press, http://press-pubs.uchicago.edu/founders/documents/a1_8_8s12.html.
14. Steven Weber, *The Success of Open Source* (Cambridge, MA: Harvard University Press, 2004). p. 1.
15. Lessig. p. 68.
16. Weber. p. 7.
17. Benkler. p. 461.
18. Andrew Lih, *The Wikipedia Revolution* (New York: Hyperion, 2009). p. 4.
19. Chris Anderson, *The Long Tail: Why the Future of Business Is Selling Less of More* (New York City: Hyperion, 2006). p. 71.
20. J. Surowiecki, *The Wisdom of Crowds: Why the Many Are Smarter Than the Few and How Collective Wisdom Shapes Business, Economies, Societies and Nations* (New York City: Doubleday, 2004).
21. Benkler. p. 470.
22. Clay Shirky, *Cognitive Surplus: Creativity and Generosity in a Connected Age* (New York City: The Penguin Press, 2010).
23. Ibid. p. 358.
24. Ibid. p. 27.
25. Gillespie. p. 29.
26. Kelly. p. 40.
27. Ibid.
28. Michael Heller, *The Gridlock Economy: How Too Much Ownership Wrecks Markets, Stops Innovation, and Costs Lives* (New York: Basic Books, 2008). p. 2.
29. Benkler. p. 463.
30. Lewis Hyde, *Common as Air: Revolution, Art and Ownership* (New York City: Farrar, Straus and Giroux, 2010). p. 47.
31. Ibid. p. 6.

32. Lessig. p. 20.
33. Benkler. p. 23.
34. Hyde. p. 185.
35. Lessig. p. 264.
36. *Free Culture: The Nature and Future of Creativity* (New York: Penguin, 2005).
37. Ibid. p. 188.
38. Hanoch Dagan, Heller, Michael, "The Liberal Commons," *The Yale Law Journal* 110, no. 549 (2001). pp. 566–568.
39. Creative Commons, "About—Creative Commons," http://creativecommons.org/about/.
40. Ibid.
41. Ibid.
42. Ibid.
43. James Boyle, *The Public Domain: Enclosing the Commons of the Mind* (New Haven: Yale University Press, 2008). p. 53.
44. Creative Commons, "Homepage," CreativeCommons.org, https://creativecommons.org/.
45. Weber. p. 2.
46. Lessig, *The Future of Ideas: The Fate of the Commons in a Connected World.* p. 13.
47. Cooper Smith, "Facebook 350 Million Photos Each Day," Business Insider, http://www.businessinsider.com/facebook-350-million-photos-each-day-2013-9; Stan Horaczek, "How Many Photos Are Uploaded to the Internet Every Minute?," Popular Photography, http://www.popphoto.com/news/2013/05/how-many-photos-are-uploaded-to-internet-every-minute; Matt Maldre, "Flickr's 1.4 Million Photos Per Day, Instagram's 40 Million Photos Per Day," MattMaldre.com, http://mattmaldre.com/2013/05/27/flickrs-1-4-million-photos-per-day-instagrams-40-million-photos-per-day/; Darrell Etherington, "Flickr at 10: 1 m Photos Shared Per Day, 170% Increase since Making 1tb Free," TechCrunch, http://techcrunch.com/2014/02/10/flickr-at-10-1m-photos-shared-per-day-170-increase-since-making-1tb-free/; Matt Brian, "Flickr Hits 6 Billion Total Photos; Facebook Does That Every 2 Months," The Next Web.
48. Rose Eleleth, "How Many Photographs of You Are out There in the World?," The Atlantic, http://www.theatlantic.com/technology/archive/2015/11/how-many-photographs-of-you-are-out-there-in-the-world/413389/.

49. Tomas David, "From the Photograph to Postphotographic Practice: Toward a Postoptical Ecology of the Eye," *SubStance* 17, no. 1 (1988). p. 62.
50. Pepper Stetler, "Franz Roh and the Art History of Photography," An Online Project of The Museum of Modern Art, New York City, http://www.moma.org/interactives/objectphoto/assets/essays/Stetler.pdf.
51. John Tagg, *The Burden of Representation: Essays on Photography and Histories, Minneapolis* (Minneapolis: University of Minnesota Press, 1988).
52. László Moholy-Nagy, *Painting, Photography, Film* (London: Lund Humphries, 1969). p. 7.
53. Susan Sontag, *On Photography* (New York City: Picador 1973). p. 24.
54. Roger Fingas, "Iphone 6, Iphone 5 s Top Most Popular Cameras Used on Flickr in 2015," appleinsider.com, http://appleinsider.com/articles/15/12/03/iphone-6-iphone-5s-top-most-popular-cameras-used-on-flickr-in-2015.
55. Lev Manovich, "Competitive Photography and the Presentation of the Self," http://manovich.net/, http://manovich.net/index.php/projects/competitive-photography-and-the-presentation-of-the-self.
56. Pierre Bourdieu, *Photography: A Middle-Brow Art* (Polity Press, 1990). p. 19.
57. Nancy Baym, danah, boyd, "Socially Mediated Publicness: An Introduction," *Journal of Broadcasting & Electronic Media* 56, no. 3 (2012).
58. José Van Dijck, "Flickr and the Culture of Connectivity: Sharing Views, Experiences, Memories," *Memory Studies* 4 (2011).
59. Rudolf Richter, Schadler, Cornelia, "See My Virtual Self: Dissemination as a Characteristic of Digital Photography—the Example of Flickr. Com," *Journal of Visual Studies* 24, no. 2 (2010). p. 172.
60. William Dutton, H., "Through the Network of Networks—the Fifth Estate," *SSRN* October (2007); Larry Strelitz, Steenveld, Lynette, "The Fifth Estate: Media Theory, Watchdog of Journalism," *African Journalism Studies* 19, no. 1 (1998).
61. Meryl Alper, "War on Instagram: Framing Conflict Photojournalism with Mobile Photography Apps," *New Media & Society* September (2013).
62. Fred Ritchin, "Photography Changes Now News Is Reported," in *Photography Changes Everything*, ed. Marvin Heiferman (New York City: Aperture, 2012). p. 177.

63. Tim Highfield, Leaver, Tama, "A Methodology for Mapping Instagram Hashtags," *First Monday* 20, no. 1 (2015).
64. Eve Forrest, "Reflections on Flickr: Everyday Photography Practices Online and Offline," EITHER/AND, http://eitherand.org/reconsidering-amateur-photography/reflections-flickr-everyday-photography-practices-/.
65. Scott McQuire, "Photography's Afterlife: Documentary Images and the Operational Archive," *Journal of Material Culture* 18, no. 223 (2013).
66. Verne Kopytoff, "At Flickr, Fending Off Rumors and Facebook," NYTimes.com, http://www.nytimes.com/2011/01/31/technology/31flickr.html.
67. Facebook Inc., "Registration Statement on Forms S-1," (Washington D.C.: United States Securities and Exchange Commission, 2012).
68. Magdalena Olaszanowski, "The 1x1 Common: The Role of Instagram's Hashtag in the Development and Maintenance of Feminist Exchange," in *Hashtag Publics: The Power and Politics of Discursive Networks*, ed. Nathan Rambukkana (New York: Peter Lang, 2015).
69. Tama Leaver, "Born Digital? Presence, Privacy, and Intimate Surveillance," in *Re-Orientation: Translingual Transcultural Transmedia, Studies in Narrative, Language, Identity, and Knowledge*, ed. John Hartley, Qu, W (Shanghai: Fudan University Press, 2015).
70. Dean, "The Unfairness of Flickr's Explore Page," Photopreneur.com, http://blogs.photopreneur.com/the-unfairness-of-flickr-explore-page.
71. Ibid.
72. Teri Evans, "Flickr Founder Caterina Fake Tells All," Business Insider, http://www.businessinsider.com/caterina-fake-on-stepping-into-the-unknown-2011-4.
73. Ibid.
74. Center for Digital Democracy, "Datamining Our "Likes" on Facebook Reveals Details About Our Personal Lives," Center for Digital Democracy, www.democraticmedia.org/datamining-our-likes-facebook-reveals-details-about-our-personal-lives-new-research.
75. Facebook Inc.
76. Aaron Brady, "World without Walls," MIT Technology Review, http://www.technologyreview.com/article/425905/world-without-walls/.
77. Natasha Singer, "Mapping, and Sharing, the Consumer Genome," NYTimes.com, www.nytimes.com/2012/06/17/technology/acxiom-the-quiet-giant-of-consumer-database-marketing.html.

78. Acxiom Corporation, "The Moment of Truth," (Little Rock: Acxiom Corporation, 2013).
79. The CIO Report, "To Facebook You're Worth $80.95," wsj.com, http://blogs.wsj.com/cio/2012/05/03/to-facebook-youre-worth-80-95/tab/print/.
80. Instagram.com, "Terms of Use," https://help.instagram.com/478745558852511.
81. Facebook, "Terms of Service," Facebook.com, https://www.facebook.com/terms.
82. Ben Tarnoff, "Neoliberalism Turned Our World into a Business. And There Are Two Big Winners," The Guardian, https://www.theguardian.com/us-news/2016/dec/13/donald-trump-silicon-valley-leaders-neoliberalism-administration?CMP=share_btn_tw%201/.
83. Joshua Porter, "Social Design Patterns for Reputation Systems: An Interview with Yahoo!'S Bryce Glass" Bokardo.com, http://bokardo.com/archives/social-design-patterns-for-reputation-systems-two/.

4

The Transformative: *Whose Network?*

The idea of the emergence of a historically distinct *network* society marches in step with the rise in importance of computer networks as mediators of social, political, and economic life. What makes these networks unique, and thus the era in which they have become ubiquitous, is their *distributed* quality. The metaphor and technical reality of the *distributed network* is, as such, posited as the pre-eminent "diagram(s) for our current social formation."[1]

As a technical-social nexus, the distributed network can be leveraged for differing political aims, both as concept and as materialized infrastructure. The propertyscape of Immaterial Exceptionalism was outlined in the previous chapter in order to show how the notion of the *distributed* can be used to argue for a model of peer-to-peer social production that promotes a shift to horizontal and participatory social relationships, based on the ideals self-dominion, self-governance, and economic autonomy. In this context, the metaphor and technical reality of the distributed network is evangelized as the harbinger of new kinds of social relations, integral to understanding what makes the age *exceptional.*

In this chapter, I will be elaborating on the parameters of a paradigmatically different propertyscape that I call "Transformative Distribution." To begin with, Transformative Distribution provides us with a critique of

P. Kalantzis-Cope, *The Work and Play of the Mind in the Information Age*, Frontiers of Globalization, https://doi.org/10.1007/978-3-319-64650-3_4

Information Exceptionalism, as it becomes the legitimizing grammar for the subsumption of the digital social by capitalist systems of appropriation. Simultaneously, Transformative Distribution provides the case for imminence within the metaphor and technical realities of distributed networks: another imagination of what makes them *transformational*. As Michael Hardt and Antonio Negri argue, "a distributed network structure provides the model for an absolutely democratic organization."[2] In contradistinction to the workings of the *exceptional distributed*, Transformative Distribution approach offers another kind of possibility, a transformative potential in a social horizon outside of capitalist production, and an imminent alternative to Neo-Liberal economic globalization.

To explore the relationship between what are supposedly dueling social imaginaries of a distributed politics, the *exceptional* and the *transformative*, I draw on vignettes from a living story, connecting several social movements, whose dynamics are accelerated by distributed networks: the Arab Spring, the activity of the hacker group Anonymous, the Occupy Wall Street movement, and the alt-right's rise in the 2016 US presidential election. In looking at the kinds of practices that distributed networks afford to these movements, I am interested to illuminate the nature of the opportunities, the unintended consequences, the possibilities of critical stasis, and the contradictory effects of the *transformational* alternatives.

The Diagnosis: Informationalization, the Virtual, and Capitalist Development

In my analysis of the propertyscape of Information Privatization I explored the ways in which the logic of rivalrousness extends itself into the production and ownership of the work and play of the mind. Moving forward to Immaterial Exceptionalism I examined an emergent post-industrial logic embedded in a non-rivalrous approach to the production and ownership of the work and play of the mind. If these first two paradigms serve as talismans for the specific logics, the negotiations between, or transitory co-existence of variations of capitalist development, then the propertyscape I now turn to, Transformative Distribution, presents us with the paradigmatic non-capitalist alternative. As with the previous chapters, I am most interested in those writing at the birth of this moment, when the internet is new. A lot of those who I am referencing are among the first generation of theorists analyzing the birth of this historical paradigm and its configuration of practices, speculating about the trajectories of our everyday lives as they become more and more interconnected with and in digital communication systems.

The defining diagnosis of the propertyscape of Transformative Distribution is grounded in an analysis of an emergent mode of capitalist development, variously called "informational capitalism,"[3] "cognitive capitalism,"[4] the "cognitive-communication economy,"[5] or simply the "current mutation of capitalism."[6] A cornerstone of this diagnosis is the historical process understood as *informationalization*, whereby the work and play of the mind is absorbed into a homogenizing concept: *information*. As Arthur Croker and Michael Weinstein explain, when "knowledge is reduced to information," it is "stripped of its lived connection to history, judgment and experience."[7] This categorization shapes the work and play of the mind into an object that is ripe to be expropriated in commodity form. In the process, the specificity of cultural and social diversity becomes submerged, replaced by a general narrative of capitalist production and innovation connected to the winds of history that have shaped the supposedly natural trajectories of capitalist development.

Informationalization also becomes the means to address critically a certain kind of post-industrial techno-scientific determinism. Croker and Weinstein provide an eloquent insight here. They use "virtuality" as a metaphor for exteriority, arguing that the question of ethics in the post-industrial age becomes subverted by de-materialization, *becoming virtual*. The *virtual* allows for the framing of a coming "technotopia" based on the premise of fulfilling the human desire for "empowerment," "the dream of being god."[8] This ideology is based on the notion that defining meaning occurs as if one operates within a social *tabula rasa*, an empty social plane where the individual is free to determine their future based simply on self-defined identity and self-constituting experience.

Within this historical context the work and play of the mind becomes a central site of political, economic, and social struggle. As Paul Virilio writes, "economic warfare" has become an "informational conflict."[9]

The work and play of the mind, Christian Fuchs' argues, becomes a "strategic economic resource."[10] Strategic in an economic sense, the work and play of the mind comes to represent immaterial capital in a post-industrial information economy. But it is also strategic in an epistemic sense, defining social meaning, representing the horizons of political, social, and economic imaginations. It establishes the parameters of our abilities to conceive alternative worlds within a post-industrial historical setting. The notion of the *distributed* becomes the centerpiece of the struggle of economic and social imagination and its grounding in the very real practices of the work and play of the mind. The dominant contestation is between an interpretation of the *exceptional distributed*, a planetary scale vision associated with the propertyscape of Information Exceptionalism detailed in the preceding chapter, and an agenda of the *transformative distributed*, which I posit, not unproblematically, as a model of counter-hegemonic social order within forces of globalization.

Transformative Distribution

The Multitude, the Social Individual, the General Intellect

During the 1990s Michel Hardt and Antonio Negri famously articulated a politics of the Multitude. Their aim was to provide the groundwork for the critique of a de-territorialized, post-industrial capitalism and its *network* logic. They also sought to illuminate how an alternative approach to the *network* as evidenced in digitally mediated modes of peer production supported the possibility of alternative forms of collective political consciousness. In this schema, the social activity of the work and play of the mind can be viewed as central to the political vision of the Multitude, as a fundamental *in-common*, and the basis of alternative counter-hegemonic globalization.

Paolo Virno offers another critical building block for understanding the life *in-common* as the basis of an ontology of the Multitude. Virno focused on a "pre-individual reality" and the meta-process that "produces singularity."[11] This *reality* and *process* is grounded in three dimensions. First, its foundation is the "pre-individual as the biological basis of the species, that is, the sensory organisms, motor skill apparatus, perception abilities."[12] Second, it is grounded in language, as language is pre-individual—"language belongs to everybody and nobody."[13] Finally, it is grounded in a history of production—"the prevailing relation of production is pre-individual." In *in-common* represents "a pre-individual reality, which is essentially historical."[14] The work and play of the mind, for Virno, is the pre-eminent "common place" that expresses these fundamental dimensions of a pre-individual social. It is the world into which we are born and represents our common humanity. An ontology of the Multitude "distances itself radically" from the Liberal tradition, where the individual is the a priori of the social, "because this individuality is the final product of a process of individualization which stems from the universal, the generic, the pre-individual."[15] We become in and through others—determined and determining; in this way, as a *social activity*, the work and play of the mind is an anchor for the ontological ordering principle of a life *in-common.*

This re-contextualizing of the individual within the social provides a footing for an interpretation of a political economy of the work and play of the mind. The analytical substance of this critique traces its legacy to two elements found in the work of Marx: the *general intellect* and the *social individual.* For Marx the general intellect represents "general scientific labor," the "natural fruit of social labor,"[16] the social individual, "general productive power," a "social body," and "the great foundation stone of production and wealth."[17] Within industrial capitalist societies, a particular logic of private accumulation is grafted onto knowledge systems, where "invention becomes a business, and the application of science to direct production itself becomes a prospect which determines, and solicits it."[18] The "worker's struggle against machinery"[19] is thus as much oriented to the machine, because it represents dead labor, as it is more broadly to a certain techno-scientific outlook. This analysis posits the subsumption of the social individual or the social body by industrial capitalism. In one respect, it can be said that this subsumption is of the "organs of the human brain."[20] In another it is the subsumption of labor to wage labor.

The above economic analysis is retooled and used to interpret the production and ownership of the work and play of the mind in a post-industrial context. The *general intellect* and the *social individual* are applied as analytical tools with which to understand the processes by which the work and play of the mind is subsumed within the specifically post-industrial mutation of capitalism. It is here that the ontology of a pre-individual social serves as a rubric for critically assessing the post-industrial political economy and the ontological foundations of a living alternative.

One main point of differentiation, as Slavoj Žižek articulates, is that "Marx failed to envisage the possibility of the privatization of the general intellect itself."[21] On one axis, privatization—as the process of subsumption—occurs at the level of formal scientific knowledge. By formal I mean the privatization of the output of research and the development in both private and public sectors via patents and copyright. On another axis, however, privatization of the general intellect—again as the process of subsumption—takes on a new shape. In the post-industrial economy, as I explored in the previous chapter, digital media capture social production, the production of our life *in-common*. This occurs, for example, via the collection of our social activity in commercial social network platforms or in the everyday use of internet browsers. This collection of social activity creates information capital of value both in the digital and in the general economy. Here we have a phenomenon of critical importance in understanding the unique character of a post-industrial mode of capitalist subsumption, whether we are talking about cultural production writ large or the communication of individuals within digital networks.

Another fundamental difference in the character of the mode of subsumption in post-industrial capitalism is explained by what Marx calls "the natural fruit of social labor," or the relationship of living to dead labor. In the industrial model of capitalist production, efficiency and surplus value are increased when labor is systematically replaced by technology. This is a key element in the distinction between the dead labor of machines and living labor. Post-industrial capitalism, however, does not aim to replace living labor with dead labor. Rather, it uses machines to extend labor into unpaid time. As Cohen writes, "the issue is not the end of work. The issue is work without end."[22] And work without recompense. At the same time, a shift occurs from living labor as "appendages to the machine," to the embodied minds of living labor merged into machines that extend and distribute cognition. Taken together, as Christian Marazzi argues, both the formal and informal aspects of the production and ownership of the work and play of the mind provide evidence of the "leaching" of "vital resources from the Multitude" that comes to "represent the new organic composition of capital."[23]

Information Privatization and Immaterial Exceptionalism ontologically define the *many* from the *one*. That is, in these schemas, the individual is the a priori of the entire social, political, and economic project, as interpreted through the *right* to the work and play of the mind. The logics of property rights, rivalrous or non-rivalrous, are centered on the individual. The distinguishing move that creates the vocabulary, social imaginary and political orientation of the propertyscape of Transformative Distribution, is one that inverts individualist political ontologies. In the case of Transformative Distribution, the *one* is now interpreted on the basis of the *many*. The *Multitude*, as a political consciousness, represents this inversion of the ontological ordering principle at the *transformative* core of the propertyscape. The general intellect and the social individual represent the social foundation of the production and ownership of the work and play of the mind. Knowledge and culture, the lifeblood of the social, are repositioned as a priori *in-common* spaces for understanding "people-as-collective" who are creating "new common knowledge."[24] Connecting the two is a politics of strategic relation; the meaning of the right to the work and play of the mind must converge with the principles of the Multitude, our life in-common. So too must our regimes for the ownership of the work and play of the mind. This convergence sits at the core of the production of the social within the logic of Transformative Distribution and underpins the possibility of an alternative model of globalization.

The Algorithmic Metaphor

The propertyscape of Transformative Distribution offers a set of normative presuppositions grounded in the bio-political dimensions of the social activity underwriting the work and play of the mind and its governance through regimes of intellectual property rights. Bio-political critiques focus on the way a vision of techno-scientific progress becomes naturalized in, and by, the workings of everyday life, mediated by information communication systems that become manifest in an algorithmic metaphor. The algorithmic metaphor then becomes one of the pre-eminent sites of normative contestation between alternative notions of the distributed: the *exceptional* and the *transformative*.

The context for the bio-political dimensions of the algorithmic metaphor to which I now turn emerged as early as 1948 with Norbert Weiner's work on cybernetics.[25] Weiner's argument is as follows: as communication systems, computing machines are, in an analytic sense, analogous to biological systems. He argues that systems such as those found in early computational machines, and their internally referential and replicating communication logics, are in fact "quite similar" to biological feedback systems such as the central nervous system, or in the information flows between the central nervous system and the "sense organs."[26] This is not to say that computers and biological systems are the same, but that there is a convergence in our techno-scientific visions of each, allowing for the information-technological and the biological to be represented according to parallel grammars. The essence of this similarity is drawn from the capacity for reflexive and synergistic logics in both the computer and the biological systems. The effect can be to produce a metaphorical conflation where everything bio-systemic is reducible to computability, and by this reasoning, bio-systems and cognitive schemas are equivalent based on their processes of computability.

An insightful analysis of this conflation of the biological and the computable at the epicenter of the algorithmic metaphor is found in Eugene Thacker's discussion of DNA research. Thacker makes a distinction between bio-informatics and bio-computing. Bio-informatics is where in experimentation "the DNA is fully digital, and the entire process takes place on and between computers … [or] bio-computing." In experimentation, "the DNA is fully biological and the entire process of computation takes place in the test tube."[27] At times this distinction is collapsed, leading to a "fundamental assumption" of an "equivalency between genetic codes and computer codes."[28] In other words, there is a conceptual conflation of biological and digital information domains. The problem raised by bio-media is that the "biological and digital domains are no longer rendered ontologically distinct, but instead are seen to inhere in each other; the biological informs the digital, just as the digital 'corporealizes' the biological."[29] Providing context for the algorithmic metaphor, this conflation suggests an epoch-defining "evolutionary implosion where technology merges with biology."[30] "It's not simply about 'the body' and 'technology' in an abstract sense, but the biological body situated by a range of techno-scientific fields."[31] As computational systems operate based on algorithmic logics, the workings of algorithms themselves begin to become naturalized, and in turn assumed to be apolitical forces in their mediation of everyday life. This conflation opens the door to a view of the algorithmic, in a very abstract sense, as being *scientific* and thus *neutral*, while in an *organic* and thus *natural* state. Contradictorily, this process humanizes digital communication technologies via the algorithm, through biology, while simultaneously scientifically de-humanizing the biological as technology within the algorithm.

Adding to the critique of post-industrial capitalist development, the algorithmic metaphor also returns our attention to the *living* aspect of labor in the information communication economy. There is a specific emphasis on what living labor means in a post-industrial age. Definitional to the post-industrial age, more and more of one's non-work lifeworld is coming to be captured and structured as information by digital information systems. These lifeworlds, pre-digital or offline, already had a kind of rhythm based on networks of communication, analogous to biological rhythms, with distinctive cycles, dependencies, and feedback loops. Each seems to have an organic basis, metaphorically at least, and embedded network logics. As these lifeworlds begin to *live* and reproduce through the mediation of digital communication systems—in social media platforms for example—their already existing patterns of interaction become intertwined with the differing algorithms that work as intermediators, serving as the social glue, connecting content and people, according to the logic of digital platforms. On the one hand, this naturalizes the subsumption of life into the algorithm, seamlessly integrated as it seems. There is no separation between the two, thus, as the very being of the social is further grafted, as *nature*, onto the algorithmic. On the other hand, the algorithm becomes abstract as the scientific expression of the social, rather than a specific logic based on defined interests. Now political economy is hidden behind an abstract force. Beyond the *living* dimensions of labor, the bio-political aspect of the algorithmic metaphor can even extend into global financial services that run on automated, rights-protected algorithms, like biological systems. These are symptoms of the same phenomenon, in which the logic of capitalist production dictates a post-industrial bio-political order.

In the propertyscape of Immaterial Exceptionalism, the metaphor and technical reality of the *exceptional distributed* is used to make the case that peer-to-peer modes of production induce a shift to horizontal, participatory, and more democratic, social relationships, as afforded by the inherent workings of distributed networks and based on the ideal of individual self-actualization. Within this normative horizon, the algorithmic metaphor adds another dimension to the normative ideal of individual self-actualization. The workings of a biological and social order, as expressed in the workings of the distributed network, naturalize a principle of self-actualization without an organizing principle of centralized or hierarchical control.

Alexander Galloway argues, "the Net is not simply a new, anarchical media format, ushering in the virtues of diversity and multiplicity, but is in fact a highly sophisticated system of rules and regulations."[32] The algorithm is where many of these rules operate. The algorithm is not natural. Nor is it apolitical. Rather, it comes to structure and management of life. But the nature of this control is often hidden by the grammar of the *exceptional distributed*. The contestation over the meaning of the distributed—*the exceptional* and the *transformative*—is in the tension that "no one controls the network, but networks are controlled."[33] The focus of the *transformative* line of argument is to de-naturalize the ideal of the distributed as being without control. This is an essential step as we think about a *transformative* potential within the operations of social lives mediated by distributed networks.

The Hack, the Gift, the Transformational Commons

The critical posture defining the propertyscape of Transformative Distribution attempts to de-naturalize, to make political, the central concepts of our time. It aims to critique the reading of the foundations of the topologies and operations of post-industrial *network* power. This is not simply a blunt critique, but a first step toward considering the possible transformation of social life, wrestled away from capitalism's evolving, shape-shifting logics. Herein lies the counter strategy of envisioning the transformative potential, of life mediated by distributed networks. It is within the *hack* and the *gift* that we find, or should look for, the alternative social imaginary, capable of bearing out the *transformative* potential of an imminent *in-common*, as the basis of an alternative institutional topology: the *transformative commons.*

The hack represents a unique kind of post-industrial political action. In the cultures of computer programming hacking is often a form of protest or resistance: an act to remove digital rights locks, or breaking into private web spaces, for instance. In the writing of McKenzie Wark we find an argument for interpreting the specific historical nature of the hack as a politics of intervention, but in a way that situates this intervention within a longer view of the agonistic nature of political action.

Wark argues that history is the product of various abstract foundations—concepts, ideas, and theories. "History is the virtual made actual, one hack after another."[34] In the world history of meaning making, each abstraction, as a hack into history, reflects the grammar of a particular worldview projected onto social life. The process whereby work and play of the mind becomes *private property* was "itself an abstraction" that produced a "legal hack" into the social fabric of human creative activity.[35] But, he argues, the logic of private property traps only "one aspect" of the transformative potential of the action of *becoming property:* "its representation and objectification" within a capitalist worldview. The outcome of private property "cannot capture the infinite and unlimited virtuality from which the hack draws its potential."[36] In other words, the singularity of *private property* forced onto the work and play of the mind restricts and constrains the unlimited generative capacity of social meaning making and the capacity to imagine other worlds that *becoming property* affords. The *transformative* potential of property hacks is to open the possibility of breaking with conceptual narratives that give meaning to oppressive institutional topologies that continue to have power and influence over social life. Thus, the political action represented by the hack establishes our essential relation to modes of production of social meaning.

The hack also establishes our relation to modes of information production. In the post-industrial age, this relation defines a new frame of class struggle, between what Wark calls the *hacker* and *vectoralist* classes.[37] The vectoralist class is "so named because they control the vectors along which information is abstracted."[38] The power of this class lies in the monopolization of intellectual property and "the means of reproducing their value—the vectors of communication."[39] The vectoralist class forces us to buy our "culture back from its owners."[40] The hacker class is primarily engaged in the work and play of the mind: a "class that makes abstractions."[41] They are knowledge workers or cultural producers of various kinds. In their relationships to the means of immaterial production, hackers come "to struggle against the forms in which abstraction is commodified and turned into the private property of the Vectoralist class."[42] To rephrase a common call: immaterial workers of the world unite! This class is united by common interests that lie in the "free circulation of information, this being the necessary condition for the renewed expression of the hack."[43] As a prognosis, "the great hacks of our time may turn out to be forms of organizing free collective expression, so that from this time on, abstraction serves the people, rather than the people serving the rulers."[44] So the hack has a doubled role as a creator and a disrupter.

The transformative potential of the hacker class is not just to motivate political action via an affinity model for ordinary people to engage critically with capitalism's economic trajectory and historical convulsions. It is also an affinity model that has the potential to transcend the labor monism of traditional Marxist accounts of class. We are presented with a framework for class unity that is being sufficiently capacious to allow scope for cultural and epistemological diversity. As Wark argues, "the hacker is not interested in mass representation, but in a more abstract politics that expresses the productivity of differences." It is these differences that "have the potential also to produce a new knowledge of class formation and action when working together with the collective experience of all the productive classes."[45]

Finally, as a mode of political action, the hack is more than a matter of addressing inequities in the production and ownership of social imaginaries; it is also a strategy for intervention. "A hack touches the virtual—and transforms the actual."[46] As our lives become further imbricated in technologies capturing, the reproduction and distributing our everyday lives, it comes as no surprise that *media* and *mediation* are the focus of intervention. The hack stimulates what Geert Lovink defines as "strategies for media activism."[47] Here we encounter the rise of new media terminology: tactical media, culture jammers,[48] guerrilla communication.[49] Lovink, marking out some of the characteristics of this logic of intervention, says that it is "born out of disgust for ideology."[50] It "celebrates disorganization."[51] "It comes with a positive attitude towards contemporary digital technology."[52] He gives examples of these kinds of technological media activism: "video art, animations, hoaxes, Wi-Fi networks, music jam sessions, Xerox cultures, grassroots robotics, street graffiti, and (don't forget!) computer code."[53]

The hack provides the conceptual tools for understanding the nature of political action and affords an historical opportunity in an age mediated by distributed networks. The transformative potential of the age is found in our imminent *in-common*: our relations to social meaning making, the labor of immaterial production, and affinity in social diversity. The *gift* and *gift economies* are then, potentially, the next step to the realization of an alternative non-capitalist model of the *transformative commons*, manifest both in already existing social practices and looking toward the creation of new social practices and relations in the future.

The primary reference point in the tradition of interpreting how social activity is mediated or regulated by gift relations is the anthropological work of Marcel Mauss. Mauss asked, "what power resides in the object given that causes its recipient to pay it back?"[54] He investigated the ways in which, in so-called primitive societies, the gift provides a centerpiece for understanding informal and formal systems of reciprocity and obligation. His work presented a critical juxtaposition to Western meta-narratives naturalizing the logic of markets to community production. In turn, this served as a critical intervention to de-naturalize the processes of alienation that arise in communities mediated by commodity production and transactional market relationships. Within studies of the social impact of digital technologies, the gift has entered the literature in counter-distinction to the transactional logic of markets. In turn, such arguments become the basis for an evolving contemporary understanding of commons-based modes of production and ownership in the digital economy.

As an historic reality of the post-industrial age, the gift economies of the *transformative commons* already exist. The internet, in fact, is heralded as the pre-eminent sign of the possibility of a gift economy. Richard Barbrook writes that "at the cutting edge of the emerging information society, money-commodity relations play a secondary role."[55] "In the absence of states or markets to mediate social bonds, network communities are instead formed through the mutual obligations created by gifts of time and ideas."[56] Peer-to-peer networks, for example, media file sharing, collaborative open software development, or collaborative wiki-based knowledge production spaces, furnish evidence to these kinds of *already existing* gift cultures. These gift cultures are essential progenitors of an alternative *transformative distributed* in life mediated by distributed networks.

In alignment with the model of affinity of the *hack*, there is no universal, singular gift economy. Rather these emerging economies are emphatically in the plural. They represent a patchwork of peer networks, embodying a multiplicity of differences brought together by shared agendas. Each has their own determination on the nature *of* exchange value, mutual coordination, and the allocation or sharing of resources.

In their relationship to formal legal property regimes, some gift economies attempt to carve out spaces of mutual cultural and informational exchange in digital social production networks without any legal regime to guarantee the terms of reciprocity. They are *permission-less*. In other words, there is no governmental or legal guarantee that underwrites their practices of sharing. This is not to say there are no relational copyright regimes, because the law of the capitalist state insists that intellectual property is private property by default. However, the regulation of the protocols of sharing and reciprocity remains entirely informal. This reading of the *transformative commons* is grounded in the recognition of its move away from formal regimes of intellectual property.

Other approaches use legal agreements to over-ride the legal default to private property to secure commons-based peer production—for instance, in the free and open source software movement, Copy-Left rights agreements, and the General Public License (GPL). These licenses preserve some element of copyright in order to secure work for the public domain, including all subsequent reuses and derivatives in the world. Richard

Stallman, the original creator of the GPL, calls this approach "pragmatic idealism."[57] What is interesting about the GPL is that it defines global rights: "The GPL created a globally de-territorialized, almost all-inclusive commons. It only excludes those users who would refuse to release their own products under the GPL license."[58] GPL licenses enable the "protection of common use-value."[59] In this instance the case for the public good potential of the *transformative commons* is grounded in the establishment of formal systems of order within state-based regimes of intellectual property.

But then there is an even more ambitious agenda for the *transformative commons*. Hardt and Negri call for a "legal theory of the common … a framework that allows for common participation in the management of these goods and services. … The common marks a new form of sovereignty, a democratic sovereignty, in which the social singularities control through their own bio-political activity those goods and services that allow for the reproduction of the Multitude itself."[60] From this arises their notion of the Commonwealth as a kind of post-national constellation, positioning a common that "exists on a different plane from the private and the public, and is fundamentally autonomous from both."[61] Here a reading of the *transformative commons* is grounded in the establishment of formal systems of order that sit above, and radically transform, state-based regimes of intellectual property.

The Propertyscape of Transformative Distribution as an Ideal Type

In the propertyscape of Transformative Distribution the a priori of the pre-individual serves as the ontological ordering principle for life *in-common*. That is, we do not use, re-use, and produce knowledge, culture, science, or art in a vacuum. Rather, we build on foundations rooted in the history of social production. Thus, life *in-common*, as represented in the production and ownership of culture and knowledge, is the expression of a deeply lived, empirical reality. The political function of the pre-individual is to position the production and ownership of the work and play of the mind as the imminent basis to reclaim the social foundations of knowledge and culture. The historical process of *becoming property*, and its *transformative potential*, is because it engenders a political consciousness that recognizes the a priori of the *in-common* as its social cornerstone. Strategically, the aim is to stimulate social movements of an alternative counter-network politics, embracing the non-hierarchal affordances of the transformative potential of life mediated by distributed networks. Moreover, in this production of solidarities, the *in-common* of *becoming property* demands a context of the global, as ideas do not end at national boundaries.

The normative presuppositions of Transformative Distribution are informed by *transformative* potential of the distributed network. The *distributed network* stimulates a phenomenological account of how power operates in the information age. The right to the work and play of the mind dictates a bio-power, revealing modes of formal and informal governance. A case is made that the *exceptional distributed* serves as the mystifying veil over this governance, via an ideology of freedom of action. This obfuscating of governance itself intimately shapes the political consciousness of the *exceptional distributed*. Freedom of action is naturalized as the logic of historical progress, and this naturalization intensified as it is ingrained within the workings of everyday life mediated by distributed networks, as if the *true nature* of the digital is indistinguishable from social life itself. The *transformative* potential of the age begins with demand to de-naturalize the teleological assumptions of this meaning of the distributed, as proclaimed by the exceptional distributed, and manifest the apolitical assertion of the algorithm. The process *denaturalization* opens the possibility of the reclaiming of our species life, our bio-power. The distributed network not only reflects a post-industrial alienation, but suggests mechanisms for reclaiming ownership of the work and play of the mind.

The institutional topology of Transformative Distribution seeks to offer a new kind of institutional imaginary: the *transformative commons* as a *transcendent geography*. This *transcendent geography* is imminent within the work and play of the mind. It is imminent in a trans-historical sense, as *becoming property* is one of the generative forces in the making of social orders. Gift cultures are thus embodiment of a *transcendent geography* of a multiplicity of social imaginations that self-constitute order around systems of mutual obligation and reciprocity. These operate with or without a formal social contract needing to express rights to the work and play of the mind. They are imminent in a very historical sense when the practice of the self-constitution in gift cultures is facilitated by distributed digital networks. These already existing social practices could foreshadow the transcendence of the operating logics of capitalist development. A patchwork of digitally supported gift cultures makes up the *transformative commons*. In fact, this multiplicity of gift cultures is essential to the *transformative* nature of elements of the *transformative commons*.

To explore these dueling models of the distributed, the *exceptional* and the *transformative*, I want to look at several examples of these kinds of *transcendent geographies*. The acceleratory force of distributed networks on social movements using digital social media has come to exemplify new geographies of collective political action. At the level of human interaction, distributed networks have aided in the production of global solidarities, or what Manuel Castells terms "communal resistance identities."[62] At the level of infrastructure, the constitution of social activity is framed by the alternative geographies that support these interactions, infrastructures of sociality that escape the default territoriality of mass communication. In these examples, we see the appearance of what we might consider alternative globalizations or responses to the dominant narratives of the global. These occur at differing scales and with differing political aims.

Distributed Social Movements

The *sine qua non* of social movements is to bring about fundamental social change. For already existing, or emerging, social movements, digital technologies act as an accelerator for communication, organization, and action. In the context of digital social movements a useful frame of reference is to explore the degree to which the movements are shaped by the operating principles of the technologies themselves. In this living story, I will provide a sampling of several social movements: the Arab Spring, the activity of the hacker group Anonymous, the Occupy movement, and the alt-right's rise in the 2016 US presidential election. I am interested in what they share in common, their use of *social media*, the relationship of these tools to the shaping of political consciousness, and their visions for social change. The logic behind analyzing what is shared across such a spectrum of seemingly disparate and politically opposed movements is to assess the transformative potential of the *distributed*, both as a metaphor for social action and as a technical reality.

As I have discussed above, the *distributed* is a contested political terrain. To frame the dueling interpretations of the *exceptional* and *transformative* distributed within the context of the forces shaping distributed networks on social movements, I will make another parallel distinction between *mainstream* and *alternative* social media. These kinds of distinctions are never simple or clean cut. But making the distinction is a necessary starting point to tease out the differing interpretations of the distributed and what is presupposed to be their inherent relationship to modes of political action. As we delve into the living stories I have selected representing social movements that have been accelerated by digital social media, the sharpness of the distinctions I am making will tend to blur, and so too the cleanness of the different meanings of the distributed network as understood by the proponents of each propertyscape.

Mainstream social media—for example, Facebook, Twitter, or Tumblr—are what we are most familiar with. The story of the evolution of these platforms generally follows a similar narrative, beginning with a start-up origin myth, typically aligned with the vision of a single or small group of creators, passing through phases of venture capital funding and the rough and tumble of the investing world, then the end game of going to market via an IPO, with success measured by capitalization. Mainstream social media in these respects are seen to be successors of the traditional mainstream media, the old guard of mass news and entertainment.

There are several shared organizational characteristics of mainstream social media. They all aim to consolidate information about your activity via a single login or identity, with the goal of creating a personalized experience for the user by reading and then catering to their preferences and desires. The nature of affinity in these spaces is essentially atomistic. The individual is the epicenter of the social, surrounded by their friends or followers. As Clay Shirky, an evangelist of the exceptionalist position that I outlined in the last chapter, writes, "collaborative production relies on shared creation, but collective action creates shared responsibility, by tying the user's identity to the identity of the group."[63] Communication within mainstream social media is regulated via codes of morality or ethics, for example, banning images of the female nipple. Despite this type of regulation, mainstream social networks present themselves as fiercely non-political, mere facilitators of the crowd.

Mainstream social media represents the ideals of the exceptional distributed in the following ways. There is a cornerstone belief in the innateness of the platform's distributed qualities, producing a disruption of social relations. At the level of *human interaction* these networks are idealized via the disruption to traditional hierarchies presented by peer communities, rooted in the expression of self-autonomy and self-actualization. At the level of *infrastructure*, these networks are idealized for their offering of freedom of interaction, personal choice, in their end-to-end qualities. They disrupt decentralized media because users are connected via devices to the network directly, without hierarchy-creating mediators. The intellectual property disruption is understood via an exceptional condition allowing the co-existence of individual dominion over ownership of content. Social activity occurs with the creation of individual intellectual property, while allowing for the right for the platform or associated third parties to use of content for commercial purposes. The infrastructure, the platform itself, is the intellectual property of the platform owners.

Alternative social media have different kinds of origin stories, rooted in pre-digital independent, DIY, and grass roots media traditions. Within a specific history of digital media, their evolution begins with email Listservs and chat rooms of the mid-1990s. The common thread among these communication technologies is the desire to use media technologies to push the boundaries of new kinds of democratic communication in modalities that shift away from corporate information channels. These moves are often understood within the rubric of struggles for open access to information and social justice. The production of these networks is frequently juxtaposed to a corporate method via the production lens of a "craft"[64] rather and the professional. The intellectual property question is interpreted via collective ownership principles of both content and infrastructure.

There are several shared organizational characteristics of alternative social media. They are generally not-for-profit. The authority over content, what can be shared, is "performed socially or by transparently delegated editors rather than by professionals or elites; decision-making that is participatory and consensus based rather than compulsory and hierarchical."[65] Alternative social media are explicitly political, oriented toward either a specific target, for example, to democratize media as a means to democratize information, or political in a more nebulosus way, to achieve the goal of decentralized, leaderless, polycentric, non-hierarchical social orders; a shift from vertical to horizontal command.[66] A distributed network logic structures social interaction and the production of affinity; a "new way of doing politics" that "involves the creation of broad umbrella spaces, where diverse organizations, collectives, and networks converge around a few common hallmarks, while preserving their autonomy and identity-based specificity."[67] Consequently, the shared organizational characteristic of alternative social networks is to afford "diverse, locally rooted struggles" the capacity to "directly link up, articulating around common objectives without compromising their autonomy or specificity, which is precisely what global justice activists mean when they talk about 'unity through diversity.'"[68]

Alternative social media represent the ideals of the transformative distributed in the following ways. Herein lies the cornerstone belief is in the innateness of the platform's distributed qualities to produce a disruption of traditional social relations. At the level of *human interaction*, the disruption depends on the platform's ability to communicate horizontally, with tools for consensus-based decision-making outside of a command structure. It is believed that alternative distributed networks "represent much more than technology and organizational form; they also provide new cultural models for radically reconstituting politics and society more generally."[69] At the level of *infrastructure* the disruption is manifest in the possibility to build an "alternative infrastructure."[70] The underlying code is often "distributed" too, in the use of already existing open source software, or by making accessible and reusable the code of software tools created. Thus, idea of *autonomous* media has emerged.

Both models of social media, *mainstream* and *alternative*, begin with a claim about there being something *innate* in the new technology itself that allows for the possible disruption of life mediated by digital social media. Nonetheless in their *constitution* of social activity, at the level of *human interaction* they present models that are oppositional, with each suggesting a different cultural logic in the model of affinity. The mainstream positions the individual as the generative basis for affinity; the alternative positions the in-common as the generative basis for affinity. These models of affinity reverberate within and from the technical *infrastructure* affording action in digitally mediated social space.

But to begin to unpack the binary of the dueling models of the exceptional and transformative, as manifest in the mainstream and alternative, these two views of the *distributed* must also be considered in an antagonistic relationship. Manuel Castells encapsulates this antagonism precisely. On one hand, we have the alternative social networks that give evidence of a "decentered form of organization and intervention, characteristic of the new social movements." Nevertheless, these are both "mirroring and counteracting the networking logic of domination in the information society."[71] The latter are represented in what I am calling mainstream social media. It is from this dialectical basis that we start to see critical fissures highlighting the distinctiveness of each model, challenging their autonomy in facilitating modes of political action.

Technologies of Dissent

The first strand in this living story and perhaps the best known is the "Occupy" movement, with its explicit stance toward the transformative potential found within capitalist crisis. Occupy emerges from several social movements shaped by both *mainstream* and *alternative* digital social media. In this and subsequent strands of the story, a particular historical milieu grounds connections between these disparate social moments, their *technologies of dissent*, the shaping effects of new technologies in the production of political consciousness, and the scope of constitutive collective political action.

To gain an insight into the production of political consciousness supported by *mainstream* social media, the scope offered by these media for political action, and the resonance of meanings between the two, I turn to the ways in which agents of the Arab Spring, specifically activists in Tunisia and Egypt, used mainstream tools such as Facebook, Twitter, and YouTube. The Jasmine Revolution in Tunisia was a revolutionary culmination point, bringing to a head decades of the "tyranny and corruption" of the Ben Ali regime.[72] While there was relative prosperity in Tunisia at the time of the uprising in comparison with many other North African states, nonetheless there were also high levels of economic and political disfranchisement. In 2011 this disfranchisement was symbolized by a 26-year-old Mohamed Bouazizi, who set himself on fire in a visceral protest against Tunisian authorities. This triggered a wave of similar suicides or attempted suicides.[73] Images and videos of these events quickly found their way onto the internet. Despite a history of internet restrictions in Tunisia, mainstream social networks became the central platforms to organize *locally* and speak *globally*. In the words of a Tunisian activist, "we could protest for two years here, but without videos no one would take any notice of us."[74] During the protest movements Tunisian activists relied heavily on Facebook to organize and disseminate information. At the time Facebook was not included within the "scope of Tunisia's online censorship."[75] Twitter also was used as a voice for protestors. Yasmine Ryan: "Twitter has been a bastion for activists. Because people can access Twitter via clients rather than going through the website itself, Tunisians could still communicate online relatively free from surveillance on the part of the regime."[76] Noureddine Miladi argues that the internet becomes a critical democratic, participatory platform for navigating issues, "the virtual space in which Tunisians debate the developments in various towns and cities."[77]

In January 2011, protesters opposing Hosni Mubarak's regime filled Egypt's Tahrir Square. The main organizing tool for the initial gathering was a Facebook page created by Wael Ghonim, a self-described "accidental activist" and then Head of Marketing for Google Middle East and North Africa.[78] Ghonim was motivated to start the page after finding an image on the internet of a young man, Khalid Mohamed Said, being beaten to death by the Egyptian police.[79] This image was the key point of leverage for the page, "We Are All Khalid Said," which became an important spark for the Egyptian Revolution. In explaining the language of the page, he says, "using the pronoun 'I' was critical to establishing the fact that the page was not managed by an organization, political party or movement of any kind. … On the contrary, the writer was an ordinary Egyptian devastated by the brutality inflicted on Khalid Said and motivated to seek justice."[80] Two minutes after setting up the Facebook page, "300 people had joined it. Three months later, that number had grown to more than 250,000."[81] The importance of the origins of these movements in mainstream social networks cannot be overstated. As Amr Gharbeia, a Tahrir Square blogger, says, "this revolution is the result of someone sending a Facebook invitation to many people."[82]

In countries like Egypt and Tunisia the focal points of media censorship were determined by a political elite. In these cases, mainstream social networks which were not easy to censor except in toto did facilitate participation and real democratic action. As an insight into the nature of political action, not only did the *distributed* qualities of these mainstream tools assist the organizers of the protests in their material appearance, they were also critical to getting a message to the world. Whether it was in the form of a YouTube video, a Tweet, or a Facebook post, these mainstream social networks became a way to bypass transitional national communication gatekeepers. A reporter from Al Jazeera noted in regard to the Tunisian revolution, "Al Jazeera heavily relied on referencing Facebook pages and YouTube in reporting the raw events, which marked a key turning point in unveiling the bloodiness and horror of the manner with which the police had been dealing with the riots."[83] Or, to quote a reporter from the Washington Post, "for days, I have been glued to Twitter, on which events in Tunisia are discussed much faster than mainstream media could report them."[84] The claims of the Arab Spring were thus amplified and able to resonate globally through use of mainstream social networks. This paints a picture of the transformative potential of the exceptional distributed, as a model of political self-actualization.

Turning to the production of political consciousness, the scope of political action, and the resonance of meanings between the two supported by *alternative social media*, I turn to the message board 4chan and the emergence of the hacker group Anonymous. 4chan, launched in 2003, is one of the largest active forums in the world with 10 million unique visitors and 705 million page views a month.[85] It is a "sprawling web of message boards on which users post images of everything from their favorite actors to their favorite bowel movements."[86] It is a primary source of the internet's characteristic viral memes and language games, an often-unseen underbelly bubbling up into contemporary mainstream culture. It is also the home to a very large community of software coders and an active hacker community. As a place holder, there are other very important demographic and sociological characteristics of 4chan users needing consideration, and I will return to this later. But for now, the take away is that, as Tim Hwang from Harvard's Berkman Center for the internet and Society argues, "it really looms big as the dark heart of the Internet. It's not common that one place generates so much."[87]

Several network characteristics make 4chan a unique space on the internet. Nothing gets archived, "threads disappear within an hour."[88] If something is going to last on the network it must be continually reposted by members. 4chan has no search functionality. Because of this lack of archiving and searchability "it's one of the last places on the Internet where you really can say anything you want and it won't come back to haunt you."[89] 4chan also has no requirement to register one's name. Nearly everyone posts under the same name, *anonymous*, with a group identity emerging under the signifier of *anons*. Here the platform's founder Christopher Poole draws a distinction with mainstream social media and their attempt to define you with vis a single identity. "Google and Facebook would have you believe that you're a mirror, but we're actually more like diamonds … look from a different angle, and you see something completely different. … Facebook is consolidating identity by making us more simple than we truly are … the fast-food approach to identity."[90] 4chan offers a space when you, under the guise of the *anon*, can become anyone, and this affordance is inherent to the transformative potential of the distributed.

As a general insight into the nature of distributed collective action afforded by 4chan, in 2009 a member decided to nominate Poole in the CNN.com/Time Person of the Year user poll. This member posted a code script on one of the 4chan message boards demonstrating how to manipulate the voting system, specifically the voting URL protocol, so that a voter could bypass the technical rules of the CNN.com voting process that limited voters through an IP blocker. This script allowed voters to "submit about 300 votes per minute from a single IP address." This has what is called a "precision hack."[91] With over 16,000,000 votes, Poole soon outpaced Barack Obama, Vladimir Putin, and Oprah Winfrey to win Time's Person of the Year. On the one hand, this kind of political action speaks to a distributed organizational and participatory power, a kind of innate decentralized, non-hierarchical, democratic power afforded by the distributed nature of the information age. On the other, it also offers grounds for a stinging critique. This was as much a poke at CNN as it was an underhand statement about the logic of crowdsourcing at the center of the digital economy, a juxtaposition to the workings of the mainstream, falsifying and undermining its logic. We also start to see a kind of ironic playfulness and satire as a key tool to undermine the mainstream system, a frequent aspect of the grammar of political action communicated by these social movements.

There are many active political movements on 4chan, though I want to focus on one, Anonymous, because of its importance in the Occupy movement. Anonymous directly emerged from 4chan. Its name, in fact, originates in "anonymous" as the naming principle of 4chan. Gregg Housh, an internet activist associated with the movement, says, the "rules of these communities spawned some of the original thinking behind the group."[92] Anonymous is a politically complex movement. "Anonymous isn't an army, or a group, per se. There aren't members." It is issue-based, forming and disappearing relational to the target. "Anonymous is nobody and nothing and nowhere."[93] The politics of Anonymous is directly related to the distributed affordances of the social aspect of this platform. We have here an anarchistic reading of participatory politics, meshed with a new, technology-driven interpretation of democratic sensibilities and political action. As argued by Mark Townsend, "ostensibly, Anonymous is a 24-hour democracy run by whoever happens to be logged on; leaders emerge and disappear depending on the target that is being attacked and the whims of members."[94]

As a precursor to the Occupy movement, and with broader connections into the propertyscape of Transformative Distribution, Anonymous is also important because it has a commonly shared position toward the privatization of intellectual property and the war on piracy. Exemplifying this war, the Motion Picture Association of America (MPAA) hired an Indian firm Aiplex Software, as "cyber hit men" to chase down copyright infringements occurring online. This contractor was rumored to have been conducting denial of service attacks (which are illegal in most countries) on torrent sites that hosted file-sharing services—such as Pirate Bay, one of the largest file-sharing sites on the internet.[95] The response of Anonymous—Operation Payback—was to shut down the websites of the MPAA and the Recording Industry Association of America (RIAA). On these and a range of other hacked websites, the following *attack message* was posted:

> Over the past years, we have borne witness to a technological revolution. The individual has become free, in the most extreme anarchistic sense, to share ideas. … There have been similar instances of such revolutions of the mind. Their effects on society are inestimably great. As in past times with the invention of the printing press, so it is today that the people embrace this revolution, this new "anarchy" of freedom to share, while their autocratic rulers seek to crush this freedom. … In spite of censorship in the form of copyright law and other restrictions, the people have succeeded in distributing content to the poor, the underprivileged and the oppressed. … Piracy democratizes knowledge and makes education affordable. … History repeats itself. There was a time when powers that be attempted to silence the printing press, the blank cassette and the recordable CD. All of these previous attempts at censorship have failed, and future attempts of this nature are doomed to failure. Indeed, the sequestration of human knowledge for the benefit of extremist capitalism is treason against the whole of humanity. All should have the right to listen to a melody, experience a plot and learn from the aggregate of human knowledge available online.[96]

This statement highlights the close linking of language articulating a freedom to communicate with the production and ownership of the work and play of the mind in the networked information economy. This issue constantly preoccupies members of these networks. Here freedom of property and communication are equated with anarchist principle, a radical expression of the distributed network and its transformative potential in the post-industrial age.

If we are to align these broad social movements with their *technologies of dissent*, what we find is that both mainstream and alterative social media can bring about *transformative* social change. Thus, the dueling models of the distributed, the *exceptional* and the *transformative*, seem here to be less dueling: they both represent an ideal of an *in-common* that can transcend national frameworks of affinity; they both provide social infrastructures that move away from state-based control of information, communication, and political action. Nevertheless, one important distinction remains and becomes apparent, opening a productive line of investigation in the context of the propertyscape of Transformative Distribution.

Mainstream social media, as the representative of the *exceptional* distributed, supports a move of *becoming public*, or bringing to visibility, constitutive collective political action. Alternative social media, as the representative of the transformational distributed, displays a move of *becoming private*, anonymous, without history, actions by anonymous actors. This thus begs the following question. If the latter is a skeleton key to open the transformative potential of the *distributed*, in contradistinction to the *exceptional*, is not the politics of anonymity counter to a healthy participatory politics? Does it reveal an emerging privatization in this alternative social media model too, pushing communication spaces into another kind of private—private actions by anonymous actors, where the social is hidden and merely circumstantial?

#OccupyWallStreet

The Occupy movement offers another vignette in the living story I am describing. With its explicit critique of capitalism, it is aligned with the *transformative* potential of the distributed network that I am associating with the propertyscape of Transformative Distribution. The original call for the movement came from one of the tactical briefings of Adbusters. Adbusters is a non-for-profit media organization founded in Vancouver in 1989.[97] Adbusters originally bought the URL used for the main website http://www.occupywallstreet.org.[98] Kalle Lasn, co-founder of Adbusters, claims that the idea for Occupy "came out of these brainstorming sessions we have at Adbusters. … We were inspired by what happened in Tunisia and Egypt and we had this feeling that America was ripe for a Tahrir moment."[99] The first tactical briefing was made available on their website, but also distributed through email lists and other mainstream social media channels. In this briefing, they spoke of the hope of a "radical democracy of the future." They also defined the target of the movement, "the greatest corrupter of our democracy: Wall Street, the financial Gomorrah of America." The briefing goes on to call for the initial occupation in New York City. "On September 17 we want to see 20,000 people flood into lower Manhattan, set up tents, kitchens, peaceful barricades and occupy Wall Street."[100]

From the initial briefing up until the first encampment in Zuccotti Park, there was a steady flow of further briefings. Two weeks out another tactical briefing announced the support of the Anonymous to the now rapidly growing movement.[101] Another tactical briefing sent ten days before the initial occupation suggested turning lower Manhattan into "an American Tahrir Square."[102] On the day before, 16 September, they sent out an Orientation Guide, using the twitter hashtag #OCCUPYWALLSTREET, detailing the time and location of the initial gathering at Zuccotti Park.

Aligned with the lessons of the Arab Spring, Adbusters spoke about a new formula of protest, "a shift in revolutionary tactics," where "we talk to each other in various physical gatherings and virtual people's assemblies."[103] Throughout the briefings is a language I have been trying to interpret via the propertyscape of Transformational Distribution—*jammers, dreamers, and horizontals*. The briefings herald a movement of "anarchic swarms."[104] In an article written for the Washington Post, Adbusters co-founders Lash and Micah White compare the Occupy Movement to the struggle of 1968. However, "this time the horizontal, open-source, peer-to-peer ways of the internet-savvy generation, living in a much more dangerous era of multiple synergetic crises, just might be able to succeed."[105] In other words there is the belief that the *distributed* qualities of the technological platform of the age provide a unique opportunity to disrupt capitalist development. As such, the movement is in deep conversation with a critique of the *exceptional distributed* model:

> For more than a decade revolutionaries and culture jammers have been paralyzed by the computer screen. Trusting the promises of technocrats

> and digital visionaries ... we've come to rely far too heavily on a particular form of Internet organizing ... we entrusted our revolution to San Francisco techies and put our faith in the methods of advertising. But we have become so dependent on digital gimmicks that our revolutionary potential is now constrained.[106]

The connection I am trying to make is as follows: from its moment of birth, with Adbusters' purchase of a website domain, the *political consciousness* of the Occupy movement is deeply imbricated in the affordances of the *distributed*, both as a metaphor and as a technical reality. As such, both in its dimensions of critique and advocacy of immanent transformative social practices, the distributed nature of a technology is presented as a key to disrupting capitalism—based on localized, grassroots, democratic, social network activism. To meet the moment on its own terms, as a politics of *transformation*, and connect to the dueling models of distributed technologies, I return to the categorization of the *mainstream* and the *alternative* as members of the Occupy movement used a mix of mainstream and alternative social media to communicate and organize.

I begin with a sample of use of the mainstream distributed social media, what I have been defining as the tools of the *exceptional distributed*. Again, this summary does not attempt to be exhaustive, but aims to provide an insight into the characteristic modes of political action.

In developing a collective consciousness, mainstream platforms like Tumblr, an image-based micro-blogging social network, were very important. One Tumblr blog, *We Are The 99%*, is of representative importance.[107] The directive was to write your personal 99% story on a sign, take a photo of yourself with that sign, and then post the image to the blog. Rebecca Rosen interprets the site as a "collaborative confessional" building a "self-service history ... with no curator and no narrator."[108] The importance of this blog cannot be overstated. As a reporter from the Washington Post said, "it's not the arrests that convinced me that Occupy Wall Street was worth covering. ... It was a Tumblr blog called, 'We Are The 99 Percent,' and all it's doing is posting grainy pictures of people holding handwritten signs telling their stories, one after the other."[109] Joanne McNeil, head curator of digital media at the New Museum in

New York City, argues that this blog informed a visual consciousness, "a kind of 'virtual reality' for the marchers by marking each of us as members of the huge social class represented by the blog."[110] Through this Tumblr page the "lives of real people" and their "unmistakable hardships" were ripe to be re-blogged and re-tweeted.

For facilitating organization and collective action, mainstream platforms like Facebook and Twitter were essential. The two earliest Facebook pages set up by the movement were *Occupy Together* and *Occupy Wall Street.* Every city across the globe with an Occupy movement had a Facebook page. The "Occupy Network" application for Facebook consolidated different Occupy sites, at one point drawing together nearly 3.5 million people.[111] These differing Occupy movement pages become the space for members to share news and personal stories and organize events. The viral nature of these pages is of course related to the sites of protest across the globe, but also must be attributed to the way Facebook is embedded within the digital social, aligning your status with that of the movement.

One of the first public calls to action came from an Adbusters status update: "Dear Americans, this July 4th dream of insurrection against corporate rule. #OCCUPYWALLSTREET."[112] The use of Twitter as a communication tool was critical too, both among protesters within the movement, and to communicate a message to world. The tweet is perfect for political messages, a communication structure that forces your message into 140 characters, the length of a pithy slogan. Such messages are also ripe for traditional media sound bites. In nearly all digital and print literature shared by the Occupy Movement, topic areas are accompanied by a hashtag, for example to talk about city-specific encampments #OCCUPYATLANTA, #OCCUPYBOSTON, and so on. A social media analytics company, Trendr, commented that "the daily volume of posts about the movement on Twitter averaged 400,000 to 500,000 a day since Oct. 7 [2011] … and there were just over 2 million Twitter posts on Nov. 15, the day the police took apart the Zuccotti Park camp."[113] Using a data set collected on November 25, Marc Smith of the Social Media Foundation concluded, "Occupy clusters look like a series of firework explosions."[114]

Two location-based social networking tools were also used—Foursquare and Meetup. Both platforms process GPS-enabled check-ins on mobile communication devices. A Foursquare check-in page also includes images posted from the site of protest, the number of other check-ins, a listing of similar local check-in locations, and a discussion space. The central Occupy page on Meetup is "Occupy Together."[115] It has similar technical affordances and in 2012 hosted 2986 communities in 2752 cities.

While I have described these mainstream social media platforms separately, they are not silos. In fact, quite the opposite, they become deeply interconnected with each other. These dependencies come to form a meta-mainstream distributed social network. All of these social networks have links to share on other pages, to become a friend or a like on Facebook, to follow on Twitter, to add tags to your posts in order to find conversation threads on Tumblr. What emerges is a common, cross platform language. For example, the Foursquare Occupy page uses a Twitter # (#OCCUPYWALLSTREET), Facebook posts on Occupy pages of the "We are the 99%" Tumblr blog, or YouTube videos of police violence. Supporting this is a growing folksonomy of tags so people can find these posts, images, videos, and conversations.

I now turn to examples of the production and uses of alternative social media by members of the Occupy movement. As a general frame, the fundamental drive to develop these networks was to gain a level of independence from mainstream distributed networks. Moreover, as mechanisms for communication, these alternative tools rose out of certain institutional critique—turning to local, grounded, participatory sites of resistance. Again, what follows is shorthand for the rich tapestry of tools that were produced during the movement.

To bolster modes of consensus decision-making, tools like People's Skype were developed.[116] Drawing upon the idea of the *people's mic*, the practice of communicating at Zuccotti Park's General Assemblies, this group developed a "phone-powered, distributed voice and voting system." You could set up account by calling a number, and then, when others can call this number, they enter the unique account number and listen to the People's Skype. This tool provides an open source communication system that assists in voting (by pressing a number) and real-time information sharing.

To foster community-based social media, platforms were developed, one example of which was the Global Square Project, an open source alternate to Facebook. One of the founding coders for this project, Ed Knuston, explains the motivation to create this social network: "We don't want to trust Facebook with private messages among activists."[117] Using a friend-of-a-friend model to ensure the security of communication within the platform, it aims to create "an open community where everyone is welcome. It is peer-to-peer, horizontal and non-hierarchical. This is a space where coders, designers, iTechs, artists, activists and philosophers are invited to collaborate together."[118] It aims to combine a grounded politics of "local squares" to one of a "global square" where "people of all nations can come together as equals to participate in the coordination of collective actions and the formulation of common goals and aspirations."[119]

To secure an autonomous infrastructure, groups developed technologies like the Freedom Tower.[120] Using peer-to-peer technologies, this project used a number of computers and routers to produce a free Wi-Fi network at Zuccotti Park. What made this unique is that it was not part of the *global internet.* Rather it created its own internal local network through which Occupiers could communicate and share information. This "private internet in a suitcase"[121] offered a model of a cooperative internet services provider and an autonomous mesh network. What makes it fundamentally different from the global internet is that it cannot be shut down by governments and is free from the influence of corporate providers of web services. The creators of this communication structure say, "we envision communications infrastructure that is owned and operated cooperatively." It is a communication structure "committed to the tenets of free information, free culture, and free society."[122]

These technological affordances of the distributed dovetail with a possibility of supporting a commons, in line with the ideals of the *transformative commons.* In Zuccotti Park there was an agenda of building an alternative economy—"OWS is a thriving commons of economic activity."[123] "Inside Zuccotti Park, and many other occupation sites, there is the production, consumption, and distribution of useful goods and services: the kitchen committee produces and distributes thousands of meals per day, the comfort committee produces clean laundry and clean bodies, the technology and open source committee is constructing a tech infrastructure, and so on."[124] This grounding gives the movement legitimacy as a site of democratic participation. Says Jodi Dean, "general assemblies are also unique settings for intense, face-to-face engagement among people who for too long have been separated behind screens, gates, and other barriers. Having broken those barriers, we now need to build our fighting strength."[125] Joanne McNeil also makes this link to the virtual: "Zuccotti Park's tenuous standing as a privately owned public park seems an inevitable metaphor for the questions of free speech, assembly, and property rights posed by so many virtual spaces."[126] Hardt and Negri's question remains, "how our movement can evolve new organizational structures that will allow the assemblies—and their highly innovative participatory model of decision-making—to survive beyond the occupations and become a permanent fixture of our emerging global society."[127]

So, what do we make of the Occupy movement's use of *mainstream* and *alternative* social media? To interpret, I will return to the *public/private* tension with which I closed the last section, where the mainstream demands a *public-ness* and the alternative a *private-ness*. But now I want to look at this tendency via the explicit critique of capitalist development that the Occupy movement represents and begin to pave a path back to the dueling visions of the distributed, the *exceptional* and *transformative*, as broader visions of the production of the social.

The first model of the production of the social, represented by mainstream social media and the *exceptional distributed*, I will call the *public–private*. On the one hand, there is this trend to the *public-ness*, with mainstream social media playing an integral role in communicating, organizing, and acting on the agenda of the Occupy movement. In constructing an *in-common*, the language of friends and followers had a semiotic effect on an emerging global social consciousness which aligns with the movement's intentions. The ability to organize collectively and communicate issues to a global audience free from the rules and regulations of the nation-state accentuates the *exceptional* qualities of mainstream distributed networks and the characteristics of the movement itself.

On the other hand, in their demand of *public-ness* mainstream distributed media reveal a contradictory trend. In this scenario, public actions become a privately owned information good. Mainstream social media extract value out of informal, communicative, social labor. Moreover, the metadata captured in the use of mainstream social media by an Occupy activist is equivalent to all such data, politically flattened into commercially valuable *information*. There are no distinctions when it comes to the substantive content of the data it captures—activity is activity, every action drawing more users into the network. It is of no consequence that the content is anti-capitalist. In fact, this anti-capitalist movement, it could be argued, is albeit inadvertently assisting in the extension of these corporate-owned platforms into our collective digital social life. At the level of social infrastructure and the making of a digital public sphere, these communication platforms are owned by private corporations. This mainstream social infrastructure is also highly centralized and part of a formal command structure: a vertical, top-down communications architecture, regulated by the content owners of the network. Data is hosted on private secure servers in data centers, and the platform itself is regulated by a mix of open standards (such as sharable calendaring) and proprietary standards (such as the platform's code). Thus, despite immediate intentions, participation in Occupy through mainstream social networks assists in the growth of information capital for these social networks and the construction of a digital public sphere that is regulated by private corporations. In this context, *becoming public* is a mystifying veil in the exceptional distributed, the trick concealing the actual privatization of apparently public activity. The effect is to create a kind of a new type of *public–private*.

The second model of the production of the social, represented by the production and use of alternative social media and the *transformational distributed*, I will call the *private–public*. On the one hand, the Occupy movement emerged as a highly visible movement contesting global capitalism. The production and use of alternative social media offers evidence of social sharing, peer production, and the commons, at both the level of meaning making and institutional order, a *transformative* way of defining the *public* as aligned with a vision of the affordances of the distributed network. This vision is something more than just about lives mediated in digital spaces. As Hardt and Negri argue, talking of the global Occupy events, "these are struggles for the common … they contest the injustices of neoliberalism and, ultimately, the rule of private property."[128]

Despite the emancipatory traces of these struggles and their aspirations, in the production and uses of alternative social media we also see a trend toward another kind of privatization. This trend is in part a response to the privatization of information in mainstream social media and its broader vision of life mediated by distributed networks represented by the exceptional distributed. The irony is, that at the level of content, if you are to ensure you are not part of the accumulation of information capital you are forced to make your personhood and activity private, to minimize the ways that economic value can be extracted from your actions. At the level of infrastructure, because global internet access points are staffed by gatekeepers in the form of internet service providers, there is a push toward alternative infrastructures that are private spaces. In these approaches to the development of alternative distributed networks, the process of anti-informationalization forces us to reconsider the future of the public and private spheres. This presents another question, this time for civics—Are secure and private networks the antithesis of an open public sphere? It is a conundrum because in taking a stance against the corporate-driven global internet one has to question what might we lose?

In another troubling irony, with the question of the *private–public sphere* still open, how distant are these alternative models from capitalism's value-extracting tentacles? Susannah Vila, co-founder of The Engine Room, an organization that researches forms of digital advocacy, argues that "the Occupy movement is not only benefiting from digital tools, but also adding to and transforming the landscape of new media available to today's advocates."[129] What does it mean when the Occupy movement gets listed by *Fast Company* magazine as one of the "50 most innovate companies of 2012"? They "embody all the traits that make a Fast Company—Disruptive. Small-d democratic. Transparent. Tech savvy. Design savvy. Local and global. Nimble. Values-driven."[130] Of course Occupy is not a company, but we see here another example of how capitalist logics can incorporate even the politics of *transformation*. Thus, even radical alternatives can be normalized within the system of capitalist order in the digitally mediated, post-industrial age. In fact, it may very well be that alternative distributed approaches also play into legitimizing the mainstream language of technology, peer production, social media, and open source. To what extent then, to take the Occupy example, is an anti-capitalist movement in fact sustaining post-industrial capitalism's future, economically and ideologically? Maybe, we could say that Transformational Distribution might fall victim to the same traps as Information Exceptionalism, casting a mystifying veil over this stage of capitalist development as it progresses undaunted.

The point of this analysis is not to discredit the Occupy movement. My aim, in part, has been to reveal the capacity of post-industrial capitalism to incorporate difference and diversity. This has been exemplified in the democratic struggles of the Arab Spring, but the capacity to absorb within its systems of value extraction is all the more poignant in the case of the incorporation of the anti-capitalist Occupy movement.

An equally worrisome lesson to be learned is that perhaps the only way one can be free of capitalist subsumption in the digitally mediated information age is to push in the direction of anti-informationalization and anti-government, toward *private information* and a *private sphere*. Does this force an alternative network politics, and its *transformative* potential, into securely bounded private spaces? And in the various degrees of embracing the anonymous and the private, does this mean that some element of the private, a *common private*, is necessary to secure a non-capitalist alternative? If so, what is the future for thinking about the public sphere, as an *in-common?* Who decides inside and outside? What would it mean to have a digital public sphere built on anonymity? Is this the true *transformative* of the *distributed*, either as a metaphor or as a technical reality?

Speech Without Regulation

In closing out this living story of *distributed* social movements I want to return to 4chan. There is not a singular connection between 4chan and Anonymous, and 4chan has since become famous for cultivating the alt-right. There is a deep association with a politics of the *distributed* and the contradictory status of the private–public.

Here we need to examine the general demographic qualities of 4chan. 4chan's millions of *anons* are generally young men who spend a large amount of their time in *virtual worlds*, for example, on message boards like 4chan, or in online gaming spaces. Their in-common is constructed around their perceived struggle with the world around them, as reflected their current conditions of life. In the most critical reading, they are "largely made up of people who have failed at the real world and have checked out of it, entering the fantasy worlds of internet forums and videos games."[131] The defining cultural characteristic of these message boards is to invert the principles of "*in real-life*," commonly named with the acronym IRL. Unlike IRL, these virtual spaces allow riskless defeat, in conversation or in games. They can also be spaces that one can assert a "power" that cannot be asserted IRL and victories within the game. Thus, the affordances of these virtual spaces can nurture a culture that "celebrates failure," while stoking an intensified "masculine competition."[132]

A particular kind of political consciousness is nurtured within one of 4chan's message boards /pol/. Made up of a mixed bag of conservatives, Ron Paul-type Libertarians, and White Nationalists, the message board /pol/ has become a communal conversation space for what is coming to be defined as the alt-right. The cornerstone of this political consciousness is a shared understanding of their social conditions via a preoccupation with gender, and in particular, manhood. Its participants paint a picture of a manhood defined by the struggle of *alphas* and *betas*. Alphas project an imaginary of physical strength, mental capacity, and financial success and betas the opposite, a reflection of the experience of many IRL and so often their reason to escape to virtual worlds. The alpha is presented as an endangered species in contemporary life. The target for this loss of manhood, the perception of reality of the life of a *beta*, is culturally attributed to "the culture of inclusion and diversity that has—in their view—infected mainstream life."[133] It is also an outcome of the failure in capitalism on its own terms, as the *alpha* is so defined by the trappings of material success. In concert, the cultural and material conditions of the *beta* reflect a loss of status for the white man in society.

While there are various degrees of critical emphasis in which these men live, there is consistency of focus in their targets and the reasons for their failures IRL. It will come as no surprise that the alt-right has become infamous for it actions that critique what they perceive to be the forces of the liberal left, forces that have stoked political correctness and the rise of the "other" at their expense. Examples include Gamergate which exposed harassment and threats of violence against women in the game development industry. Within their virtual worlds there is a belief that participation by women was "adding unwanted elements into their video games, namely things which promote gender equality."[134] There are many examples of harassment, either in asserting white identity or railing against the supposed anti-white agenda in mainstream culture. There is a constant, explicit, targeting of people of color and use of racist or derogatory language within the boards of 4chan and across the other social media that they use.[135] In their shared spaces of communication they also express a strong xenophobia based on a reading of the forces of globalization, most prominently in the politics of immigration. This serves as a prism for these men to understand their diminishing economic circumstances. A connecting thread in their scorn is political correctness, "social justice warriors" and "toxic leftism."[136] While there is no doubt a strong racist component to their *in-common*, Tara Isabella Burton argues, "the average 4chan alt-righter does not see himself as a 'real' racist, nor is racism necessarily what he would regard as his primary motivating factor. His racism is secondary to his understanding of himself as free … a masculine agent not subject to such feminized niceties as politeness and compassion."[137]

It is important to note that the scorn of these men is not solely aimed at the liberal left but at the establishment conservatives too. Their stance is also opposed to "mainstream Republicans who hold insufficiently conservative or even progressive positions on hot-button social issues like transgender rights, state use of the Confederate flag, and, especially, immigration."[138] Moreover, following the same gender-based pattern of derogatory speech, the term "cuckservative" is introduced into their lexicon, a conservative who is supposedly beholden to liberal values drawn, from "cuckold" sexual slang for the husband of an adulterous wife.[139]

In sum, the alt-right's political consciousness is tied to a culture of aggression and harassment. 4chan provides a unique space for cultivation of this political consciousness. It is important to remember the *anonymity* that defines the space. On the message boards of 4chan it is possible to harass without consequence and to express hate speech without regulation. These kinds of speech acts resonate with the "broader, deeply nihilistic ethos of chan culture."[140] Moreover, the *alpha* ideal of masculinity inspires a social logic of *one-upmanship*, again conducive to accelerating extremism. While 4chan is more than the alt-right, this movement has appropriated the general cultural characteristics of 4chan. Its defining action is the "lulz," net speak for "an evil laugh at someone's expense."[141] Its main actor figure is the troll, representing the disruption of communication via nihilistic satire. Its official mascot is Pepe the Frog, a simplistic childlike drawing of a frog. It uses memes prolifically: "to promulgate meme magic is to claim a deeper freedom in seeing the world as constructible rather than given, and the 'real' world as an un-sacred space."[142]

Enter onto the stage of history, Donald Trump. The emergence of Trump as a mainstream political force appears to be the ultimate embodiment of the alt-right. In his aggressive demeanor, focus on losers, sexual innuendo, and breaking of social norms, he is "a larger than life, walking middle finger to political correctness."[143] He is the very definition of a troll, "someone who scores rhetorical points with outrageous or controversial comments, consequences be damned."[144] He resonates naturally with the political consciousness and IRL embodiment of the alt-right. As Dale Beran argues:

> Trump the loser, the outsider, the hot mess, the pathetic joke. … Trump represents both the alpha and the beta. He is a successful person who, as the left often notes, is also the exact opposite—a grotesque loser, sensitive and prideful about his outsider status, ready at the drop of a hat to go on the attack, self-obsessed, selfish, abrogating, unquestioning of his own mansplaining and spreading, so insecure he must brag about assaulting women.[145]

There are those, mainly coming from the 4chan world, who believe that they were key figures in the rise of Trump. Pointing to a "great meme war" images that were distributed both on alternative and mainstream distributed networks, they "brag that they won the election for Trump."[146] The connection of the campaign to the 4chan message boards is also evidenced by the official communication channels of the Trump campaign sharing the memes that were organically grown on these message boards. In one of the more prominent examples, his official Twitter page retweeted a meme of himself as Pepe the Frog.[147] Furthermore, some of his official messaging tag lines for the campaign, like "Trump Train," originated in the message boards of 4chan. While the degree of explicit coordination in creating a harmonic dog-whistle can be debated, what is certain, with intent or with cynicism, is the degree to which the unique affordances of the platform of 4chan, the alt-right, and the support for Trump, historically synergized into a general social phenomenon. To make sense of the underbelly of the Trump "movement," the alt-right and its connection to a politics of the *distributed*, one needs to question whose movement in fact this is. Stephen Bannon, a strategy guru for Trump, was the previous editor of Britibart.com, which he claims to be "the platform for the alt-right."[148] The content on Britibart.com often comes from conversations found in the message boards of 4 Chan. As an emerging force of history "the alt-right now had an opportunity to inject racism, misogyny, and xenophobia into mainstream American politics. Provocative but obscure online rhetoric was quickly morphing into something more serious and powerful: the normalization of the politics of hate."[149]

I want to reconnect this movement now to the dueling models of the distributed. The 2016 US election campaign exposed two kinds of cynicism in the move from the industrial and post-industrial, represented by both the exceptional and transformative distributed. Both visions of the distributed, to various degrees, are the root cause of certain kinds of dissatisfaction with the world: economically, the loss of jobs and the global, and culturally, liberalism's recognition of gender and ethnic diversity. Supposed advances in social life did not "trickle down" to many of the members of the alt-right. But spaces like 4chan, spaces built on the principle of anonymity, become a safe harbor for ideas as they cannot be spoken in the public domain. So, this became a place for these ideas to find safety and strength, waiting for their right moment.

These actors became emboldened in their cynicism by their deep knowledge of the way communication works in an age of distributed networks. The hack is not some extreme event, but an everyday action. These hacks also operate at an intergovernmental level, the nation-to-nation hacks of political power, dominated by Russian, Chinese, and American clandestine intelligence services. At the same time, they operate at the level of general mass communication, the hack of *fake news*, or the playful disruption for extremist purposes of commercial media's profit-motivated gullibility. It is only *normies*, those outside of the 4chan community, who do not truly know how the internet works, who are unaware of this new reality.

More and more, what was obscure is becoming mainstream. Simultaneously government and everyday actors use the same tools and tricks of the trade, camouflaging who is who. Such is the nature of distributed networks and their vulnerability to manipulation by state and anti-state actors alike. In an example of this synergy, the infamous report from a British intelligence officer, supposedly containing the bombshell evidence connecting Trump to Putin, has been called a hoax, a piece of "fan-fiction" created on the /pol/ 4chan boards.[150] Whether this is true or just another "elaborate 4chan ruse" is not the point.[151] There has been enough destabilization of *truth* for these ruses to become mainstream dialog. As a result of coming into everyday consciousness, the statement and the uncertainty it creates are enough in and of itself. In this there is a mix of delusion, paranoia, and truth. The messiness of these forces is intensified by the elements of half-truth, hence the success of Trump, and Trump's embracing of the whole package, truth or not.

This final vignette of a *distributed* social movement is offered to emphasize the powerful shaping effects of technologies in the production of political consciousness and the potential scope of constitutive collective political action. The resonances of meaning between these forms of consciousness and action are coming to define the mainstream political landscape. One side calls it the unmasking and destruction of a system that no longer serves the national/populist interest of the dominant/citizen—the other regards it as anti-social, false consciousness, ideology, and propaganda. Either way, the question of *whose network* has become central. The politics and technical reality of the distributed *are* coming to define the transformative nature of the age, for better and for worse.

Whose Network?

Following the pattern established in previous chapters, I will close the chapter by attempting to make inroads into thinking of this propertyscape as a model of economic distribution, social participation, and political representation. By asking the question of *whose network*, my aim is to start to overlay an evaluative rubric of the *who*, *what*, and *how*, with a view of presenting this propertyscape as revealing a nascent model of political community.

The *who* of this nascent model of political community is ascribed to a universal global subject, a construction on a planetary scale. This global subject is the embodiment of an inherent *in-common*, the cornerstone of the political consciousness of the Multitude. Life in-common, as represented by the production and ownership of the work and play of the mind, is a viscerally lived empirical reality. Fundamentally contesting an ontology of individualism, the work and play of the mind is a universal shared place. *Distributed networks* provide an historical opening, opening a way of connecting this Multitude, through the very activities of work and play. This lays the basis for a transformative politics in the peer-to-peer affordances of the distributed network. The Multitude, and so too the transformative politics, represents another kind of globalization in the form of a post-industrial, post-capitalist, post-national constellation.

While aligning with a non-rivalrous definition of immaterial property, the substance of the *what* goes beyond the orthodox economic binary of rivalrous versus non-rivalrousness. There is something about the distributed qualities of the technological platforms for work and play that affords a different kind of approach to the *what:* the substantive meaning-making power that *becoming property* affords individuals and communities. The unique *transformative* potential of the *what* in an age of distributed networks is understood as a freedom to imagine and construct other worlds not dictated by capitalist modes of social, economic, and political production. The *transformative* potential of the *what* in an age of distributed networks is to allow for a critique of capitalist development that can move away from a labor monism, as core of a politics of affinity, to be replaced with an affinity model based on difference. *Gift* economies represent multiplicities of visions of the *what*, a move away from an economic determinism, to a more expansive understanding of what centers modes of obligation, reciprocation, social organizing principles.

The transformative response to the *how* is the transformative commons. This points to the already existing practices of peer production within distributed networks, offering an institutional alternative. At the level of infrastructure, the distributed network offers a platform supplying the means to transcend the systems of power and appropriation associated with the current mode of capitalist development. In step with this ideal of transcending the forces of capitalist development, the agenda of the transformative commons aligns with a patchwork of gift economies, a transcendent geography, where the embodiment of the work and play of the mind does not demand cultural, political, or economic uniformity of meaning. In turn the key economic potential of the transformative commons is for producers to not only own the fruits of their social activity and the platforms of that distribution, but the meanings that serve as the cornerstone of these systems of order.

When we ask *whose network*, the propertyscape reveals vulnerabilities, potentially undermining its own transformative agenda. One such vulnerability is revealed in the kinds of property alternatives offered by the propertyscape. One is to deny the character of formal and informal immaterial labor as property—freeing itself of property, as an anti-hierarchical, off-the-grid politics. The other would be to assert value for this labor as property. The political, economic, and social viability of both modes needs to be viewed in relation to a world of material production. This is for the simple reason that the material world is still economically dominated and determined, in large part, by the ownership of rivalrous property. Furthermore, there are several layers to the materiality of the digital too—it starts with the market for personal computers, as an industrial output; the cables or satellites of the global internet as sourced to various manufacturing and primary resources markets; purchased access to corporate media industry providers, and the like.

In a more general sense, there has never been anything simply *free* about the production and dissemination of the work and play of the mind. For instance, the products of scholarly knowledge have always been funded—for example, in the formal knowledge production of universities and research institutes. In other words, the work and play of the mind has been historically underwritten by the materiality of either public or private support. Thus, the denial-of-property approach produces a problem of free labor similar to that found in the paradigm of Immaterial Exceptionalism. Non-work or non-property can only be afforded to those who are not reliant on an income from this labor. To claim informal or communicative labor as property has certain implications too. While the aim might be purely pragmatic, to monetize immaterial property in order to support the livelihood of individuals and communities, nevertheless in doing so plays into the commodification and privatization of the social activity underwriting the work and play of the mind. Thus, in asking *whose network*, we also need to ask, what are the transformative limits based on this barrier of participation?

Another vulnerability for the propertyscape of Transformative Distribution is an implicit alignment of gift cultures as though there might be a natural progressive compatibility in their agendas, notwithstanding their essential plurality. What if one commons may not mesh with another, even though they share a non-market orientation? What happens when the demand to protect and defend one "gift" culture pits that gift culture antagonistically against another? At the extreme, what if these cultures are ethically mutually exclusive, based on the content of their social and political aspirations? This is the kind to tension I have been gesturing toward in this chapter though the vignettes of social movements shaped by a politics of the distributed. Does the propertyscape of Transformative Distribution trend toward another kind of privatization, a collective privatization? So, in asking *whose network*, how can distributed networks, in general, provide the ideational and institutional meaning of the *in-common* beyond groups based on gift economies?

Notes

1. Alexander Galloway, *Protocol: How Control Exists after Decentralization* (Cambridge, MA: MIT Press, 2004). p. 10.
2. Hardt. p. 88.
3. Christian Fuchs, *Internet and Society: Social Theory in the Information Age* (New York: Routledge, 2008). p. 159.
4. Matteo Pasquinelli, *Animal Spirits: A Bestiary of the Commons* (Amsterdam: Institute for Network Cultures 2008); Nick Dyer-Witheford, "Global Body, Global Brain/Global Factory, Global War: Revolt of the Value Subjects," *The Commoner* 3 (2002).

5. Christian Marazzi, "The Privatization of the General Intellect," SSRC, http://www.ssrc.org/blogs/knowledgerules/2008/02/19/the-privatization-of-the-general-intellect/.
6. Carlo Vercellone, "From Formal Subsumption to General Intellect: Elements for a Marxist Reading of the Thesis of Cognitive Capitalism," *Historical Materialism* 13, no. 36 (2007). p. 14.
7. Arthur Kroker, Weinstein, Michael, *Data Trash: The Theory of the Virtual Class* (New York City: St Martin's Press, 1994). p. 24.
8. Ibid., pp. 9–11.
9. Paul Virilio, *The Information Bomb* (Verso: New York, 2000). p. 64.
10. Fuchs. p. 159.
11. Paolo Virno, *A Grammar of the Multitude: For an Analysis of Contemporary Forms of Life* (Cambridge, MA: Semiotext(e), 2004). p. 76.
12. Ibid.
13. Ibid.
14. Ibid. p. 77.
15. Ibid. p. 76.
16. Karl Marx, "The Grundrisse," in *The Marx-Engels Reader*, ed. Robert Tucker (London: W.N Norton & Company, 1978 [1858]). p. 282.
17. Ibid. p. 284.
18. Ibid. p. 283.
19. Ibid.
20. Ibid. p. 285.
21. Slavoj Žižek, *First as Tragedy, Then as Farce* (London: Verso, 2009). p. 145.
22. Daniel Cohen, *The Nature of Capitalism in the Information Age* (Cambridge, MA: MIT Press, 2002). p. 2001.
23. Christian Marazzi, *Capital and Affects: The Politics of the Language Economy* (Cambridge, MA: Semiotext(e), 2011). p. 9.
24. Hardt. p. xv.
25. Norbert Wiener, *Cybernetics: Or Control and Communication in the Animal and the Machine* (Cambridge, MA: MIT Press, 1948).
26. Ibid.
27. Eugene Thacker, *Biomedia* (Minneapolis: University of Minnesota Press, 2004). p. 4.
28. Ibid. p. 5.
29. Ibid. p. 7.
30. Kroker. p. 20.

31. Thacker. p. 13.
32. Galloway. p. 69
33. Alexander Galloway, Thacker, Eugene, *The Exploit: A Theory of Networks* (Minneapolis: University of Minnesota Press, 2007). p. 39.
34. McKenzie Wark, *A Hacker Manifesto* (Cambridge: Harvard University Press, 2004), 09.
35. Ibid., 20.
36. Ibid., 78.
37. Ibid., 07.
38. Ibid., 29.
39. Ibid. p. 32.
40. Ibid. p. 30.
41. Ibid. p. 6.
42. Ibid.
43. Ibid. p. 81.
44. Ibid. p. 23.
45. Ibid. p. 44.
46. Ibid. p. 71.
47. Geert Lovink, *Zero Comments: Blogging and Critical Internet Culture* (New York: Routledge, 2007). p. 187.
48. Ibid. p. 202.
49. Ibid.
50. Ibid. p. 187.
51. Ibid. p. 189.
52. Ibid. p. 187.
53. Ibid. p. 189.
54. Marcel Mauss, *The Gift: The Form and Reason for Exchange in Archaic Societies* (New York: W. W. Norton & Company, 2000). p. 3
55. Richard Barbrook, "The Hi-Tech Gift Economy," First Monday, http://www.firstmonday.org/issues/issue3_12/barbrook/.
56. Ibid.
57. Richard Stallman, "Copyleft: Pragmatic Idealism," http://www.gnu.org/philosophy/pragmatic.html.
58. Jakob Rigi, "Peer to Peer Production as the Alternative to Capitalism: A New Communist Horizon" *Journal of Peer Production* 1, no. 1 (2012). p. 2.
59. Michel Bauwens, "The Political Economy of Peer Production," CTheory, http://www.ctheory.net/articles.aspx?id=499.

60. Michael Hardt, Negri, Antonio, *Multitude: War and Democracy in the Age of Empire* (New York: Penguin, 2005). p. 207.
61. *Commonwealth* (Cambridge, MA: Harvard University Press, 2009). p. 282.
62. Manuel Castells, *The Rise of the Network Society*, Information Age: Economy, Society and Culture (Cambridge, MA: Blackwell Publishers, 1996).
63. Shirky, *Here Comes Everybody: The Power of Organizing without Organizations*. p. 51.
64. Gabriella Coleman, *Coding Freedom: The Ethics and Aesthetics of Hacking* (New Haven: Princeton University Press, 2012).
65. Jeffrey S. Juris, "A New Way of Doing Politics? Global Justice Movements and the Cultural Logic of Networking," *Altermondialisme, société civile et mondialisation* 31, no. 1 (2007). p. 131.
66. Geert Lovink, "Inside Networked Movements: Interview with Jeffrey Juris," Institute of Network Cultures, http://networkcultures.org/geert/inside-networked-movements-interview-with-jeffrey-juris/.
67. Juris.
68. "Networked Social Movements: Global Movements for Global Justice," in *The Network Society: A Cross-Cultural Perspective*, ed. Manuel Castells (Cheltenham, UK: Edward Elgar, 2005). p. 347.
69. Ibid. p. 357.
70. Ted M. Coopman, "Building Resistance One Byte at a Time," National Communication Association, https://www.natcom.org/CommCurrentsArticle.aspx?id=1027.
71. Castells. p. 365.
72. Sari Hanafi, "Lessons of the Jasmine Revolution," aljazeera.com, http://www.aljazeera.com/indepth/opinion/2011/01/201111985641326468.html.
73. Mona Eltahawy, "Tunisia's Jasmine Revolution," washingtonpost.com, http://www.washingtonpost.com/wp-dyn/content/article/2011/01/14/AR2011011405084.html.
74. Yasmine Ryan, "How Tunisia's Revolution Began," aljazeera.com, http://www.aljazeera.com/indepth/features/2011/01/2011126121815985483.html.
75. Ibid.
76. "Tunisia's Bitter Cyberwar," aljazeera.com, http://www.aljazeera.com/indepth/features/2011/01/20111614145839362.html.

77. Noureddine Miladi, "Tunisia: A Media Led Revolution?," aljazeera.com, http://www.aljazeera.com/indepth/opinion/2011/01/2011116142317498666.html.
78. Jose Antonio Vargas, "Spring Awakening: How an Egyptian Revolution Began on Facebook," nytimes.com, http://www.nytimes.com/2012/02/19/books/review/how-an-egyptian-revolution-began-on-facebook.html?pagewanted=all.
79. Ibid.
80. Ibid.
81. Ibid.
82. BBC News, "Egypt Unrest: Bloggers Take Campaign to Tahrir Square," bbc.co.uk, http://www.bbc.co.uk/news/world-middle-east-12,381,295.
83. Miladi.
84. Eltahawy.
85. Vanessa Grigoriadis, "4chan's Chaos Theory," vanityfair.com, http://www.vanityfair.com/business/features/2011/04/4chan-201,104.print.
86. Monica Hesse, "A Virtual Unknown: Meet 'Moot,' the Secretive Internet Celeb Who Still Lives with Mom," washingtonpost.com, http://www.washingtonpost.com/wp-dyn/content/article/2009/02/16/AR2009021601565_pf.html.
87. Ibid.
88. Rex Sorgatz, "Macroanonymous Is the New Microfamous," fimoculous.com, http://www.fimoculous.com/archive/post-5738.cfm.
89. Grigoriadis.
90. Ben Parr, "Facebook and Google Do Identity Wrong," mashable.com, http://mashable.com/2011/10/18/chris-poole-4chan-web-2/.
91. Paul Lamere, "Inside the Precision Hack," musicmachinery.com, http://musicmachinery.com/2009/04/15/inside-the-precision-hack/.
92. Sorgatz.
93. Grigoriadis.
94. Mark Townsend, "Wikileaks Backlash: The First Global Cyber War Has Begun, Claim Hackers," guardian.co.uk, http://www.guardian.co.uk/media/2010/dec/11/wikileaks-backlash-cyber-war.
95. Ben Grubb, "Film Industry Hires Cyber Hitmen to Take Down Internet Pirates," theage.com.au, http://www.smh.com.au/technology/technology-news/film-industry-hires-cyber-hitmen-to-take-down-internet-pirates-20,100,907-14ypv.html.

96. Luis Corrons, "4chan Users Organize Surgical Strike against Mpaa," pandasecurity.com, http://pandalabs.pandasecurity.com/4chan-users-organize-ddos-against-mpaa/.
97. Michael Greenberg, "In Zuccotti Park," The New York Review of Books, http://www.nybooks.com/articles/archives/2011/nov/10/zuccotti-park/?pagination=false&printpage=true.
98. Whois.net, "Whois Information for Occupywallstreet.Org," Whois Lookup—Domain Names Search, Registration, & Availability http://www.whois.net/whois/occupywallstreet.org.
99. Mark Egan, "Who's Behind the Wall Street Protests?," Reuters.com, http://www.reuters.com/assets/print?aid=USTRE79C1YN20111014.
100. Adbusters, "#Occupywallstreet—a Shift in Revolutionary Tactics," Adbusters, http://www.adbusters.org/blogs/adbusters-blog/occupy-wallstreet.html.
101. "Anonymous Joints #Occupywallstreet," adbusters.org, http://www.adbusters.org/blogs/adbusters-blog/anonymous-joins-occupywall-street.html.
102. Ibid.
103. "#Occupywallstreet: A Shift in Revolutionary Tactics," adbusters.org, http://www.adbusters.org/blogs/adbusters-blog/occupywallstreet.html.
104. "Anarchic Swarms—the Emerging Model," adbusters.com, http://www.adbusters.org/blogs/adbusters-blog/adbusters-tactical-brief-ing-26.html.
105. Kalle Lasn, White, Micah "Why Occupy Wall Street Will Keep up the Fight," The Washington Post, http://www.washingtonpost.com/opin-ions/why-occupy-wall-street-will-keep-up-the-fight/2011/11/17/gIQAn5RJZN_print.html.
106. Micah White, "Activism after Clicktivism: How to Energize the Political Left," Adbusters, http://www.adbusters.org/magazine/93/activism-after-clicktivism.html.
107. wearethe99percent.tumblr.com, "Wearethe99percent," http://www.wearethe99percent.tumblr.com.
108. Rebecca Rosen, "The 99 Percent Tumblr: Self-Service History," the-atlantic.com, http://www.theatlantic.com/technology/archive/2011/10/the-99-percent-tumblr-self-service-history/246385/.
109. Ezra Klein, "Who Are the 99 Percent?," washingtonpost.com, http://www.washingtonpost.com/blogs/ezra-klein/post/who-are-the-99-per-cent/2011/08/25/gIQAt87jKL_blog.html.

110. Charles Peterson, "The Politics of the Poor," *Occupy: An OWS Inspired Gazette (N+1)* 1 (2011).
111. http://occupynetwork.com/.
112. Adbusters, "Dear Americans, This July 4th Dream of Insurrection against Corporate Rule," twitter.com, https://twitter.com/adbusters/status/88013043438600192.
113. Jennifer Preston, "Protesters Look for Ways to Feed the Web," nytimes.com, http://www.nytimes.com/2011/11/25/business/media/occupy-movement-focuses-on-staying-current-on-social-networks.html.
114. Peter Aldhous, "Occupy Vs Tea Party: What Their Twitter Networks Reveal," New Scientist, http://www.newscientist.com/blogs/onepercent/2011/11.
115. http://www.meetup.com/occupytogether/.
116. http://www.peoplesskype.org/.
117. Sean Captain, "Occupy Geeks Are Building a Facebook for the 99%," wired.com, http://www.wired.com/threatlevel/2011/12/occupy-facebook/all/1.
118. http://roarmag.org/2012/02/global-square-call-for-coders/.
119. Jerome Roos, "The Global Square: An Online Platform for Our Movement," roarmag.org, http://roarmag.org/2011/11/the-global-square-an-online-platform-for-our-movement/.
120. http://www.mutantspace.com/free-network-foundation-diy-technology/.
121. Sam Biddle, "Occupy Wall Street and the War to Free All Internet," gizmodo.com, http://gizmodo.com/5897109/occupy-wall-street-and-the-war-to-free-all-internet.
122. http://www.mutantspace.com/free-network-foundation-diy-technology/.
123. Maliha Safri, "Globalizing Zuccotti," *Occupy: An OWS Inspired Gazette (N+1)* 1 (2011). p. 15.
124. Ibid.
125. Jodi Dean, "Judgment," ibid. p. 37.
126. Joanne McNeil, "Occupy the Internet," ibid. p. 24.
127. Roos.
128. Michael Hardt, Negri, Antonio, "Take up the Baton," jacobinmag.com, http://jacobinmag.com/summer-2012/take-up-the-baton/.
129. Susannah Vila, "How the #Occupy Movement Is Spurring Tech Innovation," Mashable, http://mashable.com/2011/12/12/ows-tech-

innovation/?utm_source…r&utm_medium=feed&utm_campaign=Feed%3A+Mashable+%28Mashable%29.

130. Fast Company, "Occupy Movement: 50 Most Innovative Companies of 2012," Fast Company http://www.fastcompany.com/most-innovative-companies/2012/occupy-movement.
131. Dale Beran, "4chan: The Skeleton Key to the Rise of Trump," Medium.com, https://medium.com/@DaleBeran/4chan-the-skeleton-key-to-the-rise-of-trump-624e7cb798cb#.qa9nlnox0.
132. Ibid.
133. Jesse Singal, "How Internet Trolls Won the 2016 Presidential Election," New York Magazine, http://nymag.com/selectall/2016/09/how-internet-trolls-won-the-2016-presidential-election.html.
134. Beran.
135. Adrian Chen, "The Truth About Anonymous's Activism," The Nation, https://www.thenation.com/article/truth-about-anonymouss-activism/.
136. Oliver Lee, "Understanding Trump's Troll Army," Motherboard, https://motherboard.vice.com/en_us/article/understanding-trumps-troll-army.
137. Tara Isabella Burton, "Apocalypse Whatever: The Making of a Racist, Sexist Religion of Nihilism on 4chan," Reallifemag.com, http://reallifemag.com/apocalypse-whatever/.
138. Joseph Bernstein, "Behind the Racist Hashtag That Is Blowing up Twitter," Buzzfeed, https://www.buzzfeed.com/josephbernstein/behind-the-racist-hashtag-some-donald-trump-fans-love?utm_term=.qayrY9LPK#.fvrej6xlK.
139. Matthew Yglesias, "#Nrorevolt, Explained," vox.com, http://www.vox.com/2015/9/8/9276719/nrorevolt-cuckservatives.
140. Singal.
141. Chen.
142. Burton.
143. Singal.
144. Lee.
145. Beran.
146. Lee.
147. Josh Harkinson, "White Nationalists See Trump as Their Troll in Chief. Is He with Them?," motherjones.com, http://www.motherjones.com/politics/2016/11/trump-white-nationalists-hate-racism-power.

148. Sara Posner, "How Donald Trump's New Campaign Chief Created an Online Haven for White Nationalists," motherjones.com, http://www.motherjones.com/politics/2016/08/stephen-bannon-donald-trump-alt-right-breitbart-news.
149. Harkinson.
150. Tyler Durden, "4chan Claims to Have Fabricated Anti-Trump Report as a Hoax," Zero Hedge, http://www.zerohedge.com/news/2017–01-10/4chan-claims-have-fabricated-anti-trump-report-hoax.
151. Gideon Risnick, "Despite Weak Stream of Proof, 4chan Claims It Invented the Trump Golden Showers Story," The Daily Beast, http://www.thedailybeast.com/articles/2017/01/10/4chan-claims-they-invented-the-trump-golden-showers-story.html.

5

The Ecological: *Whose Nature?*

The three propertyscapes defined in this book so far have primarily connected the political action of *becoming property* to readings of the epoch-defining affordances of digital communication technologies. My final propertyscape, Ecological Decolonization, draws our attention to a different aspect of the political action of *becoming property*—how the meanings and institutions of property expand their reach into *life itself*. This is an important issue in an age of increasing anxiety about the perils of technologically modified agriculture and the challenges of the local, and of planetary environmental sustainability. In defining Ecological Decolonization, I will weave between discussions of research and political activism. These areas cross-pollinate, coming together to form a distinctive understanding of social activity and its connection to eco-systemic realities underwriting the work and play of the mind, connecting this in turn to a politics of *becoming property*. While Ecological Decolonization offers a broad critical lens, its case will be presented through an analysis of the bio-politics of food: its production, cultivation, and systems of ownership. In this essential connection to species subsistence we find its potential openings for an understanding of our material relationship to the land, seeds, and the environment, and the immaterial cultural conditions of production, sustainability, and social value.

P. Kalantzis-Cope, *The Work and Play of the Mind in the Information Age*,
Frontiers of Globalization, https://doi.org/10.1007/978-3-319-64650-3_5

The biological and cultural are essential analytical categories for understanding Ecological Decolonization's geo-politics of *life itself.* The biological is used by its proponents in some places to speak primarily of seeds, plants, and cells. The cultural is used to talk primarily of the production of individual and communal subjectivity as it relates to the natural world. The characteristic approach to the work and play of the mind of this propertyscape makes these biological and cultural frames mutually dependent. They are dependent in the ways ecosystems are integrally intertwined into cultures and in the ways culture is shaped by ecosystemic transformations, embodied in the cultivation and production of the means of human sustenance. Consequently, *life itself* is the overarching category that I will use to evoke both these aspects, each in its specificity and both in their dependency.

In some senses, Ecological Decolonization brings us back full circle to the Trade-Related Aspects of Intellectual Property Rights (TRIPS) Agreement. The TRIPS Agreement is distinctive for its global geopolitical topology. It is the symbolic manifestation of a certain kind of agenda, a globalizing universalism: legal, anthropological, and epistemological. Ecological Decolonization recognizes and interprets this phenomenon through a longer history of imperialism and colonization. It is an attempt to frame an alternative mode of social activity by naming and critiquing the political action of what I will call *ecological colonialism* and suggesting strategies for *decolonization.*

To explore and critically engage the propertyscape of Ecological Decolonization I present another selective set of living stories associated with differing applications of "geographic indications." This is a domain of intellectual property rights aimed at signaling and protecting *properties of place. Place* is embodied in a locally defined production process or good—for example, Champagne as a wine region of France, or Darjeeling tea from the region of the same name in India. Geographic indications are a unique kind of intellectual property. Here we have a domain of intellectual property that differs from the internal logic of the dominant rights regime, while existing within it. The dominant rights narrative is one of privatization, creating a rivalrous, excludable, private monopoly. Geographic indications, in contrast, are held in perpetuity; their system of ownership is collective; and their implicit anthropological assumption about innovation is based on the stability of tradition. As such, geographic indications offer a vantage point to view the ways in which eco-systems are integrally intertwined into cultures and in the ways culture is shaped by eco-systemic transformations embodied in the cultivation and production of the means of human sustenance. They also offer an example of a way to establish the cultural and eco-systemic locatedness of place in the face of a universalizing economics and cultural globalization. The connected *properties of place*, of land and human life, are seen to be inherently oppositional to forces of globalization. "Terroir is the epitomic opposite of globalization: an exemplary reflection of place and people."[1]

In the connection of these types of living stories to the propertyscape of Ecological Decolonization we are given another frame of reference on the basis of which to approach the construction of the commons: the *ecological commons*. Vandana Shiva, an intellectual lighthouse in the propertyscape of Ecological Decolonization as I am defining it here, opens our thinking to a problem. She says, "a privatized commons is no longer a commons; it is private property, either de facto or de jure. What has been called the tragedy of the commons is, in fact, the tragedy of privatization."[2] The question then arises, to what degree does the protection of alternative forms of social activity require some form of enclosure which is tantamount to creating another form of private, or whether the private in fact the antithesis of the common? Shiva makes her case for the latter. Moreover, in the context of the *properties of place* as defined by geographic indications, what are the implications of the production of *collective commons*, particularly in terms defined by readings of culture and practice?

The Diagnosis: Ecological and Epistemological Colonization

The unfolding history of global food regimes informs my reading of Ecological Decolonization, manifest today in the geo-politics of food. Following a World Systems Theory approach, my diagnosis centers on how these regimes establish, engrain, and reinforce relations of core and periphery via food systems.[3] The historical record of each regime is also symptomatic of, and referential to, broader waves of economic globalization.

The first global food regime emerges around the 1870s and lasts to the 1930s. This regime was based on the importation of "basic grains and livestock imports from settler colonies" to the core of the European Empires. This provided food for European industrial classes and, in particular, underwrote the British "workshop of the world" mantra, as the British Empire established itself as the hegemonic leader of the era.[4] The consequences for farmers in the colonial order included economic instability, forced movement of people, starvation, and famine. The effect of this food regime was to create vast *real property* displacements, in the form of land, heritage seeds, and traditional animal stocks. Layered into these displacements was an implicit epistemological colonization. Logics of food production were also imported from the imperial core. There was little regard for local agricultural methods and their grounded understandings of local ecological rhythms, or indigenous cultural moorings to the land and food production.

A second food regime begins at the close of the Second World War and extends to the 1980s. Importantly, for understanding this regime within the broader frame of transformation from an industrial to a post-industrial society, this ushers in the Green Revolution, with its logic of "Food Security." In the face of the World Food Crisis of the 1970s and its impact in higher food prices, hunger and malnutrition, the Green Revolution was presented as a definitive strategy to feed the world. In 1975 Food Security was officially defined as "the availability at all times of adequate world food supplies of basic foodstuffs to sustain a steady expansion of food consumption and to offset fluctuations in production and prices."[5] This position expresses a certain export-driven view of the global food trade. In addition, the strategies of Green Revolution and Food Security aligned with a broader techno-scientific approach to food production. This included the introduction of high yielding seeds (such as maize and rice), pesticides, and synthetic nitrogen fertilizer. These strategies also tied food production more closely to the research and development arms of multinational agri-business, ushering in an important period of post-industrial food transformation.

In this move, from the first to the second global food regime, we see an emerging pattern of ecological property dependencies. This relates to the *material aspects* of the production of food, where farms in the developing world become enmeshed in systems of seeds and fertilizers coming from a western scientific core. At the same time a particular *knowledge base* comes to underwrite the logic of food production. Seed and food technologies align with schemas of scientific progress intrinsic to the western biotechnologies themselves, connected with broader commodity systems and directed toward profit maximization. It is in this second regime that intellectual property of a rivalrous nature gains increasing importance in determining new colonial relations of core to periphery that have both *material* and *knowledge* aspects.

The third food regime begins in the 1980s and runs to the present. The accelerated, all-encompassing, colonizing processes of the third regime is marked by the rise of multinational biotechnology agri-business. As Finn Browning details, we have seen "the emergence of clusters of multinationals cooperating in achieving complete command of the food chain, from patent protection of transgenic germplasm, through chemical-assisted growing, to the collection and distribution of harvests and their processing into food."[6] Meshed into the logic of Food Security, multinational monopolies frame their research and development agendas as feeding the world, normatively buttressing their economic agendas with global trade and aid agreements. Food Security in this third global food regime represents a force that is not simply economic. As Rajeev Patel writes, in the 1990s "Food Security moved from being simply about producing and distributing food, to a whole nexus of concerns around nutrition, social control and public health."[7] Here the research agendas of corporations are buttressed by normative feedback systems, reinforced by international agencies like the World Trade Organization (WTO) and World Bank and their development agendas. In this third regime, rivalrous and exclusive definitions of intellectual property become the preeminent expression of ecological colonialism. This colonial effect is very much aligned to that of corporate globalization, with its notions of free trade and market principles.

While I focus my exploration of the Ecological Decolonization propertyscape, via a geo-politics of food, this process of ecological *colonialism*, in particular the second and third regimes, reflects a much broader systemic shift associated with the rise of biotech as an integral aspect of a post-industrial knowledge economy. In this new economy, technological, scientific, and research-driven corporations lead the way, or ride the wave, to find and patent forms of biological life. Genomic and pharmaceutical companies become extensively engaged in genetic engineering and genetic modification. In addition, as Nikolas Rose argues "the practice of medicine in most industrialized countries" becomes "colonized by the requirements of public or private health insurance, the criteria for reimbursement and in general the treatment of health and illness as merely another field for calculations of corporate activity."[8] Thus, what happens to food becomes an exemplar of phenomena also at work in other domains involving the commodification of *life itself.* If these trends are the distinguishing features of the food regimes of ecological colonialism, the response that is embodied in the propertyscape of Ecological Decolonization is presented as a direct counterpoint.

Ecological Decolonization

Nature's Rights, Subaltern Cosmopolitanism, Bio-Sovereignty

Terra nullius, Latin for *empty lands*, has been used to justify the taking of lands in colonial conquests. These lands were assumed by the new occupiers to have no recognizable pre-existing property rights. So, they were considered *empty*, regardless of those who already lived there or their actual relations to the land. Herein begins the origin story of the new world and its modern nation-states. This is further foundational evidence of the ideational and institutional power of the myth of *becoming property* in the Westphalian model.

In the contemporary post-industrial politics of the work and play of the mind, this *empty land* thesis reappears as an orientation toward *life itself.* The assumption is reproduced and expanded to "empty life, seeds and medicinal plants."[9] Life itself is then subject to the explorations of bio-prospectors who supposedly find and capture *life*. They are normatively motivated by general origin story of *becoming property* integral to the broader process of the privatization of the work and play of the mind. Drawing a connecting line between these two historical moments,

Vandana Shiva argues that such practices are implicitly premised in a belief in the inherent "passivity of the earth" and its natural assets.[10] The notion of the passivity of organic, natural matter paves the way for "the transformation of nature from a living" to a "dead and manipulable matter … eminently suited to the exploitation imperative of growing capitalism."[11]

The *empty land* thesis is not simply associated with the products of the earth. It also extends to the cultural and socio-scientific moorings of ecological materiality—in other words, to epistemological diversity. A root cause of this position is attributed to a tendency in the western scientific method to position non-western epistemological orientations as *unscientific*. This outlook in large part grounds a charge that, in western science's demand for rationality and universality on its own terms, it becomes vulnerable to breeding "a monoculture of the mind."[12] As argued by Ruth Hubbard, this reductionism is accentuated by an instrumentalism, a biodeterminism that foundationally grounds individual and communal social life in a universal biology.[13] If this defines the process of the globalization of a western epistemology, it also paves the way for a globalization of capitalist development. Western science in this schema is also seen as vulnerable to being co-opted by, and work in the service of, capitalist systems of value. Shiva argues that such a move allows capital to go "where it has never been before,"[14] paving the way for the colonial dynamic to be "extended to the interior spaces, the genetic codes, of life forms from microbes and plants to animals and humans."[15]

An important turning point in the growing authority of this empty lands thesis was the 1980 United States Supreme Court ruling *Diamond v. Chakrabarty*. This decision opened the floodgates for what is commonly referred to as the biotech century, an epoch-defining post-industrial movement. Chakrabarty was a microbiologist working for General Electric. He developed a "human-made, genetically engineered bacterium capable of breaking down multiple components of crude oil," which, as argued in the case, hosts "no naturally occurring bacteria."[16] In this ruling, the US Supreme Court was forced to decide on the ultimate patentability of living organisms. Within the US context, a tension emerged between a Constitutional mandate "to promote the progress of sciences and useful arts" and the recognition of "the fact that microorganisms are alive."[17] The decision to uphold the grant of patent was justified by the court in the following terms: this "microorganism plainly qualifies as patentable subject matter. The claim is not to a hitherto unknown natural phenomenon, but to a non-naturally occurring manufacture or composition of matter—a product of human ingenuity."[18] Here we see clearly the assertion of human domination over nature, a belief that *Man* could produce a biological entity that has no independently natural foundation, and that on this basis, this biological entity could be subsumed, alienated, and owned as private property. Aligned with the rivalrous private interpretation of the work and play of the mind is an epistemological agenda that devalues and misrecognizes the innate value of life itself, valorizing instead human ingenuity and scientific progress in the form of scientific discovery and a technological capacity to change matter.

If what has been described so far exemplifies a critical posture to what we might call *ecological colonization*, what follows is the counter argument, and the basis of an ontological ordering principle of Ecological Decolonization. The propertyscape of Ecological Decolonization is grounded in a notion of *nature's rights*. Enlightenment natural rights approaches necessarily begin with Man. They use the word *natural* metaphorically to describe original and therefore inalienable human rights.

Ecological Decolonization's ontological ordering principle, however, begins with a view of rights that exist without Man, that pre-date or prefigure Man, and as such, anthropocentric, enlightenment ontologies. Nature's rights begin with life itself. The purpose of this ontological reframing is to mirror and foreshadow an account of multiplicity and diversity that resonates within life itself. Here we are presented with a twofold interpretation of natural diversity—on the one hand, it is grounded purely biologically in the diversity of ecosystems, and on the other hand, a cultural grounding presents itself in the plurality and diversity of traditional knowledge systems, or more broadly put, epistemological diversity.

In this critical posture, western science is understood to represent a specific ontological position that displaces a natural "plural landscape of knowledge existing in the world."[19] Within a broader politics of globalization and the production of global political space, Shiva frames the problem in the following way—"'Western' is a local tradition which has been spread worldwide through intellectual colonization."[20] In this argument, there can be no ontological universalism without displacement and contestations between ontological *localisms*. Shiva turns this into a demand for "epistemological diversity, … a rigorous account of the situatedness, particularity, and constructedness of all knowledge, while rejecting relativism as an epistemological moral stance."[21] On this basis, an argument can be mounted for an ontology of nature's rights as the expression of diversity without a totalizing human nature. This ontological recasting provides a view of the innate value of the biological world. Eco-systemic diversity and value pre-date human modes of interpretation.

This ontology of nature's rights becomes grounds for a *subaltern cosmopolitanism*, as a particular kind of emancipatory politics.[22] Subaltern cosmopolitanism begins with "the recognition of the presence of a plurality of knowledge and of distinctive conceptions of human dignity and of the world."[23] It poses the challenge of "global cognitive justice" as the need to substitute "a monoculture of scientific knowledge" with varying "ecologies of knowledge," so bringing about the "decolonization of science."[24] Nature, as a generative force of social production, is not simply viewed as a blank slate or empty lands: *terra nullius*. In fact, nature informs relationships to ecological life, societal orders, and systems of meaning for participation in ownership of these lives and their outputs. Symbiotically, these domains represent a diverse range of relationships to the notion of ownership of life itself.

Translated into a geo-politics of food, this ontological recasting contests the essential premise of food *security* with one of food *sovereignty*. Raj Patel writes that the call for food sovereignty is "an active attempt to incite context-specific transformation" based on "principles of dignity, individual and community sovereignty, and self-determination."[25] Michel Pimbert argues that food sovereignty "is perhaps best understood as a transformative process that seeks to recreate the democratic realm and regenerate a diversity of autonomous food systems based on equity, social justice and ecological sustainability."[26] This has implications beyond a politics of food, weaving into broader notions of autonomous *life itself*, as integrated bio and knowledge systems. While *life itself* has material expressions, as, for example, in seed, this also stimulates a politics of the work and play of the mind, a politics of competing epistemological worldviews associated to *life itself*.

Localisms, Productivity, Environmentality

Ecological Decolonization's normative presupposition begins with a reading of the *local*. Exemplified in a geo-politics of food, we find two versions of the local: a *non-western local* represented in peasants, third world farmers, indigenous peoples, including their relationship to food systems, and plants, and a *western local* represented by small family farms, seasonal foods, community-based, and ecologically sustainable methods of production.

In the non-western context, the local defines relationships that are not simply ones of sustenance, but speaks to customs and religious practices associated with food systems. The cultural practices of peasants and indigenous peoples are held to hold an essential relationship to their local, their social lives interpreted as close to the eco-systemic rhythms of the natural world. Moreover, as a *politics of knowing*, it is argued these approaches are inherently sensitive to the particularities of local ecosystems and thus their sustainability. In these ways, non-western *locals* represent a natural plurality of peoples-in-environments, each laden with processes of subject formation intimately related to localized ecosystems and their sustainability. For these reasons, intellectual property patents and genetic engineering are pitted against cultural meanings, customs, and understandings of sustainable development that are grounded in generative fields of local social activity.

The Slow Food Movement is a perfect synthesis of the *western local*. It represents resistance not just to the industrialized food system but also to the ecological and human health ramifications of such a food system. As a *politics of knowing*, the western local is a projection of knowing what is posited to be good for the future of life itself, for example, local farms versus industrial agriculture, and the environmental impacts of local versus industrial systems of production. The symbol of the problem of intellectual property rights here is genetically modified foods and the post-industrial food system.

Together, these non-western and western visions of the local are moored in a recognition of diverse modes of production and distribution of food. Symbiotically, these represent a diverse range of cultural values embedded in the local modes of production and exchange of food, supported by locally grounded "cultural capital."[27] In these contexts, the local is not only defined in spatial terms, the domain of the nearby. It also denotes a certain temporality, a grounding in history and tradition. Nevertheless, this local normativity is wary of arguments which may nominally value differences, even admire them because they are colorfully exotic. Such a cosmopolitan ethos, De Sousa Santos argues, is vulnerable to becoming a "prime expression of the cultural logic of multi-national or global capitalism … capitalism without a homeland."[28]

Another normative proposition of Ecological Decolonization is based on a critique of what is referred to as the *production boundary*. The production boundary is an economic normative battleground—what it is to be *productive*. Capitalist modes of scientific progress normatively assign notions of the primitive and the unscientific to traditional, indigenous, or non-western epistemologies. Such thinking super-imposes a system of value over bio-life by overlaying them with already existing or future modes of commodity production and profit maximization. It institutionalizes this rationality through patents assessed by the measure of what is useful and novel, weighted by schemas of western innovation and commodity landscapes—*becoming property*. Within this system, both bio-life and non-western epistemologies are denied recognizable value because they are seen to be relatively *unproductive*. This normative construction of *unscientific* and *unproductive* legitimizes a process whereby western science parasitically feeds off *life itself*. Jack Kloppenburg argues, "Ironically, the very development of agronomically useful and novel (and therefore patentable) plant varieties has been and continues to be predicated on access by breeders to the enormous pool of biodiversity that has been produced and reproduced over the millennia by peasant farmers and indigenous peoples."[29]

The *production boundary* problem also reveals a gendered devaluation, with consequences for understanding the sustainability of life itself. Shiva argues the production boundary "is a political construct that excludes regenerative, renewable production cycles from the domain of production."[30] This "does to knowledge what the production boundary does to work: it excludes the creative contributions of women … and views them as being engaged in unthinking, repetitive biological processes." Shiva goes on to argue that, in this way historically, "creativity became the monopoly of men, who were considered to be engaged in production; women were engaged in mere reproduction or recreation."[31] This eco-feminist angle opens a normative agenda that focuses on the lives of women. The local also produces and reproduces gendered spaces, as "local economic life" and "local management of environment and health" are "usually performed by women." For example, in Asia "women produce 90 percent of the rice."[32] At the same time, this approach provides a footing upon which to critically address theories of value that prioritize principles of production over regeneration. This is part and parcel of a system of patriarchy, one that has critical effects on ecological sustainability.

The final aspect of Ecological Decolonization's defining normative presuppositions is a critique of *environmentality*. The leading proponents of this conceptual rubric are Arun Agrawal and Tim Luke.[33] Both Agrawal and Luke apply the Foucauldian notion of *governmentality* to environmental politics. Here the bio-political is embedded within a broader disciplinary modality governing *life itself* through the projection of *global development*, and the very real forces of trade liberalization, particularly the structural adjustment agenda of the 1980s and 1990s. This trade-led approach relies on precisely the logic that produced the TRIPS Agreement. Such thinking becomes the core of the IMF and World Bank's approach to third world development as it relates to the food production and supply system. In an advocacy statement from the IMF Finance and Development section, *How Free Trade Can Help The Poor*, "global trade liberalization" is discussed as a fundamental tool to "fight hunger." A report from the Gates Foundation states that this development agenda seeks to reduce "the number of people engaged in food production and instead encouraging them to get jobs in the largely urban-based manufacturing and service sectors—regardless of the social and ecological costs."[34] This kind of export-led approach ignores the fact that in the developing world, for example, in South Asia, "more than 50 percent of farmers are small producers tilling an average farm size of no more than 1.6 hectares."[35] It is also important to note that large proportions of populations in the developing world rely on small-scale production agriculture as their primary source of income.

> "The vast majority of the world's farms are small or very small. Worldwide, farms of less than 1 hectare account for 72% of all farms, but control only 8% of all agricultural land. Farms between 1 and 2 hectares account for 12% of all farms and control 4% of the land. In contrast, only 1% of all farms in the world are larger than 50 hectares, but they control 65% of the world's agricultural land."[36]

Fouad Makki argues that this mantra of global development has been "crucial in reconfiguring the global identity of ex-colonies in a way that was incorporative and universalistic yet still hierarchical."[37] Development is ideological coding for a process of re-colonization of nominally post-colonial states. These nations were promised a process in which they might become global players through agricultural and other exports. Nevertheless, assistance is only afforded to those on the path of neo-liberal transformation and, with that, a certain kind of economic dependence. Compounding this in the domain of food systems is the problem of foreign debt that leaves developing nations unable to provide support to agricultural industries, thus making them unable to compete globally against western nations whose agriculture is highly subsidized, contrary to their own neo-liberal, free-trade rhetoric. In effect, this perpetuates food dumping practices. The geo-politics of food, as an object of global trade, becomes an institutional mechanism by means of which to transform developing economies and their states. Here we see inconsistent free-trade arguments becoming the double standard for a new, informal, bio-political colonial dependency.

These normative elements dovetail in an ideal of *sustainability*. They add layers to the case for why and how the model of "neo-liberalism's Nature"[38] is unsustainable. Shiva identifies the core of the "ecological crisis and the crisis of sustainability" as privileging the new over regeneration.[39] This approach to social production, expressed in the production and ownership of the work and play of the mind, colonizes the local and misrecognizes knowledge systems by implicitly classifying them as primitive and enforces patriarchal world views. On the other hand, reclaiming the local and understanding the power of productive life outside capitalist systems of value lay the groundwork for an alternative model of social activity.

Legal Pluralism, Globalization from Below, the Bio-Commons

The concept of legal pluralism emerged in the legal scholarship of the 1970s and 1980s as a way to interpret the co-existence of western, indigenous, customary, and/or religious forms of law within colonial and post-colonial contexts.[40] Legal pluralism is defined as "a situation in which two or more legal systems coexist in the same social field."[41] This approach characteristically attempts to take into account "non-legal forms of normative ordering,"[42] focusing on the relationship between "official and unofficial forms of ordering."[43] Sally Falk Moore makes a distinction between "state law" and "a semi-autonomous social field," the latter producing its own normative orders of legal significance. While normative orders "can generate rules and customs and symbols internally," they are "vulnerable to rules and decisions and other forces emanating from the larger world."[44] There is always a co-producing dynamic between normative orders and state law, with power generally favoring the state. For this reason, legal pluralism turns its attention, as John Griffiths articulates, to a critique of "the ideology of legal centralism." It questions the proposition that the "law is and should be the law of the state, uniform for all persons, exclusive of all other law, administered by a single set of state institutions."[45] Legal pluralism's agenda is to dislodge the state as monopolistic source of law and to illuminate the power, importance, and need for the recognition of alternative normative orders within the law.

The interface of legal pluralism with the ontological ordering principle and normative presuppositions of Ecological Decolonization occurs in the processes of homogenization associated with neo-liberal economic globalization—globalization from above. At the global level, we see the production of global laws as a shaping force impacting on national laws. This process tends to homogenize a legal pluralism state-to-state, and the normative diversity within states as the law reflects cultural moorings associated with production and ownership of the work and play of the mind. This homogenization represents an attempt to bring universal order, and in the case of intellectual property rights, global law operating under the rubric of rivalrousness. The question then arises, how is it possible to maintain the constitutive capacity of already existing legal and normative orders of different peoples and communities in the face of the globalization of law and culture? In a direct sense, homogenization proceeds through the enforcement of international legal regimes. However, it is possible to mount a Gramscian argument, about the indirect hegemonic embedding associated with participation in the global political, cultural, and economic order. Direct processes of homogenization might be exemplified by TRIPS and the WTO; indirect processes by the circulation of the cultural objects the TRIPS regime sets out to defend: a movie, story, image, or in the ecological case, the genetic formation of a seed. In response, a number of networks of resistance become engaged in a counter-move whose institutional topology might be characterized as globalization from below. As food systems are the interpretive focus of the politics of *life itself*, I turn now to the politics of food, and its resistance movements, as a way of elucidating a *legal pluralism* as an alternative model of order—and the notion of food sovereignty.

The agents of this geo-politics of food are represented in networks of resistance movements, one of the most important being Via Campesina. Via Campesina, the International Peasants Network, is an "international alliance of organizations of peasant and family farmers, farm workers, indigenous people, landless peasants, and rural women and youth."[46] Via Campesina "launched the idea" of food sovereignty at the 1996 World Food Summit.[47] If the emergent industrialized and post-industrialized global food system results in taking control of the activities of local farmers through intellectual property rights in seeds and techno-scientific development, the globalization from below agenda aims to find ways to take back control. Control here is understood through a number of principles: the right to safe food; access to productive resources; possibilities of agroecological production; and the development of local markets.[48] Rajeev Patel explains that "the call is an active attempt to incite context-specific transformation within a context of universal (and defensibly humanist) principles of dignity, individual and community sovereignty, and self-determination."[49] Via Campesina defines itself as a "global, autonomous, pluralistic movement, independent of all political, economic or other denominations."[50] Taking a stance in relation to intellectual property rights, Via Campesina "opposes intellectual property over any form of life."[51] It advocates that "a moratorium be instituted on bio-prospecting … until there are mechanisms to protect the rights of our communities and to prevent and control bio-piracy."[52] It has also recommended that "a moratorium be declared on the release and trade of transgenic organisms and their derived products."[53]

The positions taken by Via Campesina are not only indicative of an alternative topology in the geo-politics of food. In a wider paradigmatic context, Via Campesina proclaims itself to be a new kind of participatory transnational organization. Advocates argue that "Via Campesina constitutes an important new space for, and agent of, transnational contention."[54] In its own words, Via Campesina operates as a "decentralized structure." It is a "grassroots mass movement whose vitality and legitimacy comes from farmers' organizations at local and national levels." It is made up of and "unites more than a hundred national and subnational organizations."[55] This transnational form of organizational power is shared between nine global regions, with an International Coordinating Committee made up of "one man and one woman" from each region.[56] Via Campesina is not only an activist network. It also seeks to provide an alternative policy platform to fight against the advancement of neo-liberal economic globalization.

As important as Via Campesina is, there have been many other community- and farmer-based organizations forming the resistance topology of Ecological Decolonization. In the non-western context, there are examples such as the Karnataka State Farmers' Association in India which "educated, debated and mobilized 200,000 farmers around the Uruguay Round draft text."[57] Or the Ghana School Feeding Program, "designed to fight hunger and reduce poverty using locally grown foodstuffs like maize, rice, soy-bean, cowpea, millet and sorghum."[58] In the western context, examples include The Peoples Grocery in Oakland, California, a community-based organization committed to the "food justice movement" and developing "community-driven solutions to food insecurity" though local bartering systems.[59]

There are also several important conjunctions between the organizational principles of these agents from below and the agenda of legal pluralism. At a legal or formal institutional level, this is reflected in a commitment to policy transformation by contesting the formal institutions of state law. In this context, state law also encompasses international law and regimes of global authority. Proponents of an alternative seek to provide a set of internal participatory governance principles in contradistinction to the realms of exclusion associated with global regimes. They engage the challenge of legal homogenization as an agent of food geopolitics. These organizations, including Via Campesina, represent a patchwork of alternative economic and legal orders. They stand in defense of local farming practices, grounded in shared cultural subject-hood. They share a politics of autonomy and self-determination characteristic institutional strategies of Ecological Decolonization. Their demands are premised on the normativity of bio-sovereignty and a set of principles of shared struggle. The institutional challenge they present is not only to the legal structures of international order. At the same time, these movements from below also posit an institutional alternative, based on notions of participation and autonomy.

If legal pluralism marks a relation to the law, we also gain entry into a distinct notion of the commons, the *ecological commons*. Ecological *colonization* manifests itself in several such enclosure movements, at a material level in land and seed ownership and at immaterial level in knowledge systems. Intellectual property rights, interpreted as private and exclusive, come to produce a unique post-industrial bio-political relation of dependence, with both temporal and spatial aspects. The temporal is associated with the rise of genetic use restriction or terminator technologies. In the development of patented "terminator" seeds, corporations have created seeds that only live through one crop cycle, thus ensuring that they must be purchased seasonally. There are also genetic use restriction technologies where crops can only express "desirable traits … when activated by the application of a proprietary chemical."[60] Through the medium of these seed types and complementary agricultural products, these biotechnologies structure "control from a distance."[61] The spatial aspects of this dynamic constitute what Jack Kloppenburg calls the "gene-scape."[62] Governance of this gene-scape is through patented seed and agricultural products. This presents hard boundaries when seeds are produced that do not cross-pollinate. There is also regulatory testing to ensure one farmer is not free riding through cross-pollination with the seeds of another. Here we witness a new bio-enclosure movement that seeks to limit the shared use of seed and farming products. Historical and ideational aspects present themselves in this kind of enclosure, as farmer identity, community identity, and subject formation constituted through the traditional processes of seed hybridization, are replaced by an annualized commodity purchase.

As an alternative model, on a biological level, the lens of the ecological commons is focused on "biological realities,"[63] grounded in our shared planetary existence. Such a foundation attempts, in direct and indirect ways, to dislodge a Westphalian understanding of community and boundaries, with a mapping of bio-community. Bruce Byers argues that "eco-regions or bio-geographical provinces are reflections, in communities of organisms, of the physical parameters of climate, soil, and topography."[64] Such a reframing opens new forms of commonality sourced in the causality of bio-life.

On a species level, biodiversity is interpreted as a common shared resource. As Shiva argues, "biodiversity has always been a local, commonly owned and utilized resource."[65] The relationship to biodiversity has been a key aspect in the production of subject-hood for indigenous and farming peoples. Here the reclaiming of the commons also speaks to knowledge systems as cultural heritage. As Shiva states, "heritage is not property at all—it is seen as a bundle of relationships rather than a bundle of economic rights."[66]

On the basis of these aspects of the ecological commons, we arrive at the agenda of food democracy as part of a broader move toward what Shiva calls "earth democracy." Food democracy, in particular, is an attempt to bring "democratic control over the food system." It "involves replacing the free trade order of corporate totalitarianism with an ecological and just system of food production and distribution."[67] Scaling up, earth democracy is "shaped by the multiple and diverse practices of people reclaiming their commons, their resources, their livelihoods, their freedom, their dignity, their identity and their peace."[68] In response to the temporal and spatial aspects of the enclosure agenda, the ecological commons comes to represent a domain for possible "self-rule and self-governance."[69] This mode of governance is sensitive to the negotiation of the universal and particular, by means of which, "living cultures recognize the multiplicity of identities in an identity of place and local community—and a planetary consciousness that connects the individual to the earth."[70] The economic aspect of this agenda is that the "commons is the highest form of economic democracy."[71] This ecological commons is the meta-institutional frame with which to understand both food sovereignty and bio-sovereignty. Its agenda is to reclaim an ecological common that has become bounded and privatized, as a consequence of ecological colonization.

The Propertyscape of Ecological Decolonization as an Ideal Type

Ecological Decolonization's ontological ordering principle of nature's rights presents an alternative rights discourse—not to begin with *Man's* inalienable rights, but *life itself*. In the face of the homogenizing forces associated with an ontology of ecological colonization, underwritten by the attempt to privatization of life itself, this ontological counter-position attempts to recognize and incorporate already existing cultural, epistemological, and biodiversity. By beginning with nature's rights, we gain the perspective to see the vast range of systems of value that operate outside of western discourses of production and value. As an ontology of social activity, the principle of nature's rights also articulates an epistemological diversity integral to a principle of the sovereignty of life itself.

There are several defining normative presuppositions in this propertyscape. The local, both western and non-western, speaks to a certain authenticity and ecological reality of scale. On this normative plane, the local is essentially understood as a natural plurality, the experience of, and dependence between, ecological and cultural lifeworlds. From here we gain insight into the normative battleground defined by the production boundary. The privatization of immaterial property labels as primitive and unscientific non-western approaches to biological life. It does so in part through the registration of patents, assigned on the basis of western-defined notions of innovation and novelty. This mode of ecological colonization rests on an empty lands thesis, misrecognizing the value of non-western epistemologies. This mode also applies a patriarchal lens to the very notion of productivity itself. The regulation of the primitive and unscientific through intellectual property rights reflects the instrumental rationality of a global environmentality. An alternative theory of value ties together this oppositional frame of normative presuppositions. For Ecological Decolonization, value is located in local bio-systems and cultures. Ecology is a self-realizing telos.

The institutional topology of Ecological Decolonization can be characterized as globalization from below. Presenting itself as a people's movement, it is grounded in a localized, ecological perspective on the world, sensitive to diversity, gender, and cultural identity. Setting this institutional agenda, legal pluralism is a strategically supportive theoretical framework. This pluralism seeks to protect biological and cultural diversity. In the legal sense, it supports diverse approaches to ownership. This is a question of framing, or "the way state law penetrates and restructures other normative orders through symbols and through direct coercion and, at the same time, the way non-state normative orders resist and circumvent penetration or even capture and use the symbolic capital of state law."[72] In these ways, legal pluralism reflects an agenda of institutional and political recognition. This is transposed into an ideal of the ecological commons, fundamentally contesting the primacy Westphalian boundaries and offering a different model of the propertyscape based on relationality of biological, epistemological, and cultural life.

Properties of Place

In addressing the effects of, and responses to, what I have called ecological colonization, researchers and commentators commonly examine the bio-politics of patents. In this living story, however, I will explore geographic indications as a unique form of the *protection* of life itself. In protecting the uniqueness of the properties of place, we see complex picture of the forces, and alternatives, to neo-liberal globalization and the propertyscape of Ecological Decolonization.

Geographic indications are protective rights assigned to products or production processes associated to specific geographic locations. On a spatial axis, the general criterion for assignment of a geographic indication is to protect a locally specific product. Such a product "yields qualities that cannot be replicated elsewhere, because place is said to be essential to the product."[73] On a process axis, as exemplified in the World Intellectual Property Organization's definition, geographic indications encompass the "qualities of a product … due to human factors that can be found in the place of origin of the products, such as specific manufacturing skills and traditions."[74]

Within the family of intellectual property rights, there are several qualities distinguishing geographic indications from other kinds of intellectual property. Unlike patents and copyright, geographic indications never expire; they are "held in perpetuity with no time limit as long as local knowledge is sustained and the indication is prevented from being generic."[75] Another distinguishing characteristic is that an individual cannot hold a geographic indication. Rather, it can only be a collective right, held by a community of practice. Geographic indications thus are a communal monopoly that "erects entry barriers on producers either within or outside the relevant geographical area."[76]

Because of the collective nature of the right, geographic indications come to represent regulatory domains often referred to as community-based orders.[77] Whether it is the production of a cheese, or wine, or other foodstuffs, community authorities ensure that products adhere to the local or traditional practices of production. For example, in France "the practice of naming wines by locality had been established for centuries and formal classifications of territory had existed for almost a century before illegal labeling and overproduction saw a gradual acceptance of the need for state enforcement through national legislation."[78] Community-based orders also regulate the boundaries of place, of who can be included as a producer in the collective right. In their totality, whether in a national or global frame, community-based orders come to represent a pluralism of non-legal regulatory orders, cultural and economic.

As we examine geographic indications as a form of *protection*, what emerges is a kind of intellectual property that is unique. With geographic indications, we have a domain of intellectual property that differs from the internal logic of the dominant regime, while existing within the dominant regime. The dominant narrative is one of privatization, creating a rivalrous, excludable, private monopoly. Geographic indications, on the other hand, are held in perpetuity, their system of ownership is collective, and their implicit anthropological assumption about innovation is based on the stability of tradition, so securing an alternative system of value, an "exceptional opportunity to utilize the power of the market to recognize and reward the products and services that convey particular traditions and uniqueness of culture and place."[79] With these *rights* we can see a possibility of securing the value of social capital, not determined singularly by rivalrousness, but represented in traditional products and their cultural practices of production. Within a broader politics of globalization, this presents a way to protect *place*, notwithstanding the forces of the universalizing culture associated with neo-liberal globalization.

A Signal of What?

The political divisions associated with interpretations of the meanings, use, and value of geographic indications within differing jurisdictional geographies offer a complex picture of the geo-politics of intellectual property. Generally, the argument that permeates the institutions and ideas of global intellectual property rights pits a global north against a global south. The dominant frame of reference is the protection of copyright and patents of northern innovation. This reflects the dominant narratives of globalization. But when it comes to geographic indications, north-south matters, but so too does another layer of core and periphery, the Old World and the New World.

I now turn to three examples of the products and production of place in order to explore these complexities: European wines, Darjeeling tea, and the Neem tree. If geographic indications are a *signaling device*, these examples offer differing insights into the nature of the signal and the geographies of life itself enmeshed in the twists and turns of history.

The first example is wine production. A wine region in France is called an appellation. The Institut National des Appellations d'Origine regulates the French Appellation of Control system. This system defines regional boundaries, for example, Burgundy, Bordeaux, the Loire Valley, and the Rhone Valley, and quality classification categories such as Regional, Communal, Premier Cru, and Grand Cru. These rules "originated from long periods of empirical experience and experimentation. The appellation system merely records and formalizes them."[80] For example, in the Bordeaux region, the classification first made in 1855 remains today. The appellation system defines both place and methods of production. On the place axis, in the case of the hills of Côte d'Or in Burgundy, for instance, "the Côte itself is a major fault scarp, dividing the Middle and Upper Jurassic limestone plateau from the Saône rift valley to the east, with the highest quality vineyards being situated on the brown calcitic or limestone soils of the gentle south-east facing slopes."[81] On the production axis, there are time-honored winemaking methods determining how far apart the vines are planted, the use of oak barrels, and the length of time a wine must age. These production and place aspects are so tightly defined that, as Tim Unwin explains, "adjacent vineyards" can be Grand Cru and the "neighbor remains a simple Appellation Communale." Cutting across both production and place is the dimension of culture. Differences are not just matters of climate and geology but the "labor of countless generations … their own distinctive human context." A geographic indication is "historical intersection between people and the environment creating a specific cultural identity."[82] Grape varieties, too, have localized ethno-botanical histories. Discussing the winemaking tradition in Portugal, Stanislawski argues, "its cultivation is immemorially important, not only as a source of livelihood, but also as part of the balance of culture which is concerned both with existence and with more subtle satisfactions as well."[83]

Tracing the flows of immigration, most new world vine varieties came with European settlement. For example, Australia has no native grape varieties. Irrespective of historical connections to the old world as the sources of cuttings and the processes of production, when these grapes are grown and wines produced in the new world, they become *generic* because they dislocated from the geographic moorings of the product. These *generic* products are often seen, economically and culturally, in warlike competition by old world producers. As a French winemaker proclaimed, "each bottle of American or Australian wine that lands in Europe is a bomb targeted at the heart of our rich European Culture."[84] The *generic* represents a struggle against the homogenizing forces of globalization, discontenting people from place. Within old world contexts a large part of the battle is the idea in Western Europe of the "vanishing peasant."[85]

The Australian wine industry is an apt reference point because it has become central player in the global wine market, intensely competing with the wines of the old world. Over and above the TRIPS Agreement, the EU has pursued, and continues to pursue, bilateral agreements designed to protect its national properties of place. One early example was the wine agreement between the EU and Australia in 1993. The Australian Minister for Primary Industry and Energy at the time noted in a speech introducing the agreement, "we have used European geographical names to denote a style of wine for more than a hundred years. Migrants often brought these names to Australia and used them to describe a familiar style of wine; the names have become generic."[86] To support and protect the non-generic aspect of Europe wines, the wine agreement led to the creation of the Australian Wine and Brandy Corporation Amendment Act 1993. In distinguishing Australian wine, the act formalized Australian wine regions in a similar way to the appellation system in France. In the same speech quoted above:

> Where does Coonawarra end and Riverina start? This question is just as relevant for Australian wine consumers as it is for the EC requirements. By defining the boundaries of our geographical indications, this bill will give greater certainty to enforcement of the label integrity program provisions of the act, which require winemakers to keep records to substantiate label claims of the vintage, variety or geographical indication of wine.[87]

So, in the same ways that European regulation marks place, regions like Hunter Valley, Coonawarra, or Barossa in Australia come to also be defined by climate, geography, and soil structure. In fact, "relying on their own regional names … the Australians have built the world's most dynamic wine industry."[88]

In the case of wine, a geographic indication is used to signal a protectionism of place, distinguishing old and new worlds. An originality of a place takes precedence over the flows of people with cultural ties to place of origin. Within a broader context this example illustrates the way in which, by protecting European products in the global marketplace, global harmonization via the legal frame of geographic indications has produced stricter definitions of localized particularity, even in the new world. In other words, global harmonization was generative of a new local; the production of the *signal* was referential to the process of harmonization. This local becomes similarly constrained by a sense of authenticity of place, culture of production. This example reveals the importance of a European local a resistance against economic globalization, a phenomenon usually presented in cases of the global south versus the global north. But it must also be noted, such harmonization has also misrecognized waves of migration, a constant phenomenon in the era of fluid globalization. Even if precisely the same knowledge is used to produce wine by families of European origin with continuous application of these practices from the old world to new world, they are denied the ability to name in similar fashion because of the particularity of place.

The second example is Darjeeling tea. Darjeeling tea represents a different kind of history of product and production-in-place. Darjeeling tea comes from the Darjeeling district in West Bengal, India. The region is made up of "87 fabled gardens that have been producing the highly prized black teas for over 150 years."[89] Although introduced by The East India Company in the seventeenth century as a more tradable commodity than Chinese Green tea, it has become more than an important regional product. As argued by the Darjeeling Tea Association, "Darjeeling tea is India's treasured Geographical Indication and forms a very important part of India's cultural and collective intellectual heritage."[90] On the place axis, the climate contributes to the unique character of the region as tea "requires at least 50 inches of rainfall annually." The fog of the valley helps to maintain "the required level of moisture." On the method axis, Darjeeling tea refers not simply to the tea comes from the Darjeeling region, but to a unique method of processing the tea. The tea goes through specific processing stages, starting from its first plucking.[91] These processes also put a premium on sustainability. In the words of promotional material created by one of the largest gardens, "we encourage and sustain an environment-friendly culture on our farms. The use of natural fertilizers has rid the soil of chemical residues, gifting the workers with safe drinking water and clean air. Renewable sources of energy such as hydro-electricity reduce carbon footprints."[92] Claims are also made about ethical labor practices:

> We care for our people as much as for that fine cup of tea. The workers are provided housing, cooking fuel, footwear, protective clothing, winter blankets and basic medical treatment free of cost. Rations are subsidized and free milk is distributed through the Infant Nutrition Program. Every child is entitled to free primary education and scholarships are provided for further training. Social security includes provident fund and pension fund, gratuity and support for dependents.[93]

Furthermore, "a unique feature of this work force is that more than 60 percent are women and the employment is on a family basis."[94] Fitting within the anti-productivist agenda, there is also a "disdain for quantity."[95] On the culture axis, religious interpretations are provided for the geographic uniqueness of Darjeeling. A report produced by the Tea Board of India explains that "the local people believe that the Himalayan range is the abode of Shanker Mahadeva and the breath of the God brings winds that cool the brow of the sun filled valley, and the mist and fog which provide the moisture. The fountain that flows from the piled hair of Shiva provides water for the crop and it thrives."[96]

In combination, "Darjeeling tea is the result of unique and complex combination of agro-climatic conditions prevailing in the region, altitude, and meticulous manufacture."[97] It is also critical to highlight the economic importance of this geographic indication for the region. The Darjeeling tea industry "employs over 52,000 people on a permanent basis, while a further 15,000 persons are engaged during the plucking season, which lasts from March to November."[98] While its identity is premised on the locality of the product, "around 98% of Darjeeling tea produced in India is exported. In 2006, the total exports of Darjeeling tea was 11.5 million kg, which fetched around Rs. 917 million (approx. US$ 20.3 million) as export earnings."[99]

In this case, a geographic indication is used to *signal* a cultural value and the defense of the identity of the community of production, so securing economic livelihoods in the domestic economy of India and the global economy. However, we must also contextualize the industry within the history of colonialism. The plantations, now called "gardens," were in fact the development of Dr. Campbell, the first colonial English Superintendent of the Darjeeling district. In 1847 "the first commercial tea gardens were planted out by the British tea interests," according to the Darjeeling Tea website. "During 1860, The Darjeeling Company was established with 4 gardens, while the Darjeeling Consolidated Tea Co. dates back to 1896".[100] So we must also be cognizant of the production of the local within often longstanding global economic structures. The economic logic of protected, local production is not simply about alternative systems of value, as the local functions as an integral part of capitalist production and distribution systems.

The final example I will present is the Neem tree. This is a tropical evergreen native to India. It is commonly referred to as India's *tree of life*, a mythical object, "mentioned in Indian texts written over 2000 years ago, and has been used for centuries by local communities."[101] On a production axis, the Neem tree is the source of a wide variety of products. For example, Neem oil is used as an insect repellent, a natural pesticide, a fertilizer, and a contraceptive.[102] The bark is even used to clean teeth. On a cultural axis, the tree is "venerated in the religions and literature of the region."[103] For all its properties, the tree is worshiped as sacred. It is known in Sanskrit as sarva-roga nivarini or "curer of all ailments." Taken as a whole the tree is a symbol of traditional knowledge.

In 1992 the chemical multinational W.R. Grace applied for a patent on an anti-fungal treatment produced from the extract of the Neem tree. W.R. Grace developed a "storage-stable version of the extract," with the Grace patent covering "processes which make the extract both more valuable to the pesticide industry and more useful to farmers."[104] Such a claim, in Vandana Shiva's words, turned the patent into "a powerful symbol of biopiracy."[105] In her view, "it was pure and simple piracy. The oil from Neem has been used traditionally by farmers to prevent fungus, it was neither a novel idea nor was it invented."[106] In opposition, Shiva among others led a global Neem campaign consisting of "an international network of patent warriors to support our national campaign. The campaign was initiated because of the intrinsic importance of Neem in our culture, agriculture and health systems."[107] The challenge was successful, and the patent claim dismissed. The Neem tree provides an example of the practices of biopiracy and bio-prospecting, how traditional knowledge becomes appropriated by private and corporate actors, and the scope for resistance. While geographic indications are used in the interests of old world industries, the "protection of geographical indications no longer is exclusively seen as an instrument to protect European values."[108] In fact, in the literature much optimism is expressed about the potentials for the use of geographic indications as a strategy for reclaiming bio-sovereignty.

In protecting the geographic indication of the Neem tree, the signal conveyed contains an element of recognition—the recognition of the scientific achievements of indigenous communities and traditional knowledge. Thus, in this living story, geographic indication provides a method, ideationally and institutionally, to secure the epistemological diversity that is represented in the Neem tree as a production object. In this way, geographic indication offers an opportunity to foster economic independence. In the words of the Neem Foundation, "the Neem tree has been recognized by the world over as a commercial opportunity. This is a welcome sign—but the bio-diversity prospects of this tree cannot be a free access to the entire world [sic]."[109]

These complex examples provide insights into how geographic indications can provide an institutional mechanism for the preservation of diverse modes of local, traditional environmental practices and cultures. As Dwijen Rangnekar writes, "to assert the necessity of GI protection is, in part, to assert the importance of local culture and tradition in the face of ever-encroaching globalization."[110] Daniele Giovannucci and Claudia Ranaboldo from the Latin-American Centre for Rural Development say that geographic indicators can be seen as an "exceptional opportunity to utilize the power of the market to recognize and reward the products and services that convey particular traditions and uniqueness of culture and place." They "can represent a form of exchange on a human-scale that represents globalization at its best by fostering respect and acknowledgement for what is intrinsically local."[111] Laurence Berard and Philippe Marchenary argue "their inscription in a place is related to their historical roots and the collective practices that produce them. In other words, they straddle space and time, and are built on shared knowledge and know-how."[112] Moreover "they exist in a broader context as an integral form of rural development that can powerfully advance commercial and economic interests while fostering local values such as environmental stewardship, culture and tradition."[113]

Nature's History

Within the complex, and as we shall see frequently problematic, examples I have provided, several insights that emerge shed light on Ecological Decolonization as a paradigmatic approach to the production and ownership of the work and play of the mind. The first emerges in the construction of the local. The examples I have offered above are grounded in the local, where the local is defined by the essential properties of place. In the case of wine regions, we encounter a history of an old world localism, and subsequently we find the creation of a new world localism. Darjeeling tea and the Neem tree similarly represent localisms of India. All are positioned as authentic and non-generic. Looking through the prism of geographic indications, the local is constructed in a dual process. On one hand, the local becomes necessarily nationalized. The state becomes the protector of this ideational domain. Geographic indications thus become intertwined in the normative purposes of the state, highlighting and protecting its regional distinctiveness. Even the TRIPS regime plays a part in this nationalizing. Article 22 grounds the products of geographic indication in the territoriality of a nation: its soils, climate, and culture. For example, the idea of "essentially attributable" central to the meaning of Article 22 historically moors this material grounding. Buttressing this is a notion of history, Article 22.2(a) refers to a "true place of origin," evoking a stable and original national source.

However, the local is only meaningful in the context of the global. A geographic indication is economically powerful within the global context. For example, "Darjeeling tea [is] a rare coveted brew which is desired globally, but is only grown in India."[114] While grounding and naturalizing products of place within the national frame, the local is also used to construct the global. Article 22.2(a) explains that naming must not "mislead the public." This opens the door to the question of who is the public? Where does it exist—in a local, a national or global frame? Both processes pose a challenge to the Ecological Decolonization ideal of the local. For Ecological Decolonization, the local is perceived as a naturalized phenomenon, associated with a particular kind of people and relationship to nature, frozen in time and place. However, Ecological Decolonization equally catches itself in a self-contradiction when it deploys the local as a political tactic, not for the sake of the local, but as a strategic ploy whose primary purpose is to negotiate global markets.

In articulating this position there is, moreover, a tendency to romanticize the local. When applied to the production and ownership of the work and play of the mind, deploying the local as a political frame can produce a number of blind spots. Economically, as Amory Starr asks, "is local food a set of policies, a consumer fad, a new market, or a social movement?"[115] Jeff Pratt points out that "the labels organic, fair trade, or local, do not in themselves reveal a great deal about the extent to which their producers have resisted or been absorbed by the corporate interests in the food industry, nor much about whether the values they embody are part of a radical or conservative political agenda."[116] There are also contradictions in positing the local as an original state. Considering the politics of food, could there be pasta in Italy without Macro Polo's travels in Asia? Would there be potatoes for fish and chips in England without the European colonization of the Americas? In other words, the local has always been in flux, continually constructed from global movements often centuries in duration, or longer. And at the political level, the construction of the local can also obscure power structures within the local. Examining the post-colonial nations of Southeast Asia, Aihwa Ong builds a detailed case of how pre-colonial political order comes to be embedded in post-colonial social production "through schemes of bio-political disciplining and pastoral care—that differently insert them into processes of global capitalism." She argues that "these gradations of governing may be in continuum, but they overlap with pre-formed racial, religious and gender hierarchies and further fragment citizenship for people who are all, nominally speaking, citizens of the same country."[117]

We also encounter the problem of ethno-biological nationalism. There is a tendency for epistemological diversity to become a nationalized phenomenon. This process is intensified in post-colonial settings where the nation-state becomes a leading advocate of a new national order, using the cultural symbols of tradition to articulate political authority, domestically and on the global stage. Here we also encounter the problem of collapsing the national, the cultural, and the biological. As Shiva argues, "we are the food we eat, the water we drink and the air we breathe."[118] In its defense of geographic indications, the post-colonial nation-state becomes the most vociferous advocate of such a position. By this move a seed or a tree are nationalized as symbolic objects, and with them the epistemologies that contextualize these objects. Naturalized bio-life thus provides a normative buffer for the nationalizing of cultural and epistemological diversity.

Yet another line of complexity draws our attention back to the production boundary. Geographic indications present an institutional mechanism with which to protect alternative systems of value based in senses of history, tradition, community, and collective personhood. They provide a mechanism to protect epistemological diversity as an expression of nature's innate multiplicity and particularity. As the French legal scholar Marie-Angele Hermitte argues:

> The difference between these two conceptions of progress: automatic, linear progress, deriving mechanically from technological change, and more complex progress, which can be satisfied by the conservation of memory and the maintaining of customs, which have arrived at a high degree of perfection, leads to what is perhaps the most profound originality of the designation of origin with respect to the other intellectual property rights.[119]

However, relationships to capitalist systems of value need to be taken into consideration. Tomer Broude argues, "in crude neo-liberal economic terms GIs could actually be said to promote free trade by facilitating full information, towards perfect market conditions."[120] In this light, geographic indications provide the necessary harmonization for decreasing *friction* in the market. The generic is viewed as a kind of commodity fraud, juxtaposed with what might be seen as the authentic commodity. The normative argument of the local-as-authentic may in fact obscure the fact of the subsumption of these domains of social production into the productionist model. In the guise of cultural protection as represented in the object of production, are we simply defining and defending the niche brand of the local in the context of global markets?

This leaves us with the final complication centering on the private. While expressed though a collective monopoly, each of the three examples represents a process of enclosure that could, in some senses, be considered to be a form of privatization. This privatization may well be necessary in order to define a protected group of people who are permitted to use a symbolic system. Nonetheless it represents another cleavage in the case for an alternative model of social activity.

Finally, while the propertyscape of Ecological Decolonization represents an attempt to ground the nature of social activity in principles of multiplicity and diversity, as the discussion above suggests, the question remains as to whether it might in fact simultaneously produce another kind of problem. Does this propertyscape implicitly produce a timeless and essentialist relationship to culture, opening the possibility of anchoring social production to a cultural frame that may reinforce historically unjust social, political, or economic divides? Nature's rights freezes an idealized history on the basis of authenticity or biological life, suggesting a natural equilibrium to which we might return. At the same time, it may present a vision of social production in the context of identity and culture that offers little scope for evolutionary change, mixing and blending.

Whose Nature?

I want to close the chapter by making inroads for thinking about this propertyscape as a model of economic distribution, social participation, and political representation. By asking the question of *whose nature*, my aim is to start to overlay an evaluative rubric of the *who*, *what*, and *how*, with a view of presenting this propertyscape as a nascent model of political community within the global system.

The *who* of this nascent model of political community is framed referentially to life itself. On the one hand, the *who* is how we understand our social lives as being relational to the realities of eco-systemic life as the cornerstone of our *natural* common bond. Such a bond pre-dates western ontologies and epistemologies of life itself. The *who* speaks to those who have been historically marginalized from the production of the *who*: indigenous people, third world peasants, women, economically marginal, unemployed, or underemployed. This systematic exclusion from the meaning making aspect of the who is a result of the logics of colonization; the misrecognition and devaluation of life itself, from the construction of the *who*.

The *what* finds its character in nature's rights. Nature, as life itself, is the ontological *a priori* that underpins diverse systems of social activity. This move lays the basis for a critique of the homogenization of knowledge, "the monoculture of the mind" that is an ancillary effect of imposing rivalrous notions of property. Nature's rights are used to construct a frame of justice grounded in principles of sustainability and diversity, contrasted with purely market-oriented production. In doing so, we may valorize alternative systems of value that are sourced in life itself. This is a *what* grounded in nature and the diversity of cultural practices in systems of ownership that collectively recognize the shared history of the cultures of production.

The critical lens of Ecological Decolonization ties its critique of epistemological homogenization to the institutional practices of legal homogenization. The decolonization of the work and play of the mind with a view to traditional, peasant or third world societies, must be based on principles of legal pluralism. Such pluralism allows for institutional recognition of diverse normative orders that appear in the form of alternative legal orderings. A lack of institutional recognition—the *empty lands* thesis—produces an enclosure effect. A focus on nature's rights brings to the fore an institutional topology of the ecological commons as an ecosystemic reality—our very being in a material sense, and in an immaterial sense our relationships to nature producing our epistemologies, worldviews, and cultures.

The ecological commons also presents a radical contestation of Westphalian principles of *man-made* global order. What ties together peoples is not their relationship as citizens in political communities, but their position as an extension of a shared biological reality. It also represents a complex engagement with institutional realities of global politics.

The nation-state is used strategically in the context of a global order. This strategic thinking reverberates in the legal pluralist agenda too. Based on research conducted in India, Shalini Randeria argues that "faced with globalization, the transnationalization of law … under the dominance of international institutions that champion the interests of global capital, legal pluralists … are beginning to discover the virtues of the state, its sovereignty and autonomy."[121] Many in the literature talk through this response in a Polanyi-like discourse of *double movement.* In Pratt's words, "rural sociologists have rediscovered Karl Polanyi, and discuss localization in terms of an embedded economy."[122] The ecological in-common is seen as a re-embedding moment.

When we ask the question of *whose nature*, several problems of framing arise. To begin with, looking at an ontology of nature's diversity, *life itself*, mapped against an agenda of legal pluralism, we are faced with a problem of moral relativism. A question remains about the relative weight afforded to normative orders before the law or how non-legal orders can maintain their differences—cultural, customary, religious, or otherwise. This raises the challenging question of mutually exclusive boundaries. For example, what are the religious components of western secular traditions, such as the way in which Judeo-Christian morality finds its way into secular law? How are these differences reconciled, and by whom?

Furthermore, in looking at the strategic interaction with the Westphalian agents of political community, we are also faced with the paradox of the *cunning state.* This notion explains a situation where "international institutions are claimed to be utterly powerless servants of their member states, and states in turn claim their powerlessness in the face of prescriptions from Washington or Geneva."[123] As the geographic indications examples presented in this chapter have brought to the fore, these debates have increasingly become nationalized. When taken up under national banners, the notion of the natural-local obscures the ways in which nations are a focal point in defense of local regimes, at times contradicting the principles of epistemological diversity. But then again, maybe these forces can be productive in transforming the *national* approach to the pluralism of culture, people, and law within their already established jurisdictional geography.

Finally, another framing danger is embryogenic in the propertyscape of Ecological Decolonization's ontology of nature and the normativity of the *local*. The local tends to create a static view of the relationship between history and culture, freezing the generative aspect of social activity. On one hand this is a consequence in part of an implicit assumption that the western is a monolithic epistemological entity. In this context, the western, marked by singular science and characteristically modern culture, is stripped of diversity or critical tensions. Western science is not seen as itself grounded in culture, connected to the material world and replete with culturally diverse interpretations and applications. On the other hand, such a view can implicitly reinforce the traditional as epistemologically static insofar as it represents a cultural snapshot of a tradition, a schema of knowledge, or a cultural object. By these means, the traditional becomes naturalized as intrinsically authentic nature. Traditional epistemologies can thereby also be denied a history or future of innovation. Rather than *living cultures*, they end up being historically trapped and static' vulnerable to reifying differences in the misrecognition of cultural change, natural adaptation, and the dynamic and changing forces of history.

Notes

1. Tomer Broude, "Taking 'Trade and Culture' Seriously: Geographical Indications and Cultural Protection in WTO Law," *BEPress Legal Series* 649 (2005). p. 19.
2. Shiva. p. 55.
3. See: Harriet Friedmann, "The Political Economy of Food: The Rise and Fall of the Postwar International Food Order," *American Journal of Sociology* 88S (1982); "International Regimes of Food and Agriculture since 1870," in *Peasants and Peasant Societies*, ed. T. Shanin (Oxford: Basil Blackwell, 1987); "The Political Economy of Food: A Global Crisis," *New Left Review* 197 (1993); "What on Earth Is the Modern World-System? Food-Getting and Territory in the Modern Era and Beyond," *Journal of World-System Research* VI, no. 2 (2000); Harriet Friedmann, McMichael, Phillip, "Agriculture and the State System:

The Rise and Fall of National Agricultures, 1870 to the Present," *Sociologia Ruralis* 29, no. 2 (1989); Phillip McMichael, "A Food Regime Genealogy," *The Journal of Peasant Studies* 36, no. 1 (2009).
4. p. 141.
5. L. and Payne Joy, P.R., "Food and Nutrition Planning, Nutrition Consultants' Reports," (Rome: FAO, 1975).
6. Finn Bowring, "Manufacturing Scarcity: Food Biotechnology and the Life Sciences Industry," *Capital & Class* 27, no. 79 (2003). p. 109.
7. Rajeev Patel, "Grassroots Voices: Food Sovereignty," *The Journal of Peasant Studies* 36, no. 3 (2009). p.
8. Nikolas Rose, *The Politics of Life Itself: Biomedicine, Power, and Subjectivity in the Twenty-First Century* (Princeton: Princeton University Press, 2007). p. 11.
9. Vandana Shiva, *Biopiracy: The Plunder of Nature and Knowledge* (Cambridge: South End Press, 1997). p. 4.
10. Ibid. p. 46.
11. Ibid. p. 47.
12. *Monocultures of the Mind: Perspectives on Biodiversity and Biotechnology* (New York City: Zed Books, 1993). p. 12.
13. Ruth Hubbard, "Human Nature," in *Biopolitics: A Feminist and Ecological Reader on Biotechnology*, ed. Vandana Shiva (New York City: Zed Books, 1988). p. 28.
14. Shiva, *Biopiracy: The Plunder of Nature and Knowledge*. p. 45.
15. Ibid. p. 3.
16. *Diamond V. Chakrabarty* 447 U.S. 303 (1980). p. 306.
17. Ibid. p. 306.
18. Ibid. p. 310.
19. Boaventura De Sousa Santos, Arriscado Nunes, Joao, Meneses, Maria, "Opening up the Cannon of Knowledge and Recognition of Difference," in *Another Knowledge Is Possible: Beyond Northern Epistemologies* ed. Boaventura De Sousa Santos (New York City: Verso, 2008). p. xxxvii.
20. Shiva, *Monocultures of the Mind: Perspectives on Biodiversity and Biotechnology*. p. 10.
21. De Sousa Santos. p. xxxxi.
22. Ibid. p. xxv.
23. Ibid. p. xl.
24. Ibid. pp. xlviii–xlix.

25. Rajeev Patel, "Global Fascism, Revolutionary Humanism and the Ethics of Food Sovereignty," *Development* 48, no. 2 (2005). p. 81.
26. Michel Pimbert, "Towards Food Sovereignty," *Sustainable Agriculture, Biodiversity and Livelihoods: International Institute for Environment and Development* 141, no. November (2008). p. 5.
27. See: Jeff Pratt, "Food Values: The Local and the Authentic," *Critique of Anthropology* 27, no. 3 (2007).
28. De Sousa Santos. p. xxiii.
29. Jack Kloppenburg, "Impeding Dispossession, Enabling Repossession: Biological Open Source and the Recovery of Seed Sovereignty," *Journal of Agrarian Change* 10, no. 3 (2010). p. 372.
30. Shiva, *Biopiracy: The Plunder of Nature and Knowledge*. p. 61.
31. Ibid. p. 44.
32. Arze Glipo, "Agreement on Agriculture and Food Sovereignty: Perspectives from Mesoamerica and Asia," *Hbf Policy Paper for Cancún* (2003). p. 18.
33. See: Tim Luke, "On Environmentality: Geo-Power and Eco-Power in the Discourses of Contemporary Environmentalism," *Cultural Critique* 31 (1995); Cori Hayden, *When Nature Goes Public: The Making and Unmaking of Bioprospecting in Mexico* (Princeton: Princeton University Press, 2003).
34. Pimbert. p. 2.
35. Glipo. p. 3.
36. globalagriculture.org, "Industrial Agriculture and Small-Scale Farming," globalagriculture.org, http://www.globalagriculture.org/report-topics/industrial-agriculture-and-small-scale-farming.html.
37. Fouad Makki, "The Empire of Capital and the Remaking of Centre-Periphery Relations," *Third World Quarterly* 25 (2004). p. 155.
38. Hayden.
39. Shiva, *Biopiracy: The Plunder of Nature and Knowledge*. p. 42.
40. M. B Hooker, *Legal Pluralism: An Introduction to Colonial and Neo-Colonial Laws* (Oxford: Clarendon Press, 1975).
41. Sally Engle Merry, "Legal Pluralism," *Law & Society Review* 22, no. 5 (1988). p. 870.
42. Ibid.
43. Ibid. p. 873.
44. Sally Falk Moore, "Law and Social Change: The Semi-Autonomous Social Field as an Appropriate Subject of Study," ibid.7, no. 719 (1973). p. 720.

45. John Griffiths, "What Is Legal Pluralism?," *Journal of Legal Pluralism* 24 (1986). p. 3.
46. Peter Rosset, "Food Sovereignty and the Contemporary Food Crisis," *Development* 51, no. 4 (2008). p. 469.
47. Via Campesina, "The International Peasant's Voice," viacampesina.org, http://viacampesina.org/en/index.php/organisation-mainmenu-44.
48. See: Wilhemina Quaye, "Food Sovereignty and Combating Poverty and Hunger in Ghana," *Tailoring Biotechnologies* 3, no. 2 (2007). Peter Rosset, "Moving Forward: Agrarian Reform as a Part of Food Sovereignty," in *Promised Land: Competing Visions of Agrarian Reform*, ed. Michael Courville, Patel, Raj, Rosset, Peter, (Oakland: Food First Books, 2006); *Food Is Different: Why We Must Get the WTO out of Agriculture* (New York City: Zed Books, 2006); "Food Sovereignty and the Contemporary Food Crisis."
49. Rajeev Patel, "Global Fascism, Revolutionary Humanism and the Ethics of Food Sovereignty," ibid. 48, no. 2 (2005). p. 81.
50. Pimbert. p. 6.
51. Via Campesina, "The Position of Vía Campesina on Biodiversity, Biosafety and Genetic Resources," *Development* 44, no. 4 (2001). p. 49.
52. Ibid. p. 48.
53. Ibid. p. 51.
54. Rajeev Patel, "International Agrarian Restructuring and the Practical Ethics of Peasant Movement Solidarity," *Journal of Asian and African Studies* 41, no. 71 (2006). p. 89.
55. Saturnino Borras Jr., "La Vía Campesina: An Evolving Transnational Social Movement," *Transnational Institute* TNI Briefing Series, no. No 2004/6 (2004). p. 1.
56. Via Campesina, "The International Peasant's Voice."
57. Patel, "International Agrarian Restructuring and the Practical Ethics of Peasant Movement Solidarity." p. 73.
58. Quaye. p. 76.
59. Peoples Grocery, "About Us," peoplesgrocery.org, http://www.peoples-grocery.org/about/.
60. Bowring. p. 137.
61. Quaye. p.
62. Kloppenburg. p. 368.
63. Bruce Byers, "Ecoregions, State Sovereignty and Conflict," *Security Dialogue* 22, no. 1 (1991). p. 65.

64. Ibid. p. 65.
65. Shiva, *Earth Democracy: Justice, Sustainability and Peace.* p. 41.
66. Ibid.
67. *Stolen Harvest: The Hijacking of the Global Food Supply* (Cambridge, MA: South End Press, 2000). p. 117.
68. *Earth Democracy: Justice, Sustainability and Peace.* p. 5.
69. Ibid. p. 11.
70. Ibid.
71. Ibid. p. 5.
72. Merry. p. 881.
73. Kal Raustiala, Munzer, Stephen, "The Global Struggle over Geographic Indications," *The European Journal of International Law* 18, no. 2 (2007). p. 338.
74. "About Geographic Indications," available at: http://www.wipo.int/about-ip/en/about_geographical_ind.html.
75. Pradyot Ranjan Jena, Grote, Ulrike, "Changing Institutions to Protect Regional Heritage: A Case for Geographical Indications in the Indian Agrifood Sector," *Development Policy Review* 28, no. 2 (2010). p. 7.
76. Rangnekar, "The Socio-Economics of Geographic Indications: A Review of Empirical Evidence from Europe," UNCTAD–ICTSD Project on IPRs and Sustainable Development Issue Paper No. 8, May 2004, at 15.
77. Warren Moran, "Rural Space as Intellectual Property," *Political Geography* 12, no. 3 (1993). p. 264.
78. Ibid.
79. Daniele Giovannucci, Ranaboldo, Claudia "Markets and Geographical Indications of Origin," (Latin-American Center for Rural Development 2008). p. 1.
80. Moran. p. 266.
81. Tim Unwin, *Wine and the Vine: An Historical Geography of Viticulture and the Wine Trade* (London: Routledge, 1991). p. 13.
82. Ibid. p. 1.
83. D. Stanislawski, *Landscapes of Bacchus: The Vine in Portugal* (Austin: University of Texas Press, 1970). pp. 4–5.
84. Quoted in: Broude. p. 1.
85. Henri Mendras, *The Vanishing Peasant: Innovation and Change in French Agriculture* (Cambridge, Mass.: MIT Press, 1970).
86. Commonwealth of Australia, "House of Representatives Hansard," *29 September* (1993). p. 1342.

87. Ibid.
88. The Economist, "Protecting Names: The European Union's List of Sacrosanct Trade Names May Not Fend Off Imitators," *The Economist*, July 31 2003.
89. Darjeeling Tea Association, "Darjeeling, a Paradise," Darjeeling Tea Association, http://www.darjeelingtea.com/protection/paradise.asp.htm.
90. "Protection of Darjeeling Tea," Darjeeling Tea Association, http://www.darjeelingtea.com/protection/geographical.asp.htm.
91. Ranjan Jena.
92. *Ambootia, "Ambootia,"* http://ambootia.com/.
93. Ibid.
94. Darjeeling Tea Association, "The Present Scenario," Darjeeling Tea Association, www.darjeelingtea.com/growth/present.asp.htm
95. "Darjeeling, a Paradise."
96. Tea Board of India, "Darjeeling Tea: A Quest for Intellectual Property Rights," (Kolkata: Tea Board of India, 2010).
97. Darjeeling Tea Association, "Darjeeling, a Paradise."
98. "The Present Scenario."
99. Ranjan Jena. p. 13.
100. http://www.darjeelingtea.com/growth/beginning.asp.htm.
101. Neem Foundation, "Patents on Neem," neemfoundation.org, http://www.neemfoundation.org/neem-articles/patents-on-neem.html.
102. John Vidal, "Granting Community Theft," The Guardian, http://www.guardian.co.uk/environment/2003/sep/08/wto.fairtrade3.
103. Neem Foundation.
104. Emily Marden, "The Neem Tree Patent: International Conflict over the Commodification of Life," *Boston College International and Comparative Law Review* 22, no. 2 (1999). p. 279.
105. Vandana Shiva, "Free Tree," The Hindustan Times, India, http://www1.hindustantimes.com/nonfram/090600/detOPI01.htm.
106. The Hindu, "India Wins Neem Patent Case," The Hindu, http://www.hindu.com/2005/03/09/stories/2005030902381300.htm.
107. Shiva, "Free Tree."
108. Marion Panizzon, "Traditional Knowledge and Geographical Indications: Foundations, Interests and Negotiating Positions," in *NCCR Trade Working Paper* (Geneva: Swiss National Centre of Competence in Research, 2006). p. 35.
109. Neem Foundation.

110. Raustiala. p. 339.
111. Daniele Giovannucci, Josling, Tim, Kerr, William, O'Connor, Bernard, Yeung, May "Guide to Geographical Indications: Linking Products and Their Origins," (Geneva: International Trade Centre, 2009). p. 21.
112. Laurence Berard, Marchenay, Philippe, "Local Products and Geographical Indications: Taking Account of Local Knowledge and Biodiversity," *International Social Science Journal* 187 (2006). p. 109.
113. Giovannucci. p. 4.
114. Darjeeling Tea Association, "Protection of Darjeeling Tea."
115. Amory Starr, "Local Food: A Social Movement?," *Cultural Studies ↔ Critical Methodologies* 10, no. 6 (2010). p. 480.
116. Pratt. pp. 285–86.
117. Aihwa Ong, "Graduated Sovereignty in South-East Asia," *Theory, Culture & Society* 17, no. 55 (2000). p. 62.
118. Shiva, *Earth Democracy: Justice, Sustainability and Peace*. p. 5.
119. Translated and Quoted in: Berard. p. 114.
120. Broude. p. 16.
121. Shalini Randeria, "Legal Pluralism, Social Movements and the Post-Colonial State in India: Fractured Sovereignty and Differential Citizenship Rights," in *Another Knowledge Is Possible: Beyond Northern Epistemologies*, ed. Boaventura De Sousa Santos (New York City: Verso, 2007). p. 43.
122. Pratt. p. 289.
123. Randeria. p. 43.

6

Conclusion: *Whose Property?*

The propertyscapes whose terrains I have explored in this book serve as origin stories, historical records, that illuminate dominant contemporary alternatives in the politics of the work and play of the mind. I have been arguing that within their models for *becoming property*, each offers an essential insight into alternatives of constitutive collective political action, relative to the historical affordances of a post-industrial information age, and the lived realities of global space. In trying now to draw some summary conclusions from this analysis I return to the normative thrust of the project, to identify an emancipatory potential within the global politics of the production and ownership of the work and play of the mind.

The kind of emancipatory potential I am interested in relates to my own historical diagnosis. One aspect of this historical diagnosis centers on the ways in which the work and play of the mind remains under pressure and continues to be subsumed by capitalist logics of production. In my analysis of all four propertyscapes, I have sought to reveal the complicated edges and shape-shifting forms of these processes. This can be seen, for example, in the enclosures of knowledge via copyright laws, the commodification of everyday life in the production of the social in digital communication networks, and the patenting by biological life. Each of

P. Kalantzis-Cope, *The Work and Play of the Mind in the Information Age*,
Frontiers of Globalization, https://doi.org/10.1007/978-3-319-64650-3_6

these examples embodies the evolving logic of capitalism inveigling itself in diverse domains of social life. My working hypothesis has been that the production and ownership of the work and play of the mind is the under-represented epicenter for understanding the nature of the revolution in social life that is the so-called information age, as well as a productive site to think of possible paths forward.

Another aspect of my historical diagnosis centers on what I consider to be a worrying trend: a rejection of the *global* and a resurgent nativism in the current geo-political climate. This is worrying insofar as it is not simply a rejection of varying models of globalization per se, but a rejection of the move toward models of affinity, and institutions of binding quality, that reflect the nature of our global social interdependence. The propertyscapes outlined in this book raise clear arguments about the opportunities and effects of social interdependence in global space, as lived realities, and projected ideals. They also reveal cracks in their edifices, spaces in which a nativist misdiagnosis of the global project grows, and new spaces of injustice shaped by the misdiagnosis.

Claims to the work and play of the mind occur in grounded social practices. Each site offers a unique place to investigate the framings of global political life, bounded by or in opposition to disembodied flows of culture and knowledge. The speculative component of the book has been centered on political community, as a kind of constitutive collective political action. Because *becoming property* and *political community* are similarly generative, theoretical moorings, each process comes to demand an institutional form of some shape: a law, regime, or common set of accepted norms, this is where my diagnosis dovetails with the strategic agenda in the form of a prognosis. The agenda I propose aligns with the challenge posed by Nancy Fraser: "overcoming injustice means dismantling institutionalized obstacles that prevent some people from participating on a par with others, as full partners in social interaction."[1] The question of *whose property* locates this prognosis in a demand to *design* a new political geography from the *nascent* potentials, new opportunities for political communities as modes of collective political action, representing fundamental, democratic-constitutive acts, emerging from the contradictory ground of our contemporary propertyscapes.

Strategic Dilemmas

The first section of each chapter constructed ideal types of each propertyscape. My aim was not to cultivate an assumption that each had a monolithic conceptual identity. Nor was I trying to assert that the propertyscapes were mutually exclusive when they play out in the lifeworlds of the work and play of the mind. Rather, the opposite is true. There is a persistent reality, both at the philosophical/theoretical level and at the social/empirical level in which the propertyscapes often co-produce and synergize each other. For all their differences in terms of paradigm and practice, the different propertyscapes govern the social life of the work and play of the mind simultaneously, either in relative autonomy from each other or in striking and at times contradictory relations of co-dependency. In terms of my diagnosis of our present condition, strategic dilemmas emerge from each propertyscape, in and of themselves. Other dilemmas emerge from intersections with each other. Knowing which path forward might be most generative in the layered fog of these propertyscapes is at times difficult to determine.

The strategic dilemma evidenced in the propertyscape of Information Privatization reveals itself in the confluence of free trade and free speech, visible so clearly in the living story of the Great Firewall. In this living story the *global* internet is used as a battering ram to construct a global communication market. *Becoming property*, in this case private property, becomes a principle of global economic and moral right in the production of global political space, private interests attempting to take the beach head in the framing of a global economic space. Given the character of immaterial goods, neo-liberal democratic principles can become deeply interwoven within a politics of speech itself. Free speech then takes on an economic character. The meaning of democracy becomes interchangeable with the workings of free market equilibrium. In turn, the market metaphor becomes elevated to be a meta-narrative of the global internet, inducing a conclusion that the internet may be singularly coded with a vision of democracy, as a manifestation of principles of neo-liberal capitalist development. In turn this assumption, often unintendedly, reifies the market metaphor, dangerously evacuating any democratic possibility from digital communication networks as the basis of a global common platform of human interaction. The strategic dilemma here is as follows: if the internet will be a central platform for economic, social, and political life, how can we construct principles of communicative democracy without being complicit in the extension of this *market metaphor* in global space?

With the propertyscape of Information Exceptionalism we are offered our first alternative to this global movement of privatization. Exceptionalists advocate a different model of the normative foundations and economic character of the work and play of the mind. They argue that the digital age has presented an exceptional opportunity to produce as peers, to validate knowledge democratically, and to be financially rewarded for one's personhood. These affordances uncover an alternative system of meanings of personal responsibility, community civics, and non-rivalrous economic motivation. *Becoming property*, in this case becoming non-rivalrous property, is the paradigmatic act of freedom. Giving away the work and play of one's mind, and motivated by the allure of participating in this new social horizon, cultural creators become agents of history. As digital networks are de-territorialized, so is the imaginary of political space of this new age. This is a seductive alternative as the grammar of the *exceptional* throws a mystifying veil over the operations of capitalist subsumption of everyday life and creative labor. An ideal of participation comes to be used as something like the Weberian protestant ethic. It is an impulse to undertake immaterial labor without payment for some normative good. A creator will work for the speculative ideal of personal success validated by social recognition. This provides a normative underpinning of private decisions to cede immaterial property to a *commons*. The strategic dilemma is as follows: can we leverage the affordances of the age, the distributed nature of social, political, and economic organization that new technologies afford, without our actions being imbricated in the same forces of mystification? What kind of commons does not make us complicit in the privatization and commodification of the work and play of the mind in global space?

Transformative Distribution responds to this strategic dilemma. To approach the dilemma, the political action of *becoming property* is framed by the fundamentally shared experience of social life, expressed in the work and play of the mind. The work and play of the mind powerfully represents an essential *in-common* reflecting social practice and a deeply lived empirical reality. The act of *becoming property*, mediated by *distributed networks*, provides a historical opening. It promises to be a wellspring of a transformative social imaginary, the basis of an alternative model of constitutive collective political action oppositional to capitalist development. The unique *transformative* potential of the age is understood as a freedom of imagination, to imagine and construct other worlds not dictated by capitalist modes of social, economic, and political production. But as I explored in the living story, in the use of digital social media by radical democratic or anti-capitalist movements, such as the Occupy movement, we are presented with a similar dilemma faced by Information Exceptionalism. The action of consumer and radical alike furnish metadata for the pool of information capital, calling into question the transformative potential of the distributed network, as a social organizational principle. How can the transformative principles be reconciled with the scraping of social activity metadata for commercial purposes? And as for the alternative, what are the implications for the scope of an in-common, if the alternative of anti-information is to push into private spaces and become anonymous actors? Again, what can be taken from the affordances of the age, without being coded with co-producing the forces of mystification, even when the actions are pointed toward the transformative potential of age? How do we grapple with the shape-shifting forces of capitalist development in global space?

Finally, another kind of strategic dilemma reveals itself in the propertyscape of Ecological Decolonization. Ecological Decolonization gives us a different starting point: nature's rights. Nature's rights pre-date *man's* co-producing normative, epistemological, and economic schemas for framing the work and play of the mind. In their incarnations in multinational corporations and Western science, these are seen to be intrinsically colonizing, leading to an ecological crisis. The challenge of supporting epistemic and cultural colonialism is framed in a case for legal pluralism at the interface of legal and customary orders. In this interface a notion of cognitive justice is infused into an agenda of institutional recognition. Geographic indications, for instance, exemplify a way justice can be achieved, offering an institutional defense for epistemological and biological diversity in the reclamation of a bio-sovereignty. Nevertheless, the strategic dilemma is as follows: to protect local production systems in the broader context of local knowledge and life, a static view of culture emerges, offering little scope for change and development in the production practices of local, indigenous, or third world peoples. There also arises a danger of ethno-botanical nationalism and a tendency to romanticize the local within the institutional frame of the nation-state. Paradoxically, the very practices that Ecological Decolonization sets out to protect then become ripe to be colonized by capitalist systems of appropriation on the world market, whether in the form of niche cultural products, production process, or plant types.

My interest in the work and play of the mind was initially sparked by how these essential aspects of social life afford a unique insight into the thick political complexities of our time. Too often the responses to the kinds of strategic dilemmas listed above come singularly from within the contextual literatures of each propertyscape: *privatization* within legal studies; *exceptionalism* and *the transformative* in media and communication studies; and *the ecological* within post-colonial and development studies. My purpose in framing ideal types with considerable breadth, and animating these with living stories, was to view these propertyscapes from as wide a perspective as possible. I also wanted to see how the strategic dilemmas of each move into the other.

This book is an attempt to offer a different way of approaching these strategic dilemmas, and with this, a way to interpret the formation of political community around the work and play of the mind in the information age. In trying to shift from diagnosis to prognosis, the *disembodied* and *embodied* nature of the work and play of the mind opens an opportunity to reframe how we interpret global space and the kind of alternatives that history may now afford. My working hypothesis has been that the lens of political community can give us the conceptual and practical tools to approach this strategic quagmire, by addressing in this case the obstacles to emancipating the work and play of the mind.

The Who, What, and How of Political Community

The initial impetus for this investigation began with a historical event, the ratification of the TRIPS Agreement in 1994. In its scope and breadth, this global regime was the cause for grave concern. Historically, the social bargains at the core of the meaning of the right to property operated within national sovereignties and territorialities. These meanings were not only ingrained in the domain of social activity, but also imbricated in the broader meaning of the legitimacy and moral purpose of the nation-state. And this was the cause of the *grave concern*: did these shifting tides produce a vulnerability for capitalist development to exploit? What kind of vision of the global space did the agreement represent, global rules for private gain?

But TRIPS was as much a reaction to changing circumstances as it was visionary. It was a response to emerging social realities of interdependent lives in global space and to an awakening of alternative ways of understanding the right to the work and play of the mind. In a broader historical view, the forces that prompted the Agreement also prompt a kind of *strategic optimism*.

One of the speculative hypotheses of my project has been that, at the very least, each of the four emergent propertyscapes presented speaks in its own way to shifting tides of Westphalian political community. This takes the form of the erosion of the autonomy and authority of the nation-state to regulate the work and play of the mind from above and below. In the most general sense the work and play of the mind can longer be confined by, or fit neatly into, borders of the nation-state. But, this may lead to a more ambitions claim: what if, embedded in all four models for *becoming property* are the germinating elements for *becoming political community?* In each propertyscape, as a constitutive collective political act of *becoming*, could there be traces of nascent political communities, either as theoretical propositions or as empirical phenomena? Equally, if there are not the traces of nascent political communities, what does this tell us about the limits of political community as constitutive collective political action?

There was a distinct rationale for wanting to approach the work and play of the mind via the frame of political community. This was deeply connected with the normative thrust of this project. My thinking has been that the notion of political community gives us a grammar with which to pivot from *diagnosis* to *prognosis*. To open up the legacy concept of *political community* I needed to strip back its meaning, to expand its utility as a conceptual and practical tool. I need to take if off the shelf and dust off the telos of the nation-state. If this book is to make a methodological contribution, it is to offer an approach to seeing political community not as static givens but as something that is in a continual state of production and reproduction. Propertyscapes *generate* political communities. The tripartite rubric—ontological ordering principles, normative presuppositions, and institutional topology—offers a framework that is designed to be sufficiently capacious to account for both current and emerging alternate configurations of political community, as constitutive collective political action.

There was another rationale for approaching the work and play of the mind via the lens of political community. Essential to their legitimacy, political communities represent models and institutionalized processes through which to express the meaning and deliver the substance of *social justice*. My reasoning in the tripartite rubric finds its conceptual pedigree within Nancy Fraser's *who*, *what*, and *how* of approaching the question of social justice, in what she, and I, consider to be an age riddled with crises of *misframing*. This problem of *misframing* serves as the motivation for prognosis, and that too has been integral to my questioning. My move toward prognosis aligns with Fraser's evaluative criteria in her principle of the *parity of participation*:

> According to this radical democratic interpretation of the principle of moral worth, justice requires social arrangements that permit all to participate as peers in social life. Overcoming injustice means dismantling institutionalized obstacles that prevent some people from participating on a par with others, as full partners in social interaction.[2]

In pivoting toward prognosis, I will begin to tie together the evaluative bread crumbs left at the end of each chapter. That is, for whom does each propertyscape seek to secure economic benefit, allow into social participation, and frame political representation?

The first layer of evaluative comparison pertains to the *who*: whose work and play is demanding of equal consideration; what is the scale of concern? This framing of the *who* is found in the ontological ordering principle of *becoming property*.

In the propertyscape of Information Privatization the *who* is negatively defined in relation to specific historical reality, a leakage in the market of *information* demanding a global subject needing to abide by consistently applied rules, so ascribing a globally shared meaning to the right of the work and play of the mind. Contextualized within a longer ontological thesis of *becoming property* in a material context, it is positively defined via an assertion of this universal global subject in the context of rivalrous property. Private property is a necessary monopoly of the *inventor* as the assertion and protection of personal dominion, or the person who purchases the fruits of their labor or the time of their labor. This ontological framework is essential for the very belief in the market as a model of global political economy. In asking who is afforded equal concern, the *who* is determined in the context of the incomplete project of capitalist development in global space. The construction of the *who* reveals the need for the institutionalization of order, regulating and protecting the not-so-natural operations of the market. Taken as a nascent model of political community, the framing of the *who* is imposed via international law and the synergizing of national regulatory logics to the order of private property in this domain of social activity.

In the propertyscape of Information Exceptionalism the *who* is framed by what appears at first glance to be a fundamentally different approach, to the economic character and social utility of the work and play of the mind. Within a longer ontological view, the economic character of the work and play of the mind is associated to its essential non-rivalrousness. Its social utility is found in a claim of the natural and inalienable right to the work and play of the mind of individuals. These principles dovetail in a principle of self-determination and self-dominion as the basis of our politics of action. Within our current historical condition the technical social structure of distributed networks accelerates non-rivalrousness and intensifies the power of the claim of individuals to the work and play of the mind as *makers* of their own culture. In asking who is afforded equal concern, in this context, the *who* is a politics of self-autonomy; the right to make, to be creative, is asserted on a planetary scale. Taken as a nascent model of political community, in this framing of the *who*, the act of *becoming property* reveals a self-awakening of individuals who self-generate their politics of community.

In the propertyscape of Transformative Distribution, the *who* is framed within a longer ontological view of the work and play of the mind as an essential place of *in-common* based on pre-individual legacies of knowledge and culture. In this framing, the politics of communality has a different starting point. It is a politics of *reclamation*. Becoming property is not simply about an individual *making* order, but the collective reclaiming of social order and the work and play of the mind, from the clutches of capitalist development. Within the context of historical affordances of distributed communication systems, we are also offered a transformative potential in the framing of the *who*, based on new principles of affinity. Order centered on gift relations allows for a *who* that supports the reclamation of authentic identities, not determined by relation to capitalist modes of production. Taken as a nascent model of political community in the framing of the *who*, the act of *becoming property* allows for a framing of the *who* that ranges from an inherent *in-common* at a planetary scale to the authenticity of life grounded in the local and the particular.

Finally, in the propertyscape of Ecological Decolonization the *who* is framed by an ontology of rights that exist outside of, or that prefigure, western ontologies. They do not begin with *Man*'s inalienable rights, but *life itself*. This ontological position attempts to recognize and incorporate already existing cultural and epistemological orientations and biodiversity. In asking who is afforded equal concern, we begin with a different starting point for the *who*, one that has equal concern for nature itself. This *who* speaks to those who have been historically marginalized from the production of the imperialist who: indigenous people, third world peasants, women, the economically marginal, unemployed, or underemployed. This systematic exclusion from the meaning-making aspect of the who is a result of the logics of colonization. This reflects a misrecognition and devaluation of life itself in the construction of the *who* in other systems of meaning and configurations of political community.

What is striking in all four propertyscapes is that the project of the *who* operates today at a planetary scale. That is, politics is constituted at the level of a universal global subject. In the propertyscapes of Information Privatization, Information Exceptionalism, and Transformative Distribution the scale of concern, and politics of relation, is understood via the thickening interconnectedness of global communication platforms and the birth of the internet. For Ecological Decolonization, our relation to life itself is inherently planetary. This shared view of the scale of contemporary ontological ordering principles is in part tied to manifest realities of global life. In part, it is also a projection of how players defining each propertyscape approach the realty of our shared life, as a speculative, future-creating enterprise.

The second layer of evaluative comparison pertains to the *what*. This *what* encompasses a projection of the meaning of social justice in each nascent model of political community. It connects to the unique historical synergy of the technological affordances of the age and reflects distinctive perspectives on the work and play of the mind. This *what* finds its footing in the normative presuppositions of each propertyscape, which themselves mirror anthropological assumptions about the nature of human motivation.

In the propertyscape of Information Privatization, its central anthropological assumption is aligned with the motivational basis of rivalrousness. One would opt into or in submit oneself to this propertyscape to the extent that one allowed their personhood to be framed in a market-based identity. Here, status orders are driven by the profit motive, regulated by a promise of supply and demand equilibrium, and rewarded by the promise (if mostly the unreality) of material affluence. As a model of economic redistribution, we get a *laissez-faire*, trickle-down approach to economic development. The individual can fulfill the destiny of their market-based economic futures. Such private motivations generate the hidden hand of the social, congealing as human progress.

In the propertyscape of Information Exceptionalism the anthropological assumption is cast as *altruistic* motivation, ceding the work and play of the mind to the commons. One would opt in to reveal the recognizable *self* through the work and play of the mind. This self is an *individual* who acts and produces, whose most fundamental motivation is self-actualization. This happens in the act of ceding their activity of the commons. As they cede their labor, the self participates in the constitution of the *collective-self*, in which the validation of social activity emerges as a consequence of a community accreditation where ratings of *likes*, *re-tweets*, *shares* serve as a myriad of reputational referenda, the invisible hand of the *crowd*. One opts in, making of one's work and play of the mind non-rivalrousness because rivalrousness blocks opportunities for self-actualization, restricting audiences to the fruits of one's labor.

Frictionless movement of information is idealized as being the exceptional market condition of cognitive association. This idea of free association connects with a principle of our economic future, as economic self-determination. As part of the awakening of the self, being able to define the *what*—to be "in" and "out" of the market—is central to this anthropological assumption.

In the propertyscape of Transformative Distribution its key anthropological assumption is grounded in a different kind of reading of our sociality, beginning with an historical fact, an *in-common* at the very root our species being. Here one would opt in, in order to participate in the production of communal identities as represented in gift economies. The *gift* comes to represent the production of identities that are not relational to, or determined by, capitalist status orders. Motivation is thus recast in an authentic actualization of community, based on alternative status orders of obligation and reciprocity. Moreover, emanating from a Marxist legacy, this position nevertheless tries to resolve orthodox labor monism, while still recognizing that there is a political economy of the work and play of the mind. The gift aims to foster social ecologies free from the logic of capitalist development, where systems of value can be established that have autonomous and self-determined redistributive qualities.

Finally, in the propertyscape of Ecological Decolonization, anthropological assumptions of human motivation are brought into the scope of critique that connect human life with nature. Rather and putting *man* at the center of making their world, motivation is recast via human relations to biological life and eco-systemic rhythms. One would opt in to this principle of recognition based on meanings grounded in the natural diversity of ecological systems and cultural moorings that relate to the earth in non-productionist ways. These are things that have frequently been misrecognized as valueless by colonialism. This model of economic redistribution finds fault with accounts of human motivation that privilege production over regeneration. The problem of contemporary ecological crisis, in this perspective, needs to be recast within such a motivational logic.

In the varying *what* projections of the operating logics supporting the *normative presuppositions* of each approach to the work and play of the mind, we find reasons why one would submit to, opt in, or recognize, one *becoming property* thesis or another. The normative presuppositions are aspirational, serving to motivate and legitimize the constitutive collective political action of *becoming property*. They motivate actors within history. In these propertyscapes we see the normativity of the work and play of the mind as fundamentally originating in principles of recognition. This *anthropological assumption* drives as the rationale for opting in, the constitutive collective political action itself. This essential process of *recognition* defines the agenda for economic redistribution, symbiotically connected to the assumption about the nature of human motivation. This is an important point to consider in the pivot toward prognosis: how does the ideal of *opting in*, as a constitutive act imbricated with an anthropological assumption about human motivation, reveal nature of each propertyscape?

The final layer of evaluative comparison pertains to the *how*. How does each propertyscape frame global space? What is its jurisdictional geography and associated model of political representation? What kind of social contract does it offer? Explicitly approaching each propertyscape as a nascent model for the production, and form, of political community, I want to start to unpick the incomplete, problematic, contentious aspects of these as modes of *political community*, representing alternative kinds of post-industrial social contract.

The model of political community nascent within the propertyscape of Information Privatization scales up from national to global order. Formally, the TRIPS agreement is quite comprehensive. It defines rights and responsibilities of nations and their citizens, including the characteristics of rights holders, multilevel enforcement, and the right to confiscate property. The Agreement has a broad shaping effect on the agendas of global development bodies, meditating the forces of this global law on the embodied work and play of the mind. As the scope of this social activity is so expansive, from a poem to a vaccine, TRIPS can apply in spaces where the presence of the agreement is not immediately apparent, across a very wide global range. As a jurisdictional geography, at a micro scale, it protects very narrow interests: the sovereignty of corporations, owners of the work and play of the mind understood legally to be akin in their rights to be like people. At a macro scale it does not produce, nor is generative of any formal citizen rights or responsibilities at the global level. As a model of political representation, the nation-states, or national industries, act as the representatives of the work and play of the mind; our interests understood in a very Westphalian way, as the interest of nationalized industry.

As a kind of social contract this projection of global law, easily mistaken by its normative authority as global *public law*, protects very narrow private interests. In the need for order, we are given evidence of the need for capitalism to institutionalize global space. The free market is not some given, but requires the making of legal order, hence this incursion into global space framing actors and actions. However, there is a fundamental participatory deficit in the kind of social contract offered by this propertyscape. The TRIPS/WTO model offers only diffused participation within the formal bodies of the institution: your state acts as your representative. Thus, the democratic accountability that had been originally associated with the *real* property bargain, defining the social contract of the nation-state, is distanced from the embodiment of the work and play of the mind. The agreement gives us a kind of global social contract that is both more formal and more elusive: formal in the reach of its regulatory authority privatizing global space; illusive in the diffused system of democratic accountability. This model of the social contract presents shallow globalization, a post-industrial "information feudalism."[3] It rightly provokes a critique of globalization, as the operating logic of processes of capitalist expansion. Maybe this is a marker of the final victory of capitalism in the Cold War, further consolidating control in the hands of capital? But then again, maybe the demand for order cuts both ways. In asking *whose property* in this frame of reference, an opportunity also arises, to consider the possibility of a global framework that affords genuine political representation.

The model of political community nascent within the propertyscape of Information Exceptionalism scales up in principle, but down in practice. It scales up in a universalized reading of the sovereignty of the individual and scales down by presenting easy-to-use contracts in the making of this order. As a jurisdictional geography, the *exceptional commons* is a de facto public domain, aggregated as a collection of individual contracts. It operates within the legal regulatory order of nation-states. As a model of political representation the act of contractualism is the placeholder for the new kind of democratic spirit: self-dominion, self-governance, and an ideal of a cooperation that also guarantees one's ability to exit. It is a model of political representation that universalizes the *maker's right*, supporting an unfettered ability to *opt in* and/or *opt out*.

Taken as a kind of social contract, the *exceptional commons* promises to protect a *public domain* of the work and play of the mind. Nevertheless, apart from the interpretation of the acts of *making* and *exiting*, this framing of the *public domain* is antagonistic at best, and intentionally blind at worst, to the broader political economy that the embodied work and play of the mind is empirically situated. Its fatal flaw is to frame the work and play as *exceptional*, while its embodiment in labor and objects reflects a materiality where the uncontested *norm* is capitalist order and as such remains rivalrous property. This materiality inherently restricts those who can *opt in*, presenting an enfeebled notion of the *public*. Compounding this restricted nature of this construction of the public, the *exceptional commons* does not attempt to provide capital that reinvests in labor. Nor does it guarantee an income in times of unemployment. With the *exceptional commons*, we are presented with a model that for these reasons does not support any kind of socially sustainable or authentically democratic horizon. Its model of political community idealizes both individualism and markets as a condition for true self-realization and human empowerment. This reflects on an impoverished imaginary of the *public* and a hollowing out of the social responsibilities that for some time had been assumed by the modern nation-state. In fact, the modality of the exceptional commons can be cast as a species of the privatization of services that is a pillar of neo-liberal capitalist efficiency. Finally, while supposedly contesting the Westphalian construction of political space, it very much needs it for its existence, as each contract is situated within the regulatory framework of state-based regulatory authority.

When we ask *whose property*, this nascent political community situates the work and play of the mind in a precarious position. Its idealization of the opt in, reducing the *exceptional* to an economic character, leaves the embodiment of the work and play of the mind vulnerable to exploitation. It is corrosive as a model for the global, as it produces a new kind of core and periphery, those who can opt in and opt out, a *creative class*, those who are afforded the benefits of the age.

The model of political community nascent within the propertyscape of Transformative Distribution also scales up in principle, but down in practice. On the one hand, scaling up, the Multitude is very much a post-national vision. The living labor of the work and play of the mind is the embodiment of an essential in-common, producing and informed by the *general intellect* as the disembodied, de-territorialized flows that resist the Westphalian framing of global space. But on the other hand, social relations centered on the gift are localized. They are localized not simply as geographic entities, but in terms of the scope of practice, or shared mutually defined systems of affinity and reciprocity. The organizational principles of the distributed network supposedly afford a kind of framing that can be universalized, but still respecting the ability to determine one's own meanings. As a jurisdictional geography, with the *transformative commons* we are offered two kinds of alternatives for framing order. One leverages contract law, in a similar way to the exceptionalist model. Another that rejects the legal contract altogether, and this rejection is an act integral to the organization meaning of the order. The *transformative commons* is the culmination of the patchwork of gift economies, with or without formal contracts defining them. This model of the commons does not universalize the demand for order, but nonetheless is connected in the explicit or implicit rejection in social practices of the logics of post-industrial capitalism. As a model of political representation, posited as a radical democratic alternative, the *transformative commons* centers the struggle for political representation, not just in the shared management of the work and play of the mind, but in the meanings that would underwrite such an order. This political representation is based on the principle of difference, allowing for a move away from economic reductionism in the model of political representation.

Taken as a kind of social contract the *transformative commons* foregrounds the in-common and supports the production of a multiplicity of *socialites*. But there is equivocation in the *with* or *without* contract models. In the *with* contract model, there are similar predicaments to those of the exceptional commons. Again, there is an inherent restriction on who can readily give away their work and play, their creative labor. In the *without* contract model, an anarchic approach adds another kind of vulnerability to the resilience of social organization in global space. Without some form of centralized order to protect the rights of these communities, to scale up, what are the safeguards that will protect participants in the push and pull of global space? Who will adjudicate between these communities when they come into contact? Are we too dependent on moral relativism? Does this state of affairs calcify difference in a way that leaves no room for shared affinities?

So once again, when we ask *whose property*, this nascent political community situates the work and play of the mind in a precarious position. While setting out to do so, it does not comprehensively resolve the embodied and disembodied labor problem of the *exceptional*. Whose *property is* still determined by who can afford to give away property or who may benefit from the giving in ancillary markets. Those able to participate, the agents of this political community, might be no different to the creative class of exceptionalism. This may become corrosive as a model for the global, as a consequence of this economic flaw in the area of participation. But it might also be corrosive in the calcification of a politics of difference that does not allow for wider models of affinity, at times undermining its own ontological premise of the in-common.

Finally, the model of political community nascent in the propertyscape of Ecological Decolonization offers a very different frame for order. What essentially ties together peoples is not their relationship as citizens in nation-states, but bio-natural realities. This framing emphasizes the *local*, as a cultural logic inherently sensitive to these eco-systemic realties. The global in many ways co-produces the meaning of the local. As a jurisdictional geography, the *ecological commons* represents a kind of re-embedding movement. This is because its looks to the sovereignty of life itself, a bio-sovereignty, that pre-dates *man*. As a framing of global space, the ecological commons, in a general sense, seeks to contest the homogenizing power of national and international law on the diverse practices of the work and play of the mind. As a model of political representation, it is tactical and strategic in its engagement, demanding representation from already existing models of political organization and national and international levels. It also introduces the idea of a collective monopoly to support relationships to knowledge, culture, and ecological realties.

As the basis of a kind of social contract the *ecological commons* is a frame that demands a reconstitution of Westphalian political space. It also demands a reconsideration of how we think of the very basics of *productionist* accounts of human development. Finally, in the agenda of legal pluralism, there is a demand for inclusivity in political representation, within already established orders: national and international. Nevertheless, contrary to its premise, this model of the social contract does not singularly demand a reconstitution of Westphalian political space. Rather, it may in fact reinforce the role of the state in global space as mediating these demands.

These propertyscapes that I have described are real, living frames that give context both to the embodied and to the disembodied flows of the work and play of the mind. As much as they are real, they are also speculative. They are various ways of asking us to *opt in*. In other words, each propertyscape is asking us to make decisions about the kind of world we want to live in. In fact, we may inadvertently opt in an out of these models, simply as actors constituting history through our everyday action.

The leap of faith by those readers who have joined me on this journey was to allow that propertyscapes might be generative of models of political community. These propertyscapes have not produced political communities, in any traditional sense. One could say there is nothing *nascent* here other than a politics of intellectual property. But my persistent counter question has been, if these real propertyscapes do not tell us anything about the constitutive collective political action that implicates the connection between property and political community, maybe this reflects a more concerning dilemma about the persistent misframing of lived realties of our contemporary age. My working hypothesis has been that being able to see the *nascent* is essential to the emancipatory potential of the work and play of the mind, and the future framing of political community as modes of collective political action. These may yet represent fundamental, democratic-constitutive acts.

In presenting each propertyscape as generative of models of political community, I believe, a pattern becomes apparent. The idea of modern political community, formerly codified in the nation-state, had until the information era settled into a grammar of a shared experience of history or sense of cultural belonging, manifest institutionally in constitutional sovereignty, normatively underwritten by notions of democratic accountability. In those times, the formation of political community arose as a constitutive act out of a kind of propertyscape of material property. But this propertyscape represented a more expansive kind of social bargain, represented by the construction an essential space in the modern political community: the public. The four propertyscapes I have been describing in this book, and their nascent models of political community, do not generate a full conception of, or shared institutions for, a *public* that matches the realities of global space. We do not yet see signs of the emergence of a *global public*. However, it is critically important to strategize how we can *remake* order. My prognosis looks to the construction of this *global public* that goes beyond all four propertyscapes of the information age. In the words of Nancy Fraser, what is "the possibility of new-institutions of post-Westphalian democratic justice."[4] The demand of *whose property?* speaks to this challenge.

Whose Property?

The framing of a *public* has been traditionally understood, and guaranteed, within the nation-state. The modern nation-state constituted the *public*, as an abstract as well as an institutional manifestation. The question of what the *public* means, as read through the right to the work and play of the mind, begs an alternative imaginary for political community, revealing the shape of the requirements for a post-Westphalian political community. In these final paragraphs, I want to set a course for prognosis, beginning with a speculative enterprise, toward a *global public* grounded in a generative response to the question of *whose property*. The opportunity for this has a lot to do with the social platform that defines the age: the internet.

When asking *whose property*, the *who* of a *global public*, must be at a planetary scale. The disembodied flows of the work and play of the mind offer an imminent social imaginary for our in-common. Our species interdependence today demands this scale. The experience of our lives connected to, or impacted by, the flows of information via the internet is a pre-eminent mechanism for the integration of these realities and demands. I would argue that the ontological ordering of the *global public* must combine our pre-individual realties within the ecological framing of life itself. We produce and share content that has a long pre-digital history, but what we do in *digitizing* is a fundamental constitutive act. But the internet is not just bits and bytes. It is a material thing with an ecological footprint in the production of its objects: cables, devices, platforms, equipment, and the labor that supports these realities, from miners of rare metals to software technicians. The question of *who counts* for equal consideration in an ontological ordering principle for the *global public* thus must include the in-common of the social individual, and an ecological context, both material and immaterial.

When responding to the question of *whose property*, addressing the *what* in the form of the mechanisms for sustaining a just global public sets our course in the following ways. As a model for recognition, it must allow us to look back in recognition of culture and identity, as particular disembodied and embodied histories. But we must also be able to look forward, not Orientalizing culture as static, but seeing all cultures as dynamic and ever evolving, within a framework of justice. Aligned with Fraser's transformative remedies, this *global public* must be able to "destabilize" identities "to make room for future regroupments."[5] As a projected ideal, the *global public* must be able to encompass the planetary scale that is at its ontological core. A global identity must be on par with national, local, familial, or personal identity. These particularized identities are then the *vernacular* of a mutually shared global frame. Furthermore, a *global public* must provide the security for the right to regroup identities. It must equally provide boundaries for sanctioning the kinds of speech that undermine the in-common of a global public in the same ways hate speech is illegal in the jurisdictional geographies of the nation-state. If we apply this logic to the internet, the challenge is how to develop a model for recognition that takes advantage of the ways it can support distributed models of cultural formation, but in ways that also protect and defend against injustice based on misrecognition, discrimination, or the whims of moral relativity devoid of any formal democratic feedback loop capable of matching the ontological scale of a global public.

A model of redistribution must begin with the question *not* of why, in an economic sense, the work and play of the mind should be *free*, but *how*. And if it is to be free (as in "freedom"), what are the conditions for this freedom. When looking at the internet, the argument for why the work and play of the mind should be *free* too often is used as the motivation for one to give away their work and play of the mind ("free" as in, at no charge) to an economy that extracts financial value from this act with no just recompense. This is a hollow economic freedom. As Fraser argues, a politics of redistribution must "redress unjust distribution by transforming the underlying political-economic structure."[6] We must continually remind ourselves that there was nothing ever economically *free* about the production of the work and play of the mind. Its *materiality* always has to be paid for in one way or another. The *public* nature of the work and play of the mind has historically been supported by the economic input of the nation-state in public institutions such as universities, public libraries, or public media. Thus, in a model of *just* economic redistribution, for a global public we would need to consider how we deliver on this ideal of the *free*.

Finally, when asking *whose property*, to approach the *how*, I begin with Fraser's call to "challenge the deep grammar of frame-setting."[7] Aligning with the ontological ordering principle of a *global public*, the *how* must begin with an a priori *global in-common*, which in itself challenges the Westphalian framing of global space. But we must steer away from the assumption that an institutional in-common is a natural extension of this ontological principle. Nor is it something that logically or necessarily follows. Even when we look at earlier models of the *commons*, these can also be conceived as enclosure movements of sorts—enclosures of spaces for community activity. Thus, the institutional *in-common* is the fact an outcome of the production of the webs of norms and rules in a process of perpetual historical negotiation. We often speak of *global society*, but in an abstract way. Missing are institutions that are built from principles of popular sovereignty, shared affinities, and rules of binding quality that might produce and protect a *global public*.

Nancy Fraser argues that "overcoming injustice means *dismantling* institutionalized obstacles that prevent some people from participating on a par with others, as full partners in social interaction"[8] (emphasis added). The aim of my speculative frame of the *global public* is to adopt a variant of this approach. Rather than *dismantling*, let us re-embed social power to create institutions that supersede, re-frame, such "institutional obstacles." This then becomes a demand to *design* a new political geography, directing our attention to the *nascent* potentials, new opportunities for political communities as modes of collective political action, representing fundamental, democratic-constitutive acts, and such political institutions that they may need to sustain them.

In an unexpected way, the conclusion I come to, or rather the cornerstone of the next stage of this project, pertains to internet governance. Could this be the *place* where a post-Westphalian political community emerges, one that can constitute a *global public?* To date, internet governance has found its ideal in the logic of exceptionalism. This model supports a radically decentralized vision for the co-constitution of social contracts. The pre-eminent act of freedom is to *opt in*. It defines its exceptionality as a social space not regulated by the traditional authority of the modern nation-state, a place for the neutral framing of global space. But it is not neutral, far from it. As I have argued and shown above, its political, economic, and social power operates in a regulatory manner. Furthermore, I have argued that the self-governing participatory thesis, often found in presentations on the unique historical affordances of the internet, misdirects what might be another kind of emancipatory potential in the constitutive act of the disembodied and embodied work and play of the mind, *becoming property*.

To think about internet governance, framing post-Westphalian political community in order to secure a *global public* would demand us to consider several questions. What is the relation between internet service providers and free access to the internet? Who secures access to a global public? If the internet is considered to be a public infrastructure, then who pays for this infrastructure? If it is a shared labor space, how do we ensure social services in times of unemployment or need? Is there possible redistributive opportunity via possible taxation model? Who determines the rules of the space, in a truly democratic participatory way, not just those who can opt in via their economic advantage? Can we see the work and play of the mind as a collective monopoly, but on the planetary scale, as a public institution? Then, we must measure these ideals against the model of the welfare state, as electoral democracy was born from these kinds of questions.

If guaranteeing property rights was one of the foundational acts of the creation of the modern nation-state as a political community, at the very least the changes I have analyzed in this book undermine the sovereign integrity of the nation-state, and with it the very foundations of the Westphalian frame. This opens new opportunities for political communities as modes of constitutive collective political action, representing fundamental, democratic-constitutive acts. I want to argue for a reclamation of political community as a tool for political action—to remember its social democratic potential.

Whose property? now turns into a question about the emancipatory potentials in emergent political communities as acts of political agency. This is productive for thinking about social justice in the post-industrial information age. The production and ownership of the work and play of the mind is a fertile site for such institutional imagination. It challenges and dilemmas a motivation for constitutive collective political action—the constitution of the *global public*.

In the human labor process, the domains of material and immaterial production both begin with the work and play of the mind. In an earlier modernity, political struggles over the social meaning and ownership of material property took precedence over immaterial property. In a post-industrial information age, however, struggles over immaterial property might have more pressing consequences in the extension of capitalist systems of appropriation into our individual and social lives. The struggle over the meaning of the right to the work and play of the mind is the pre-eminent political struggle of our era, crossing domains immaterial and material production, and will likely remain so for future generations.

Notes

1. Ibid.
2. Ibid.
3. Drahos.
4. Fraser, "Reframing Justice in a Globalizing World." p. 85.
5. "From Redistribution to Recognition? Dilemmas of Justice in a 'Post-Socialist' Age." p. 84.
6. Ibid.
7. Ibid. p. 81.
8. Ibid. p. 73.

Bibliography

Acxiom Corporation. "The Moment of Truth." Little Rock: Acxiom Corporation, 2013.

Adbusters. "Anarchic Swarms—the Emerging Model." adbusters.com, http://www.adbusters.org/blogs/adbusters-blog/adbusters-tactical-briefing-26.html.

———. "Anonymous Joints #Occupywallstreet." adbusters.org, http://www.adbusters.org/blogs/adbusters-blog/anonymous-joins-occupywallstreet.html.

———. "Dear Americans, This July 4th Dream of Insurrection against Corporate Rule." twitter.com, https://twitter.com/adbusters/status/88013043438600192.

———. "#Occupywallstreet—a Shift in Revolutionary Tactics." Adbusters, http://www.adbusters.org/blogs/adbusters-blog/occupywallstreet.html.

———. "#Occupywallstreet: A Shift in Revolutionary Tactics." adbusters.org, http://www.adbusters.org/blogs/adbusters-blog/occupywallstreet.html.

Albright, Madeleine. "Sustaining Democracy in the Twenty-First Century." In *The Rostov Lecture Series*. School of Advanced International Studies, Johns Hopkins University, 2000.

Aldhous, Peter. "Occupy Vs Tea Party: What Their Twitter Networks Reveal." New Scientist, http://www.newscientist.com/blogs/onepercent/2011/11.

Alper, Meryl. "War on Instagram: Framing Conflict Photojournalism with Mobile Photography Apps." *New Media & Society* September (2013).

P. Kalantzis-Cope, *The Work and Play of the Mind in the Information Age*, Frontiers of Globalization, https://doi.org/10.1007/978-3-319-64650-3

Ambootia. "Ambootia." http://ambootia.com/.
Anderson, Chris. *The Long Tail: Why the Future of Business Is Selling Less of More.* New York City: Hyperion, 2006.
Appaduria, Arjun. *Modernity at Large: Cultural Dimensions of Globalization.* Minneapolis: University of Minnesota Press, 1996.
Baker, James. "America in Asia: Emerging Architecture for a Pacific Community." *Foreign Affairs* 70, no. 5 (1991/92).
Barbrook, Richard. "The Hi-Tech Gift Economy." First Monday, http://www.firstmonday.org/issues/issue3_12/barbrook/.
Bauwens, Michel. "The Political Economy of Peer Production." CTheory, http://www.ctheory.net/articles.aspx?id=499.
Baym, Nancy, danah, boyd. "Socially Mediated Publicness: An Introduction." *Journal of Broadcasting & Electronic Media* 56, no. 3 (2012).
BBC News. "Egypt Unrest: Bloggers Take Campaign to Tahir Square." bbc.co.uk, http://www.bbc.co.uk/news/world-middle-east-12381295.
Beibei, Bao. "How Internet Censorship Is Curbing Innovation in China." The Atlantic, http://www.theatlantic.com/china/archive/2013/04/how-internet-censorship-is-curbing-innovation-in-china/275188/.
Benkler, Yochai. *The Wealth of Networks: How Social Production Transforms Markets and Freedom.* New Haven: Yale University Press, 2007.
Beran, Dale. "4chan: The Skeleton Key to the Rise of Trump." Medium.com, https://medium.com/@DaleBeran/4chan-the-skeleton-key-to-the-rise-of-trump-624e7cb798cb-.qa9nlnox0.
Berard, Laurence, Marchenay, Philippe. "Local Products and Geographical Indications: Taking Account of Local Knowledge and Biodiversity." *International Social Science Journal* 187 (2006).
Bernstein, Joseph. "Behind the Racist Hashtag That Is Blowing up Twitter." Buzzfeed, https://www.buzzfeed.com/josephbernstein/behind-the-racist-hashtag-some-donald-trump-fans-love?utm_term=.qayrY9LPK-.fvrej6xlK.
Biddle, Sam. "Occupy Wall Street and the War to Free All Internet." gizmodo.com, http://gizmodo.com/5897109/occupy-wall-street-and-the-war-to-free-all-internet.
Borras Jr., Saturnino. "La Vía Campesina: An Evolving Transnational Social Movement." *Transnational Institute* TNI Briefing Series, no. No 2004/6 (2004).
Bourdieu, Pierre. *Photography: A Middle-Brow Art.* Polity Press, 1990.
Bowring, Finn. "Manufacturing Scarcity: Food Biotechnology and the Life Sciences Industry." *Capital & Class* 27, no. 79 (2003).

Boyle, James. *The Public Domain: Enclosing the Commons of the Mind.* New Haven: Yale University Press, 2008.

Brady, Aaron. "World without Walls." MIT Technology Review, http://www.technologyreview.com/article/425905/world-without-walls/.

Braithwaite, John, Drahos, Peter. *Global Business Regulation.* Cambridge: Cambridge University Press, 2000.

Brian, Matt. "Flickr Hits 6 Billion Total Photos; Facebook Does That Every 2 Months." The Next Web.

Broude, Tomer. "Taking 'Trade and Culture' Seriously: Geographical Indications and Cultural Protection in Wto Law." *BEPress Legal Series* 649 (2005).

Burton, Tara Isabella. "Apocalypse Whatever: The Making of a Racist, Sexist Religion of Nihilism on 4chan." Reallifemag.com, http://reallifemag.com/apocalypse-whatever/.

Business Software Alliance. "About Us." Business Software Alliance, http://www.bsa.org/about-bsa.

Byers, Bruce. "Ecoregions, State Sovereignty and Conflict." *Security Dialogue* 22, no. 1 (1991).

Calinoff, Jordan. "Beijing's Foreign Internet Purge." *Foreign Policy*, 2010.

Captain, Sean. "Occupy Geeks Are Building a Facebook for the 99%." wired.com, http://www.wired.com/threatlevel/2011/12/occupy-facebook/all/1.

Castells, Manuel. *The Rise of the Network Society.* Information Age: Economy, Society and Culture. Cambridge, Mass.: Blackwell Publishers, 1996.

Center for Digital Democracy. "Datamining Our "Likes" on Facebook Reveals Details About Our Personal Lives." Center for Digital Democracy, http://www.democraticmedia.org/datamining-our-likes-facebook-reveals-details-about-our-personal-lives-new-research.

Chang, Gorden. "China's 'Internet Plus' Strategy, a Net Minus." Frobes, http://www.forbes.com/sites/gordonchang/2015/04/19/chinas-internet-plus-strategy-a-net-minus/-6f5734227ac4s.

Chen, Adrian. "The Truth About Anonymous's Activism." The Nation, https://www.thenation.com/article/truth-about-anonymouss-activism/.

Chen, George, Dickinson, Steve, Schleshiner, Qiang, Xiao, Creemers, Rogier, Wertime. "China's Great Firewall Is Rising." Foreign Policy, http://foreign-policy.com/2015/02/03/china-great-firewall-is-rising-censorship-internet/.

Chen, Liyan. "Alibaba Claims Title for Largest Global Ipo Ever with Extra Share Sales." Forbes, http://www.forbes.com/sites/ryanmac/2014/09/22/alibaba-claims-title-for-largest-global-ipo-ever-with-extra-share-sales/-e57f7bf7c26d.

China Internet Network Information Center. n.d. "Statistical Report on Internet Development in China. China Internet Network Information Center. http://www1.cnnic.cn/IDR/ReportDownloads/201302/P020130221391269963814.pdf.

Chow, Ow Wei. "Songs About 'Mother' at the Verge of Being 'Harmonised': Propagation of Resistance against the Great Firewall of China." In *Music and Mind*, edited by Jahnichen Gisa, Made, Mantle Hood, Chinthaka, Meddegoda. Selangor: Universiti Putra Malaysia, 2014.

Clinton, Hillary. "Remarks on Internet Freedom." United States Department of State, http://www.state.gov/secretary/rm/2010/01/135519.htm.

Cohen, Daniel. *The Nature of Capitalism in the Information Age*. Cambridge, Ma.: MIT Press, 2002.

Coleman, Gabriella. *Coding Freedom: The Ethics and Aesthetics of Hacking*. New Haven: Princeton University Press, 2012.

Collins-Chase, Charles. "The Case against Trips-Plus Protection in Developing Countries Facing Aids Epidemics." *University of Pennsylvania Journal of International Law* 29, no. 3 (2008).

Commonwealth of Australia. "House of Representatives Hansard." *29 September* (1993).

Coopman, Ted M. "Building Resistance One Byte at a Time." National Communication Association, https://www.natcom.org/CommCurrentsArticle.aspx?id=1027.

Corrons, Luis. "4chan Users Organize Surgical Strike against Mpaa." pandasecurity.com, http://pandalabs.pandasecurity.com/4chan-users-organize-ddos-against-mpaa/.

Creative Commons. "About—Creative Commons." http://creativecommons.org/about/.

———. "Homepage." CreativeCommons.org, https://creativecommons.org/.

Dagan, Hanoch, Heller, Michael. "The Liberal Commons." *The Yale Law Journal* 110, no. 549 (2001).

Darjeeling Tea Association. "Darjeeling, a Paradise." Darjeeling Tea Association, http://www.darjeelingtea.com/protection/paradise.asp.htm.

———. "The Present Scenario." Darjeeling Tea Association, http://www.darjeelingtea.com/growth/present.asp.htm.

———. "Protection of Darjeeling Tea." Darjeeling Tea Association, http://www.darjeelingtea.com/protection/geographical.asp.htm.

David, Tomas. "From the Photograph to Postphotographic Practice: Toward a Postoptical Ecology of the Eye." *SubStance* 17, no. 1 (1988).

De Sousa Santos, Boaventura, Arriscado Nunnes, Joao, Meness, Maria. "Opening up the Cannon of Knowledge and Recognition of Difference." In *Another Knowledge Is Possible: Beyond Northern Epistemologies* edited by Boaventura De Sousa Santos. New York City: Verso, 2008.

Dean. "The Unfairness of Flickr's Explore Page." Photopreneur.com, http://blogs.photopreneur.com/the-unfairness-of-flickr-explore-page.

Dean, Jodi. "Judgment." *Occupy: An OWS Inspired Gazette (N+1)* 1 (2011).

Deere, Carolyn. *The Implementation Game: The Trips Agreement and the Global Politics of Intellectual Property Reform in Developing Countries.* Oxford: Oxford University Press, 2009.

Diamond V. Chakrabarty 447 U.S. 303 (1980).

Drahos, Peter. "Bits and Bibs: Bilateralism in Intellectual Property." *The Journal of World Intellectual Property* 4 (2001).

Drahos, Peter, Braithwaite, John. *Information Feudalism: Who Owns the Knowledge Economy?* New York: W. W. Norton & Company, 2003.

Durden, Tyler. "4chan Claims to Have Fabricated Anti-Trump Report as a Hoax." Zero Hedge, http://www.zerohedge.com/news/2017-01-10/4chan-claims-have-fabricated-anti-trump-report-hoax.

Dutton, William, H. "Through the Network of Networks—the Fifth Estate." *SSRN* October (2007).

Dyer-Witheford, Nick. "Global Body, Global Brain/Global Factory, Global War: Revolt of the Value Subjects." *The Commoner* 3 (2002).

Egan, Mark. "Who's Behind the Wall Street Protests?" Reuters.com, http://www.reuters.com/assets/print?aid=USTRE79C1YN20111014.

Eleleth, Rose. "How Many Photographs of You Are out There in the World?" The Atlantic, http://www.theatlantic.com/technology/archive/2015/11/how-many-photographs-of-you-are-out-there-in-the-world/413389/.

Eltahawy, Mona. "Tunisia's Jasmine Revolution." washingtonpost.com, http://www.washingtonpost.com/wp-dyn/content/article/2011/01/14/AR2011011405084.html.

Endalk. n.d. "Ethiopia: Netizens Outraged as Ethiopia Steps up Internet Censorship." GlobalVoices.org, https://globalvoices.org/2012/04/27/ethiopia-netizens-outraged-as-ethiopia-steps-up-internet-censorship/.

Etherington, Darrell. "Flickr at 10: 1m Photos Shared Per Day, 170% Increase since Making 1tb Free." TechCrunch, http://techcrunch.com/2014/02/10/flickr-at-10-1m-photos-shared-per-day-170-increase-since-making-1tb-free/.

Evans, Teri. "Flickr Founder Caterina Fake Tells All." Business Insider, http://www.businessinsider.com/caterina-fake-on-stepping-into-the-unknown-2011-4.

Facebook. "Terms of Service." Facebook.com, https://www.facebook.com/terms.

Facebook Inc. "Registration Statement on Forms S-1." Washington D.C: United States Securities and Exchange Commission, 2012.

Fast Company. n.d.. "Occupy Movement: 50 Most Innovative Companies of 2012." Fast Company. http://www.fastcompany.com/most-innovative-companies/2012/occupy-movement.

Fingas, Roger. n.d. "Iphone 6, Iphone 5s Top Most Popular Cameras Used on Flickr in 2015." appleinsider.com, http://appleinsider.com/articles/15/12/03/iphone-6-iphone-5s-top-most-popular-cameras-used-on-flickr-in-2015.

Forrest, Eve. "Reflections on Flickr: Everyday Photography Practices Online and Offline." EITHER/AND, http://eitherand.org/reconsidering-amateur-photography/reflections-flickr-everyday-photography-practices-/.

Fraser, Nancy. "Abnormal Justice." *Critical Inquiry* Spring (2008).

———. "From Redistribution to Recognition? Dilemmas of Justice in a 'Post-Socialist' Age." *New Left Review* 212, no. July–August (1995).

———. "Reframing Justice in a Globalizing World." *New Left Review* 36, no. Nov–Dec (2005).

Friedmann, Harriet. "International Regimes of Food and Agriculture since 1870." In *Peasants and Peasant Societies*, edited by T. Shanin. Oxford: Basil Blackwell, 1987.

———. "The Political Economy of Food: A Global Crisis." *New Left Review* 197 (1993).

———. "The Political Economy of Food: The Rise and Fall of the Postwar International Food Order." *American Journal of Sociology* 88S (1982).

———. "What on Earth Is the Modern World-System? Food-Getting and Territory in the Modern Era and Beyond." *Journal of World-System Research* VI, no. 2 (2000).

Friedmann, Harriet, McMichael, Phillip. "Agriculture and the State System: The Rise and Fall of National Agricultures, 1870 to the Present." *Sociologia Ruralis* 29, no. 2 (1989).

Fuchs, Christian. *Internet and Society: Social Theory in the Information Age*. New York: Routledge, 2008.

Fukuyama, Francis. *The End of History and the Last Man*. New York: Maxwell Macmillan International, 1992.

Galloway, Alexander. *Protocol: How Control Exists after Decentralization*. Cambridge, Ma: MIT Press, 2004.

Galloway, Alexander, Thacker, Eugene. *The Exploit: A Theory of Networks*. Minneapolis: University of Minnesota Press, 2007.

Garvie, Jon. "Trading Free Speech." *Index on Censorship* 4 (2007).

Gillespie, Tarleton. *Wired Shut: Copyright and the Shape of Digital Culture*. Cambridge: MIT Press, 2007.

Giovannucci, Daniele, Josling, Tim, Kerr, William, O'Connor, Bernard, Yeung, May "Guide to Geographical Indications: Linking Products and Their Origins." Geneva: International Trade Centre, 2009.

Giovannucci, Daniele, Ranaboldo, Claudia. "Markets and Geographical Indications of Origin." Latin-American Center for Rural Development 2008.

Glipo, Arze. "Agreement on Agriculture and Food Sovereignty: Perspectives from Mesoamerica and Asia." *Hbf Policy Paper for Cancún* (2003).

globalagriculture.org. "Industrial Agriculture and Small-Scale Farming." globalagriculture.org, http://www.globalagriculture.org/report-topics/industrial-agriculture-and-small-scale-farming.html.

Greenberg, Michael. "In Zuccotti Park." The New York Review of Books, http://www.nybooks.com/articles/archives/2011/nov/10/zuccotti-park/?pagination=false&printpage=true.

Griffiths, John. "What Is Legal Pluralism?". *Journal of Legal Pluralism* 24 (1986).

Grigoriadis, Vanessa. "4chan's Chaos Theory." vanityfair.com, http://www.vanityfair.com/business/features/2011/04/4chan-201104.print.

Grubb, Ben. "Film Industry Hires Cyber Hitmen to Take Down Internet Pirates." theage.com.au, http://www.smh.com.au/technology/technology-news/film-industry-hires-cyber-hitmen-to-take-down-internet-pirates-20100907-14ypv.html.

Hanafi, Sari. "Lessons of the Jasmine Revolution." aljazeera.com, http://www.aljazeera.com/indepth/opinion/2011/01/2011119856413264668.html.

Hardt, Michael, Negri, Antonio. *Commonwealth*. Cambridge Ma.: Harvard University Press, 2009.

———. *Multitude: War and Democracy in the Age of Empire*. New York: Penguin Books, 2004.

———. *Multitude: War and Democracy in the Age of Empire*. New York: Penguin, 2005.

———. n.d. "Take up the Baton." jacobinmag.com, http://jacobinmag.com/summer-2012/take-up-the-baton/.

Harkinson, Josh. "White Nationalists See Trump as Their Troll in Chief. Is He with Them?" motherjones.com, http://www.motherjones.com/politics/2016/11/trump-white-nationalists-hate-racism-power.

Hayden, Cori. *When Nature Goes Public: The Making and Unmaking of Bioprospecting in Mexico*. Princeton Princeton University Press, 2003.

Heller, Michael. *The Gridlock Economy: How Too Much Ownership Wrecks Markets, Stops Innovation, and Costs Lives*. New York: Basic Books, 2008.

Hesse, Monica. "A Virtual Unknown: Meet 'Moot,' the Secretive Internet Celeb Who Still Lives with Mom." washingtonpost.com, http://www.washingtonpost.com/wp-dyn/content/article/2009/02/16/AR2009021601565_pf.html.

Highfield, Tim, Leaver, Tama. "A Methodology for Mapping Instagram Hashtags." *First Monday* 20, no. 1 (2015).

Hooker, M. B. *Legal Pluralism: An Introduction to Colonial and Neo-Colonial Laws*. Oxford: Clarendon Press, 1975.

Horaczek, Stan. "How Many Photos Are Uploaded to the Internet Every Minute?" Popular Photography, http://www.popphoto.com/news/2013/05/how-many-photos-are-uploaded-to-internet-every-minute.

Hubbard, Ruth. "Human Nature." In *Biopolitics: A Feminist and Ecological Reader on Biotechnology*, edited by Vandana Shiva. New York City: Zed Books, 1988.

Hughes, Christopher, R. "China and the Globalization of Icts: Implications for International Relations." *New Media & Society* 4, no. 2 (2002).

Human Rights Watch. "Race to the Bottom: Corporate Complicity in Chinese Internet Censorship." New York City: Human Rights Watch, 2006.

Hyde, Lewis. *Common as Air: Revolution, Art and Ownership*. New York City: Farrar, Straus and Giroux, 2010.

Information Office of the State Council of the People's Republic of China. n.d. "The Internet in China." Information Office of the State Council of the People's Republic of China, http://news.xinhuanet.com/english2010/china/2010-06/08/c_13339232.htm.

Instagram.com. "Terms of Use." https://help.instagram.com/478745558852511.

International Intellectual Property Alliance. "About the International Intellectual Property Alliance." International Intellectual Property Alliance, http://www.iipa.com/aboutiipa.html.

———. "New Economic Study Shows U.S Copyright Industries Pass $278 Billion Mark and Account for over 3.5 Million U.S Jobs." Washington D.C: International Intellectual Property Alliance, 1996.

Internet Live Stats. "Internet Users in China." http://www.internetlivestats.com/, http://www.internetlivestats.com/internet-users/china/.

Internet Society of China. n.d. "Public Pledge of Self-Regulation and Professional Ethics for China Internet Industry." Internet Society of China, http://www.isc.org.cn/20020417/ca102762.htm.

INTERPOL. "Database on International Intellectual Property." INTERPOL, http://www.interpol.int/Public/FinancialCrime/IntellectualProperty/DIIP/Default.asp.

Isaac, Mike. "Facebook Said to Create Censorship Tool to Get Back into China." NYTimes.com, http://www.nytimes.com/2016/11/22/technology/facebook-censorship-tool-china.html.

Jefferson, Thomas. "Thomas Jefferson to Isaac Mcpherson." University of Chicago Press, http://press-pubs.uchicago.edu/founders/documents/a1_8_8s12.html.

Joy, L. and Payne, P.R. "Food and Nutrition Planning, Nutrition Consultants' Reports." Rome: FAO, 1975.

Juris, Jeffrey S. "Networked Social Movements: Global Movements for Global Justice." In *The Network Society: A Cross-Cultural Perspective*, edited by Manuel Castells. Cheltenham, UK: Edward Elgar, 2005.

———. "A New Way of Doing Politics? Global Justice Movements and the Cultural Logic of Networking." *Altermondialisme, société civile et mondialisation* 31, no. 1 (2007).

Kalantzis-Cope, Phillip. "Geopolitical Structuring in the Age of Information: Imagining Order, Understanding Change." *Alternatives: Global, Local, Political* (2017).

———. "Whose Data? Problematizing the 'Gift' of Social Labour." *Global Media and Communication* 12, no. 3 (2016).

Kelly, Kevin. *New Rules for the New Economy*. New York: Viking, 1998.

Klein, Ezra. "Who Are the 99 Percent?" washingtonpost.com, http://www.washingtonpost.com/blogs/ezra-klein/post/who-are-the-99-percent/2011/08/25/gIQAt87jKL_blog.html.

Kloppenburg, Jack. "Impeding Dispossession, Enabling Repossession: Biological Open Source and the Recovery of Seed Sovereignty." *Journal of Agrarian Change* 10, no. 3 (2010).

Kluver, Randolph. "Us and Chinese Policy Expectations of the Internet." *China Information* 19 (2005).

Kopytoff, Verne. "At Flickr, Fending Off Rumors and Facebook." NYTimes.com, http://www.nytimes.com/2011/01/31/technology/31flickr.html.

Kroker, Arthur, Weinstein, Michael,. *Data Trash: The Theory of the Virtual Class*. New York City: St Martin's Press, 1994.

Lamere, Paul. "Inside the Precision Hack." musicmachinery.com, http://musicmachinery.com/2009/04/15/inside-the-precision-hack/.

Lasn, Kalle, White, Micah "Why Occupy Wall Street Will Keep up the Fight." The Washington Post, http://www.washingtonpost.com/opinions/why-occupy-wall-street-will-keep-up-the-fight/2011/11/17/gIQAn5RJZN_print.html.

Leaver, Tama. "Born Digital? Presence, Privacy, and Intimate Surveillance." In *Re-Orientation: Translingual Transcultural Transmedia, Studies in Narrative, Language, Identity, and Knowledge*, edited by John Hartley, Qu, W. Shanghai: Fudan University Press, 2015.

Lee, Oliver. "Understanding Trump's Troll Army." Motherboard, https://motherboard.vice.com/en_us/article/understanding-trumps-troll-army.

Lessig, Laurence. *Free Culture: The Nature and Future of Creativity*. New York: Penguin, 2005.

———. *The Future of Ideas: The Fate of the Commons in a Connected World*. New York: Vintage, 2002.

Li, Xuan, Correa, Carlos, ed. *Intellectual Property Enforcement: International Perspectives*. Cheltenham: Edward Elgar, 2009.

Lih, Andrew. *The Wikipedia Revolution*. New York: Hyperion, 2009.

Lovink, Geert. "Inside Networked Movements: Interview with Jeffrey Juris." Institute of Network Cultures, http://networkcultures.org/geert/inside-networked-movements-interview-with-jeffrey-juris/.

———. *Zero Comments: Blogging and Critical Internet Culture*. New York: Routledge, 2007.

Luke, Tim. "On Environmentality: Geo-Power and Eco-Power in the Discourses of Contemporary Environmentalism." *Cultural Critique* 31 (1995).

Makki, Fouad. "The Empire of Capital and the Remaking of Centre-Periphery Relations." *Third World Quarterly* 25 (2004).

Maldre, Matt. "Flickr's 1.4 Million Photos Per Day, Instagram's 40 Million Photos Per Day." MattMaldre.com, http://mattmaldre.com/2013/05/27/flickrs-1-4-million-photos-per-day-instagrams-40-million-photos-per-day/.

Manovich, Lev. "Competitive Photography and the Presentation of the Self." http://manovich.net/, http://manovich.net/index.php/projects/competitive-photography-and-the-presentation-of-the-self.

Marazzi, Christian. *Capital and Affects: The Politics of the Language Economy*. Cambridge, Ma.: Semiotext(e), 2011.

———. "The Privatization of the General Intellect." SSRC, http://www.ssrc.org/blogs/knowledgerules/2008/02/19/the-privatization-of-the-general-intellect/.

Marden, Emily. "The Neem Tree Patent: International Conflict over the Commodification of Life." *Boston College International and Comparative Law Review* 22, no. 2 (1999).

Marx, Karl. "The Grundrisse." In *The Marx-Engles Reader*, edited by Robert Tucker. London: W.N Norton & Company, 1978 [1858].
Maskus, Keith. *Intellectual Property Rights in the Global Economy*. Washington D.C: Institute for International Economic, 2000.
Maskus, Keith, Reichman, Jerome. "The Concept of Public Goods in the Expanding Knowledge Economy." In *International Public Goods and Transfer of Technology under a Globalized Intellectual Property Regime*, edited by Keith Maskus, Reichman, Jerome. Cambridge: Cambridge University Press, 2005.
Mauss, Marcel. *The Gift: The Form and Reason for Exchange in Archaic Societies*. New York: W. W. Norton & Company, 2000.
May, Christopher. *The Global Politcal Economy of Intellectual Property Rights: The New Enclosures*. London: Routledge, 2010.
———. *The World Intellectual Property Agenda: Resurgence and the Development Agenda*. New York: Routledge, 2007.
May, Christopher, Sell, Susan. *Intellectual Property Rights: A Critical History*. Ipolitics: Global Challenges in the Information Age. Edited by Renee Marlin-Bennett London: Lynne Rienner Publishers, 2006.
McMichael, Phillip. "A Food Regime Genealogy." *The Journal of Peasant Studies* 36, no. 1 (2009).
McNeil, Joanne. "Occupy the Internet." *Occupy: An OWS Inspired Gazette (N+1)* 1 (2011).
McQuire, Scott. "Photography's Afterlife: Documentary Images and the Operational Archive." *Journal of Material Culture* 18, no. 223 (2013).
Mendras, Henri. *The Vanishing Peasant: Innovation and Change in French Agriculture*. Cambridge, Mass.: MIT Press, 1970.
Merry, Sally Engle. "Legal Pluralism." *Law & Society Review* 22, no. 5 (1988).
Miladi, Noureddine. "Tunisia: A Media Led Revolution?" aljazeera.com, http://www.aljazeera.com/indepth/opinion/2011/01/2011116142317498666.html.
Min, Jiang. "Authoritarian Informationalism: China's Approach to Internet Sovereignty." *SAIS Review* 30, no. 2 (2010).
Moholy-Nagy, László. *Painting, Photography, Film*. London: Lund Humphries, 1969.
Moore, Malcolm. "Ai Weiwei Starts New Openness Campaign." The Telegraph, http://www.telegraph.co.uk/news/worldnews/asia/china/8159401/Ai-Weiwei-starts-new-openness-campaign.html.
Moore, Sally Falk. "Law and Social Change: The Semi-Autonomous Social Field as an Appropriate Subject of Study." *Law & Society Review* 7, no. 719 (1973).

Moran, Warren. "Rural Space as Intellectual Property." *Political Geography* 12, no. 3 (1993).

Murray, Ruby. "China's Digital Natives Behind with the Great Firewall." thesaturdaypaper.com.au, https://www.thesaturdaypaper.com.au/2016/01/23/chinas-digital-natives-behind-with-the-great-firewall/14534676002803.

Musungu, Sisule, Dutfield, Graham. "Multilateral Agreements and a Trips-Plus World: The World Intellectual Property Organisation (Wipo)." In *TRIPS Issue Papers*, edited by Geoff Tansey. Geneva: Quaker United Nations Office, 2003.

Neem Foundation. "Patents on Neem." neemfoundation.org, http://www.neemfoundation.org/neem-articles/patents-on-neem.html.

Nordin, Astrid, Richaud, Lisa. "Subverting Official Language and Discourse in China? Type River Crab for Harmony." *China Information* 28, no. 1 (2014).

Okediji, Ruth. "Public Welfare and the Role of the Wto: Reconsidering the Trips Agreement." *Emory International Law Review* 17, no. 2 (2003).

Olaszanowski, Magdalena. "The 1x1 Common: The Role of Instagram's Hashtag in the Development and Maintenance of Feminist Exchange." In *Hashtag Publics: The Power and Politics of Discursive Networks*, edited by Nathan Rambukkana. New York: Peter Lang, 2015.

Ong, Aihwa. "Graduated Sovereignty in South-East Asia." *Theory, Culture & Society* 17, no. 55 (2000).

Open Democracy. "The Great Firewall of China." Open Democracy., http://www.opendemocracy.net/print/2524.

Oyelaran-Oyeyinka, Banji, Sampath, Padmashree. *Latecomer Development: Innovation and Knowledge for Economic Growth*. New York: Routledge, 2010.

Panizzon, Marion. "Traditional Knowledge and Geographical Indications: Foundations, Interests and Negotiating Positions." In *NCCR Trade Working Paper*. Geneva: Swiss National Centre of Competence in Research, 2006.

Parr, Ben. "Facebook and Google Do Identity Wrong." mashable.com, http://mashable.com/2011/10/18/chris-poole-4chan-web-2/.

Pasquinelli, Matteo. *Animal Spirits: A Bestiary of the Commons*. Amsterdam: Institute for Network Cultures 2008.

Patel, Rajeev. "Global Fascism, Revolutionary Humanism and the Ethics of Food Sovereignty." *Development* 48, no. 2 (2005).

———. "Grassroots Voices: Food Sovereignty." *The Journal of Peasant Studies* 36, no. 3 (2009).

———. "International Agrarian Restructuring and the Practical Ethics of Peasant Movement Solidarity." *Journal of Asian and African Studies* 41, no. 71 (2006).

Peoples Grocery. "About Us." peoplesgrocery.org, http://www.peoplesgrocery.org/about/.

Peterson, Charles. "The Politics of the Poor." *Occupy: An OWS Inspired Gazette (N+1)* 1 (2011).

Pimbert, Michel. "Towards Food Sovereignty." *Sustainable Agriculture, Biodiversity and Livelihoods: International Institute for Environment and Development* 141, no. November (2008).

Porter, Joshua. "Social Design Patterns for Reputation Systems: An Interview with Yahoo!'S Bryce Glass" Bokardo.com, http://bokardo.com/archives/social-design-patterns-for-reputation-systems-two/.

Posner, Sara. "How Donald Trump's New Campaign Chief Created an Online Haven for White Nationalists." motherjones.com, http://www.motherjones.com/politics/2016/08/stephen-bannon-donald-trump-alt-right-breitbart-news.

Pratt, Jeff. "Food Values: The Local and the Authentic." *Critique of Anthropology* 27, no. 3 (2007).

Preston, Jennifer. "Protesters Look for Ways to Feed the Web." nytimes.com, http://www.nytimes.com/2011/11/25/business/media/occupy-movement-focuses-on-staying-current-on-social-networks.html.

Quaye, Wilhemina. "Food Sovereignty and Combating Poverty and Hunger in Ghana." *Tailoring Biotechnologies* 3, no. 2 (2007).

Randeria, Shalini. "Legal Pluralism, Social Movements and the Post Colonial State in India: Fractured Sovereignty and Differential Citizenship Rights." In *Another Knowledge Is Possible: Beyond Northern Epistemologies*, edited by Boaventura De Sousa Santos. New York City: Verso, 2007.

Ranjan Jena, Pradyot, Grote, Ulrike. "Changing Institutions to Protect Regional Heritage: A Case for Geographical Indications in the Indian Agrifood Sector." *Development Policy Review* 28, no. 2 (2010).

Raustiala, Kal, Munzer, Stephen. "The Global Struggle over Geographic Indications." *The European Journal of International Law* 18, no. 2 (2007).

Richter, Rudolf, Schadler, Cornelia. "See My Virtual Self: Dissemination as a Characteristic of Digital Photography—the Example of Flickr.Com." *Journal of Visual Studies* 24, no. 2 (2010).

Rigi, Jakob. "Peer to Peer Production as the Alternative to Capitalism: A New Communist Horizon ". *Journal of Peer Production* 1, no. 1 (2012).

Risnick, Gideon. " Despite Weak Stream of Proof, 4chan Claims It Invented the Trump Golden Showers Story." The Daily Beast, http://www.thedailybeast.com/articles/2017/01/10/4chan-claims-they-invented-the-trump-golden-showers-story.html.

Ritchin, Fred. "Photography Changes Now News Is Reported." In *Photography Changes Everything*, edited by Marvin Heiferman. New York City: Aperture, 2012.

Roos, Jerome. "The Global Square: An Online Platform for Our Movement." roarmag.org, http://roarmag.org/2011/11/the-global-square-an-online-platform-for-our-movement/.

Rose, Nikolas. *The Politics of Life Itself: Biomedicine, Power, and Subjectivity in the Twenty-First Century*. Princeton: Princeton University Press, 2007.

Rosen, Rebecca. "The 99 Percent Tumblr: Self-Service History." theatlantic.com, http://www.theatlantic.com/technology/archive/2011/10/the-99-percent-tumblr-self-service-history/246385/.

Rosset, Peter. *Food Is Different: Why We Must Get the WTO out of Agriculture*. New York City: Zed Books, 2006.

———. "Food Sovereignty and the Contemporary Food Crisis." *Development* 51, no. 4 (2008).

———. "Moving Forward: Agrarian Reform as a Part of Food Sovereignty." In *Promised Land: Competing Visions of Agrarian Reform*, edited by Michael Courville, Patel, Raj, Rosset, Peter. Oakland: Food First Books, 2006.

Ryan, Yasmine. "How Tunisia's Revolution Began." aljazeera.com, http://www.aljazeera.com/indepth/features/2011/01/2011126121815985483.html.

———. "Tunisia's Bitter Cyberwar." aljazeera.com, http://www.aljazeera.com/indepth/features/2011/01/20111614145839362.html.

Safri, Maliha. "Globalizing Zuccotti." *Occupy: An OWS Inspired Gazette (N+1)* 1 (2011).

Sell, Susan, K. "Intellectual Property and the Doha Development Agenda". In *The WTO after Hong Kong: Progress in, and Prospects for, the Doha Development Agenda*, edited by Donna Lee, Wilkinson, Rorden,. London: Routledge, 2007.

———. *Private Power, Public Law: The Globalization of Intellectual Property Rights*. Cambridge Studies in International Relations. Cambridge: Cambridge University Press, 2003.

Shirky, Clay. *Cognitive Surplus: Creativity and Generosity in a Connected Age*. New York City: The Penguin Press, 2010.

———. *Here Comes Everybody: The Power of Organizing without Orgaizations*. New York City: Penguin Press, 2008.

Shiva, Vandana. *Biopiracy: The Plunder of Nature and Knowledge*. Cambridge: South End Press, 1997.

———. *Earth Democracy: Justice, Sustainability and Peace*. Brooklyn: South End Press, 2005.

———. "Free Tree." The Hindustan Times, India, http://www1.hindustantimes.com/nonfram/090600/detOPI01.htm.

———. *Monocultures of the Mind: Perspectives on Biodiversity and Biotechnology*. New York City: Zed Books, 1993.

———. *Stolen Harvest: The Hijacking of the Global Food Supply* Cambridge, MA: South End Press, 2000.

Simonite, Tom. "Browser Plug-in Punches an Unfixable Hole in China's Great Firewall." MIT Technology Review, https://www.technologyreview.com/s/543711/browser-plug-in-punches-an-unfixable-hole-in-chinas-great-firewall/.

Singal, Jesse. "How Internet Trolls Won the 2016 Presidential Election." New York Magazine, http://nymag.com/selectall/2016/09/how-internet-trolls-won-the-2016-presidential-election.html.

Singer, Natasha. "Mapping, and Sharing, the Consumer Genome." NYTimes.com, http://www.nytimes.com/2012/06/17/technology/acxiom-the-quiet-giant-of-consumer-database-marketing.html.

Smith, Cooper. "Facebook 350 Million Photos Each Day." Business Insider, http://www.businessinsider.com/facebook-350-million-photos-each-day-2013-9.

Sontag, Susan. *On Photography*. New York City: Picador 1973.

Sorgatz, Rex. "Macroanonymous Is the New Microfamous." fimoculous.com, http://www.fimoculous.com/archive/post-5738.cfm.

Stallman, Richard. "Copyleft: Pragmatic Idealism." http://www.gnu.org/philosophy/pragmatic.html.

Stanislawski, D. *Landscapes of Bacchus: The Vine in Portugal*. Austin: University of Texas Press, 1970.

Starr, Amory. "Local Food: A Social Movement?". *Cultural Studies ↔ Critical Methodologies* 10, no. 6 (2010).

State Council Information Office. "Provisions on the Administration of Internet News and Information Services." State Council Information Office., http://www.china.org.cn/business/2010-01/21/content_19281869.htm.

Sterling, Bruce. "Web Semantics: Popular Chinese Internet Slang Expressions and Acronyms." Wired.com, https://www.wired.com/2010/09/web-semantics-popular-chinese-internet-slang-expressions-and-acronyms/.

Stetler, Pepper. "Franz Roh and the Art History of Photography." An Online Project of The Museum of Modern Art, New York City, http://www.moma.org/interactives/objectphoto/assets/essays/Stetler.pdf.

Strafella, Giorgio, Berg, Daria. "A Decade of Blogging in China." University of Nottingham, https://blogs.nottingham.ac.uk/chinapolicyinstitute/2015/08/31/a-decade-of-blogging-in-china/.

Strelitz, Larry, Steenveld, Lynette. "The Fifth Estate: Media Theory, Watchdog of Journalism." *African Journalism Studies* 19, no. 1 (1998).

Sullivan, Jordan. "China's Weibo: Is Faster Different?". *New Media & Society* 16 (2014): 1.

Sung, Wook Kim, Douai, Aziz. "Google Vs. China's "Great Firewall": Ethical Implications for Free Speech and Sovereignty." *Technology in Society* 34 (2012).

Surowiecki, J. *The Wisdom of Crowds: Why the Many Are Smarter Than the Few and How Collective Wisdom Shapes Business, Economies, Societies and Nations.* New York City: Doubleday, 2004.

Tagg, John. *The Burden of Representation: Essays on Photography and Histories, Minneapolis.* Minneapolis: University of Minnesota Press, 1988.

Tarnoff, Ben. "Neoliberalism Turned Our World into a Business. And There Are Two Big Winners." The Gaurdian, https://www.theguardian.com/us-news/2016/dec/13/donald-trump-silicon-valley-leaders-neoliberalism-administration?CMP=share_btn_tw%201/.

Tea Board of India. "Darjeeling Tea: A Quest for Intellectual Property Rights." Kolkata: Tea Board of India, 2010.

Thacker, Eugne. *Biomedia.* Minneapolis: University of Minnesota Press, 2004.

The CIO Report. "To Facebook You're Worth $80.95." wsj.com, http://blogs.wsj.com/cio/2012/05/03/to-facebook-youre-worth-80-95/tab/print/.

The Economist. "Big Data, Meet Big Brother: China Invents the Digital Totalitarian State." TheEconomist.com, http://www.economist.com/node/21711902/.

———. "Protecting Names: The European Union's List of Sacrosanct Trade Names May Not Fend Off Imitators." *The Economist*, July 31 2003.

The Hindu. "India Wins Neem Patent Case." The Hindu., http://www.hindu.com/2005/03/09/stories/2005030902381300.htm.

The World Bank. "2010 World Development Indicators". Washington D.C.: The World Bank, 2010.

Townsend, Mark. "Wikileaks Backlash: The First Global Cyber War Has Begun, Claim Hackers." guardian.co.uk, http://www.guardian.co.uk/media/2010/dec/11/wikileaks-backlash-cyber-war.

Tsui, Lokman. "An Inadequate Metaphor: The Great Firewall and Chinese Internet Censorship." *Global Dialogue* 9, no. 1 (2007).

U.S Copyright Office. "Executive Summary, Digital Millennium Copyright Act, Section 104 Report." copyright.gov, http://www.copyright.gov/reports/studies/dmca/dmca_executive.html.

Unwin, Tim. *Wine and the Vine: An Historical Geography of Viticulture and the Wine Trade*. London: Routledge, 1991.

US Government. "Digital Millennium Copyright Act (Dcma)." edited by 105th United States Congress, 1998.

Van Dijck, José. "Flickr and the Culture of Connectivity: Sharing Views, Experiences, Memories." *Memory Studies* 4 (2011).

Vargas, Jose Antonio. n.d. "Spring Awakening: How an Egyptian Revolution Began on Facebook." nytimes.com, http://www.nytimes.com/2012/02/19/books/review/how-an-egyptian-revolution-began-on-facebook.html?pagewanted=all.

Vercellone, Carlo. "From Formal Subsumption to General Intellect: Elements for a Marxist Reading of the Thesis of Cognitive Capitalism." *Historical Materialism* 13, no. 36 (2007).

Via Campesina. "The International Peasant's Voice." viacampesina.org, http://viacampesina.org/en/index.php/organisation-mainmenu-44.

———. "The Position of Vía Campesina on Biodiversity, Biosafety and Genetic Resources." *Development* 44, no. 4 (2001).

Vidal, John. "Granting Community Theft." The Guardian, http://www.guardian.co.uk/environment/2003/sep/08/wto.fairtrade3.

Vila, Susannah. n.d. "How the #Occupy Movement Is Spurring Tech Innovation." Mashable, http://mashable.com/2011/12/12/ows-tech-innovation/?utm_source...r&utm_medium=feed&utm_campaign=Feed%3A+Mashable+%28Mashable%29.

Virilio, Paul. *The Information Bomb*. Verso: New York, 2000.

Virno, Paolo. *A Grammar of the Multitude: For an Analysis of Contemporary Forms of Life*. Cambridge, Mass.: Semiotext(e), 2004.

Wark, Mckenzie. *A Hacker Manifesto*. Cambridge: Harvard University Press, 2004.

Watts, Jonathan. "China's Secret Internet Police Target Critics with Web of Propaganda." The Guardian, http://www.theguardian.com/technology/2005/jun/14/newmedia.china—article_continue.

wearethe99percent.tumblr.com. "Wearethe99percent." http://www.wearethe99percent.tumblr.com/.

Weber, Steven. *The Success of Open Source*. Cambridge, Ma.: Harvard University Press, 2004.

Weiwei, Ai. "Ai Weiwei: The Internet Vs. The Chinese Government." Big Think: Smarter, Faster, http://bigthink.com/experts-corner/dispatches-from-the-police-state-nil-1-the-internet-is-constantly-putting-the-chinese-government-on-trial.

———. "China's Censorship Can Never Defeat the Internet." The Guardian, http://www.guardian.co.uk/commentisfree/libertycentral/2012/apr/16/china-censorship-internet-freedom.

White, Micah. "Activism after Clicktivism: How to Energize the Political Left." Adbusters, http://www.adbusters.org/magazine/93/activism-after-clicktivism.html.

Whois.net. "Whois Information for Occupywallstreet.Org." Whois Lookup—Domain Names Search, Registration, & Availability http://www.whois.net/whois/occupywallstreet.org.

Wiener, Norbert. *Cybernetics: Or Control and Communication in the Animal and the Machine*. Cambridge, Ma.: MIT Press, 1948.

World Customs Organization. "Global Congress Combating Counterfeiting and Piracy: Outcomes and Recommendations." World Customs Organization, http://www.ccapcongress.net/Recommendations.htm.

World Trade Organization. "Agreement on Trade Related Aspects of Intellectual Property Rights." World Trade Organization, http://www.wto.org/english/tratop_e/trips_e/t_agm0_e.htm.

Wu, Tim. "The World Trade Law of Censorship and Internet Filtering." *Chicago Journal of International Law* (2006).

Yang, Goubin. "A Chinese Internet? History, Practice, and Globalization." *Chinese Journal of Communication* 1, no. 6 (2012).

———. "Technology and Its Contents: Issues in the Study of the Chinese Internet." *The Journal of Asian Studies* 70, no. 4 (2011a).

———. "Technology and Its Contents: Issues in the Study of the Chinese Internet." *The Journal of Asian Studies* 40, no. 4 (2011b).

Yglesias, Matthew. n.d. "#Nrorevolt, Explained." vox.com, http://www.vox.com/2015/9/8/9276719/nrorevolt-cuckservatives.

Zhang, Feng. "The Rise of Chinese Exceptionalism in International Relations." *European Journal of International Relations* 12, no. 2 (2011).

Zhang, Lena. "Behind the 'Great Firewall': Decoding China's Internet Media Policies from the Inside." *Convergence: The International Journal of Research into New Media Technologies* 12, no. 3 (2006).

Zhang, Zhan, Negro, Gianluigi. "Weibo in China: Understanding Its Development through Communication Analysis and Cultural Studies." *Communication, Politics & Culture* 46 (2013).

Zizek, Slavoj. *First as Tragedy, Then as Farce*. London: Verso, 2009.

Index[1]

[1]Note: Page number followed by 'n' refers to note.

P. Kalantzis-Cope, *The Work and Play of the Mind in the Information Age*, Frontiers of Globalization, https://doi.org/10.1007/978-3-319-64650-3

CPSIA information can be obtained
at www.ICGtesting.com
Printed in the USA
LVOW13*2346071117
555378LV00012B/224/P

9 783319 646497